James Pye has taught in comprehensive and special schools, supervised student teachers, and taught adult 'returners'. Since writing has become his chief occupation, he has worked part-time in a variety of settings—running a befriending scheme and other voluntary work in a psychiatric hospital, for instance. After completing this book—in its argument a sequel to his first book, *Invisible Children* (also in Oxford Paperbacks)—he became mature students adviser at Oxford Polytechnic.

Second Chances

*

Adults Returning
to Education

*

JAMES PYE

Foreword by Willy Russell

Oxford   New York

OXFORD UNIVERSITY PRESS

1991

Oxford University Press, Walton Street, Oxford OX2 6DP

Oxford New York Toronto
Delhi Bombay Calcutta Madras Karachi
Petaling Jaya Singapore Hong Kong Tokyo
Nairobi Dar es Salaam Cape Town
Melbourne Auckland

and associated companies in
Berlin Ibadan

Oxford is a trade mark of Oxford University Press

First published 1991 as an Oxford University Press paperback

British Library Cataloguing in Publication Data
Data available
ISBN 0-19-212990-2

Library of Congress Cataloging in Publication Data
Pye, James.
Second chances : adults returning to education / James Pye.
p. cm.
Includes bibliographical references and index.
1. Adult education—Great Britain—Case studies. I. Title.
374'.941—dc20 LC5256.G7P94 1991 91-11366
ISBN 0-19-212990-2

Typeset by Columns of Reading
Printed in Great Britain by
Biddles Ltd.
Guildford and King's Lynn

To the memory of Pat Aspinall and Ellen Dowdall

Acknowledgements

I cannot thank the people I interviewed enough. They gave me very generous amounts of time. All have influenced this book even if their accounts have not been included. Meeting returners—and members of their families—has been inspiring; and unfailingly and continually interesting. Several of those I interviewed have now become friends whose advice has been invaluable in the later stages of this book's creation.

I would also like to thank the following for their interest, or advice, or help, or all three:

Susie my wife, whose editorial instinct led me away from an early false trail, Sarah Feilden, Desmond and Barbara Vowles, Kay Wood, Nigel Evans, Christine Park, John Parker, Maria Pratico, Katherine Hughes.

Willy Russell's play, *Educating Rita*, has encouraged countless people to return to education. So when he offered to begin this book, it was as if a band were being joined by an orchestra. I am very grateful to him.

I did not see or read the play again while I was working on this book. I think I was superstitiously afraid of being influenced, or of feeling redundant. I loved the play when I first saw it. Now that I have read it again, I realize how perfectly it found the centre of its subject. But I should not have worried. If I had watched the film of *Educating Rita* every fortnight of this book's early life, I could only have been encouraged. Rita herself would have made me laugh, kept me going, criticized me usefully, and confirmed the richness of the words spoken by the people in this book, because their experience echoes her own. Speaking for all returners I should thank her as well as her creator.

Foreword
by Willy Russell

Reading these pages, and the vivid testimonies within, I was struck, as I have been by other experiences, by a deep sense of how state education gives a terrible return on its investment. Can I prove this? No. I am not a statistician, nor sociologist, nor politician nor part of any other species which has a vested interest in proving this or that with these or those figures or facts. I am merely a member of this English society and have witnessed its education from the various perspectives of pupil, part-time student, mature student, parent, teacher, writer in residence and casual observer. As such my views are a mixture of subjective/objective, my evidence largely anecdotal and my conclusion a mere sense that something is badly wrong. A *sense* of something cannot be proven or disproven just as a poem cannot be 'proven' or otherwise. But a sense can be true—as a poem can be true. For me it has long been blindingly true that state education fails the majority of its clients—even that minority which appears to have done well by this system. I assert that this minority, well served though they appear to have been, could have done even better whilst the vast majority could have done much better indeed. Some, from that majority, appear vividly in these pages. But we know, from conversations with friends, acquaintances, relations, strangers at bus-stops and in check-out queues that for every one in this book there are a thousand others who will tell you that they failed at their education or that their education failed them. How can it be that a system which takes up so much of our national expenditure and draws upon so much of the best of the intellectual vision and specialist knowledge available, can so consistently fail so many? Could it be that we are backing the wrong horse? Or, perhaps, backing a horse at all when the horse is no longer central to our culture?

On reading the manuscript for this book I found that it rekindled all sorts of fundamental and exhausting questions with which I have intermittently grappled for the past twenty-five years or so. These questions were not directly to do with 'returners' but were aimed again and again at why anyone should ever need to return. Education should never have been allowed to become something that has a definite beginning and a definite end. The very concept of 'returning' should not be one we recognize because education itself should be ongoing, without beginning or end. I realize immediately, of course, that already I am in danger of becoming vulnerable—of sounding an unrealistic utopian note here. But is it really hopelessly utopian to suggest that education and life itself should be woven indelibly together? Difficult, yes, difficult to grapple with because it is a simple idea and the simple idea is most often the most profound, and radical. Difficult, then, but not impossible, as the many eloquent voices in this book testify. Like all of them, I once experienced education as hell on earth, but ultimately, found in it my own salvation.

The Willy Russell Story

In 1967 I was, of all things, a ladies hairdresser. I was no good at the job. I hated it. By the time I'd finished with them, the customers hated me. Like hundreds of thousands of people in this country I'd been 'no good at school' and had drifted into a job, because if you're 'no good at school' you have to pay the price and take whatever you can get. I suppose that's fair enough. I'm not moaning about it. Even if I'd been given the chance of going back to being a kid again and having a crack at school again, I still wouldn't have taken advantage of it. When I was at school I simply didn't want to learn the vast majority of what they wanted to teach—and nothing can be taught if there's no desire to learn. I could read and did read a lot. Reading was a pleasure and was never, for me, consciously associated with school or learning. I played football, ran and wrestled and talked with my mates and learned when I was about thirteen, how to play a few chords on the guitar, and speculated endlessly on the intoxicating mystery of girls. What time was there for learning? What desire was there for learning when learning had nothing to do with reality? You might think that someone learning to play the guitar might take an interest in music lessons, but wanting to play rock and roll has little in common with a demented music teacher hell-bent on bludgeoning us into liking 'Dashing Away With The Smoothing Iron' or 'Riding Down From Bangor On An Eastern Train'.

I didn't know it then, I didn't know it for years and years, but my experience at school was doomed from day one.

It was a largely futile experience because two cultures were in constant conflict. Of course this was never explicit, and it was only when I became a teacher myself that I realized that schools assume and reflect a middle class culture with literacy at its heart, whilst kids from working class families are part of a culture which has not literacy, but oracy at its heart. The languages are different, and yet still, today, schools try to teach working class kids without addressing the fact that the school speaks with one tongue and the kid speaks another. And implicit in this process is the message that the language of the school is the valid *Language* whilst the language, the working class idiom of the kid, is valueless, is base.

I wanted to learn

Like thousands of others who left school bemused, confused and apparently apathetic, I sensed that inside I was capable. I sensed that I was valuable. But I couldn't prove it. The facts were there, massed against me—Maths: the teacher's comments on my final report: 'We consider it an achievement if William manages to get the date right.' Woodwork: 'Wood and William are best kept apart. His attempts at making a guitar would seem rather ambitious when in four long years he has not yet learnt how to use a tenon saw.' PE: 'The pursuit of physical excellence is not for one who wears winkle pickers and smokes Capstan Full Strength.'

On and on the relentless indictment rolled, the one star in an otherwise black sky, being the favourable comment from my English teacher. In summary, at the bottom of the report the headmaster had written: 'William will obviously not go far in life. Perhaps this is just as well for, given his knowledge of Geography, he would surely get lost.'

For years I'd believed their opinion of me—but in 1967, in the hairdresser's shop where I'd worked for nearly five years, things were beginning to happen. Chiefly, I was beginning in a fumbling stumbling sort of way, to realize that I wanted to learn, I wanted to know and to do more than I ever would in my role as a hairdresser. I wanted to do a job in which I could contribute something more than a mediocre perm or a tint.

At night time, away from the trap of the shop, I'd begun to sing and perform in folk clubs and I'd met people who tried to persuade me that I had the ability to do other things if that's what I desired. They talked about going into social work or teaching and their talk of such things both fascinated and terrified me.

'Yes,' I'd think in an unguarded moment, 'yes, that's what I want to do. That's what I could do.' And then I'd be overwhelmed by doubt and insecurity. Me? A teacher? The mere thought was ludicrous. And so, the next morning I'd be back at the perm trolley or the shampoo basin, depressed, frustrated, full of resentment for my poor innocent customer whose only crime was in wanting a beehive hair-do or a silver rinse.

I was so terrified

The situation eventually became impossible. As ludicrous as it was to imagine I might go into teaching, it was even more ludicrous to imagine I might go on shampooing and setting for another forty years. I went to some friends and said, 'OK how do I do it, how do I become a teacher?' When they uttered the infamous phrase 'five O levels', I went into a dead faint. I had one already, English Language, but four more? Four O levels! Four O levels represented the North Face of the Eiger with Everest grafted on top of it. I ran straight back to the shop, told myself I loved hairdressing and that I could be a satisfied human being. But I wasn't. I wanted more. I was cursed with the desire for something else, something unattainable. The girl I was later to marry suggested a sort of compromise—why didn't I take one O level at night school and, so to speak, test the water. Walking into Kirkby College of Education clutching *Animal Farm*, *Henry the Fifth*, and Browning's poetry, riddled with fear and uncertainty, the smells common to all educational buildings—making me feel sick with memories of school. In the classroom with twenty others—all of them looking sure and poised and confident. There was a break for tea and coffee down the corridor. I was so terrified, felt so conspicuous and exposed I just sat at the desk, clutching it, pretending I wasn't thirsty when in truth I was craving for a drink of tea. It was all a mistake. I'd never be able to do it. I wouldn't come back. It was too late for me and I'd better start accepting the fact. And anyway, I hated Shakespeare—that's why I'd never read it or seen it. And that book about pigs, I mean pigs. Who the hell would write a book about pigs? I'd packed in after the first three pages. And then he was saying—this teacher—it isn't about pigs at all. Well it is, on the surface. But below that, it's about the Russian revolution. Oh, so the pigs are like, like symbols of people in the revolution? Yes. The book is what's known as an allegory.

I wrote down the word—allegory. And then my understanding of its definition—a story that looks as though it's about one thing but is also about another. On the bus, going home, reading, making perfect sense now out of something which I'd dismissed because I'd been afraid. Going home and straight to bed to read right through this great book.

At nine the next morning I walked in to the shop, a self-appointed expert on the work of George Orwell, with particular reference to *Animal Farm*. As I enthused over the book, my worried and anxious customers exchanged glances of dismay.

'What's got into him? I think I preferred him when y' couldn't get a bleedin' word out of him.'

'Pigs! a book about soddin' pigs. He must've been drinkin' perm lotion.'

'Pigs! He must be thinkin' of goin' into butchery.'

'He already has—have y' seen my hair?'

And so for the best part of a year my long suffering customers had to cope with my conversion and new-found beliefs.

As is often the case with converts, passion and belief in the new discovery invariably send restraint and common sense straight out the window. No sooner had I come to grips with Browning than I would be reciting 'Oh To Be In England' or 'My Last Duchess' to startled and disbelieving shampoos and sets.

In love

Fifteen years later I still squirm with embarrassment when I recollect the excesses brought about by my meeting with O level literature. My only excuse is that starvation prompted gluttony. I'd passed the exam. I'd tested the water and found that I could at least paddle in it. But now I wanted to swim. I had fallen in love with studying. I still had a vague idea of becoming a teacher but what I really wanted most of all was the study itself. I loved learning and more than anything else in the world I wanted to be a student, a proper, all day long, seven days a week student. I wanted to be with other students, with people who were eager to soak up anything and everything. I wanted to be with open and questioning minds. Flushed with my success in O level literature, convinced that I'd proved my dedication and commitment to learning, I began the process of applying for a *Grant*.

Catch 22

I might have learnt a little about Browning and Shakespeare, but a double first with honours wouldn't have equipped me with skills necessary for filling in a Grant Application Form. You see, what I wanted to do was obtain a grant in order to go to a college for a year, in order to do 'O', and possibly 'A' levels. At Lancashire Education Office, in Preston, she said to me 'Well y' better fill the form in.'

'Erm, yes, er I have.'

'Oh. Well why are you here?'

'Well, because, y' see, the form that I filled in doesn't seem to allow for the sort of course I want to take, an' you sent it back.'

'What sort of course is that?'

'O and A level. For a year.'

'We don't give grants for that.'

'Why?'

'Well, people who take O level courses, like at sixth form colleges are younger than eighteen, aren't they? An' so they're supported by their parents.'

'Yeh, but I'm twenty. I'm gettin' married soon an' my parents can't support me.'

'Twenty? Twenty an' y' wanna take O levels . . . what for?'

'I just y' know . . . do.'

'Well y' should've took them at school shouldn't y'? We can consider a grant if you're takin' a degree course or teacher trainin'.'

'But I can't do that yet.'

'Why not?'

'I haven't got enough O levels.'

'Well y'll have to get them won't y'?'

'Well I would do, I want to, but you won't give me a bloody grant!'

'Don't you get abusive with me. It's not your God-given right to have a grant you know. Grants are discretionary.'

'I'm sorry, I just, I mean it's been months now an' I'm just like gettin' nowhere fast an' . . .'

Finally she told me I was in catch twenty-two. They only gave grants for designated courses, designated courses required minimum entry requirements of five 'O' levels. I didn't have the 'O' levels so could not get on a designated course. There were no designated O level courses and so I couldn't get a grant.

I left the offices and travelled home feeling deeply ashamed. I felt dirty. I had been made to feel like a beggar. Without the means to support myself whilst studying, and without the aid of a grant, I would not be able to become a student. I resigned myself, but determined to take at least one positive step—leave hairdressing. When I broke the news to my customers, they wept with joy.

I went to work at a warehouse in the Bear Brand factory—40 long and boring hours every week for £12. The conditions were as I have found them in any factory, anti-human. I remember that the windows were painted over so that we would not be distracted from our work by looking out at a tree

or the sky. That factory overlooking Woolton Golf Course
often put me in mind of some verse from Victorian England:

> The Mill is so near the Golf Links
> That almost every day
> Children look up from their work
> And see the men at play.

Bear Brand was a dump but at least it wasn't a trap in the
way that the hairdressing shop had been. I knew that I could
walk out of the factory at a moment's notice.

Whilst at Bear Brand I got married and moved from Kirkby
to Broadgreen. Somebody pointed out to me that as I now
came under the jurisdiction of Liverpool and not Lancashire
Education Authority, I could re-apply for a grant. I did. It was
Preston all over again. The only change was the accent.

'But we don't do grants for O Level courses—we don't do
them. An' anyway, y' should've done them at school. Schools
are for O Levels an' we don't give grants for goin' to school.'

I had to accept it, I was never going to get a grant. After
some hasty consultation with my wife, we established that if
we took in some lodgers, we'd be able to manage without me
earning for a year. I was assured that even if the authority
would not give me a grant, they would at least pay my college
fees. With that and the lodgers, I would be able to afford to
take a course.

I sat on one side of a table in a room in a Further Education
College in Liverpool, opposite me was the principal. I had not
said a word. He glanced up from my papers, dismissed them
and began 'And would you like to tell me why I should let you
come to this college? You wasted your time and your teachers'
time when you were at school. Quite simply son, if you think
you're going to waste my time and the time of my staff, you'd
better think again.'

Faced with such open hostility I fell to bits. To have
organized the whole financial situation and be faced with this
brick wall, left me reeling. I could not say a word in my own
defence. If I tried to speak I would, for the first time in ten
years or so, have cried with frustration and a sense of injustice.
I just got up and started to leave. I had to get away from him,
but he wouldn't let me alone. He followed me to the door and

shouted 'You want O levels, you do them the hard way sonny, do them at night school.'

Fighting for my life

I wanted to scream and to pin him against the wall and tell him that time was running out for me, that night school wouldn't be fast or intense enough for me. I wanted to tell him that I was now a different person from the kid at school. But I just ran. And as I ran the pain turned into anger, the frustration turned into purpose and the self pity turned into outrage. At the Education Office I said to her calmly 'I have nothing against you but I am fighting for my life, it is that important. And I want to talk to someone who will understand. Now. Please.'

She turned and went out of the door. A man appeared and without pause for breath I told him I would no longer be treated as a leper just because I'd been no good at school. I told him that I would not have my dignity stripped from me every time I tried to return to education. I told him I had a right to be helped by him and his department. I told him that I paid rates and national insurance, that I was a human being. I probably threw in The Gettysburg Address and 'Oh To Be In England' for good measure.

When I'd finished, he stared hard at me and very quietly said—'Get out!' I punched the wall. He was telling someone to 'phone the police, I was ripping down a small handbill which had been pinned to the wall I'd punched. I tried to hold it in front of his face and demanded to know why, when I'd asked and asked I'd not been told about this place mentioned on the hand bill. So many times I'd asked about colleges that ran the sort of course I was looking for and so many times I'd been told the only college was the one from which I'd just came. And there, on his wall was a college in Childwall advertising the very course I'd been seeking. I left before the arrival of the law, jumped a bus, found Childwall Hall County College, ran down the drive, found the secretary's office and said 'Please, I know I've got no appointment but, please can I see the Principal?'

The Vice Principal sat me down in an armchair, passed me a

cup of tea and just said talk. 'What about?' 'About yourself, what brought you here.'

Two hours later I walked out with the promise of a place in September.

I didn't have a sense of victory, a feeling that I'd won. I walked back down that drive with feelings only of gratitude and relief. I suddenly, and for the first time in my life, felt that I had a future.

In July, I was informed by the Education Authority that they would not pay my fees at college. But it didn't matter. I was determined to start college in September, determined to find the money to pay the fees, and I did. But, as they say, that's another story. . . .

Contents

Part I: Lives

Part II: Brief Lives: An Access Course

Part III: Themes and Conclusion

PART I

Lives

1

Introduction

This book is about people who go back into education in adult life. For the sake of brevity, I refer to them as 'returners'. Like Willy Russell, their schooling cheated most of them. Much later, to their astonishment, they discover abilities they never knew they possessed.

Returners are everywhere. One may just have serviced your washing machine, leaving to attend a seminar for his part-time degree course at polytechnic. Bored at the till, the woman who checked your groceries last Saturday morning may be another. My first book, *Invisible Children*, led me to meet several. They were good analysts of the shortcomings of schools. One impulse for this book was to talk to many more, so that I could build on my critique of schooling. State schools lack the power to do what they set out to do. This book explores that weakness in returners' testimony. My first book was about the profligate neglect of children teachers do not see. This book is about more comprehensive disservice, and rests on the premiss that—despite so-called reforms—schools are being weakened rather than strengthened. Each of the stories a returner tells here is being repeated, again and again, in schools today.

Returners begin to succeed when they meet optimism and interest from their teachers. I write about Kerry in *Invisible Children*. She left school with no qualifications. Teachers at school took no interest in her. Depressed, divorced, with a young child and no job, she went at the age of 24 to a college of further education after she saw an advertisement about classes in literacy and numeracy. Perhaps if she got some help with basic English and maths, she thought, she might be able to go for a better sort of job: her last had been as a telephonist.

First she met the vice-principal:

He was easy to talk to, and he listened. I could tell he was really interested in me, and not just doing his job. He got round to what subjects I liked. I said biology. He told me I had to do maths and English, but he said I ought to do another subject, so we decided on sociology. So he put me down for four O levels!

The vice-principal's ordinary interest made it possible to accept his mad suggestion. She passed those O levels, with very good grades. From the start, she warmed to her English teacher:

Instead of implying, I am a teacher, and I'm better than you, she said, I'm a bit scared because this is my first lesson. I want you to ask anything you need to find out; we'll get to know each other this lesson, and begin work next. Then she came over to talk to me. She put me at my ease.

She was full of admiration: I didn't quite know what I'd done that was so wonderful. Jan who taught me sociology was brilliant too. Again, she talked to me. She was a good friend all the way through, and Rosa, who was in charge of the mature students—she was really nice, she wanted to know about your home life and things like that.

The first day was so good I couldn't wait till the next.

Time and again, returners echo this account. Dubiously, they await the appearance of their first teacher, on the first day of their return. Some expect nothing worse than impatience. Others expect the teacher as terrorist, exploding their confidence, ambushing them with sarcasm. Others still expect boredom: a droning voice from the front. But nearly all expect distance. They expect a teacher not to be interested in them, not to want to know them.

When returners meet the opposite their education can begin. They tell this blunt but forgotten truth: teachers are very important. But teachers today are demoralized because they are being asked to do the impossible. As new responsibilities accumulate—many, in schools, associated with the National Curriculum—teachers have less and less time to know pupils as individuals, and make the sort of relationships that returners find so important. Policy at present ignores the importance of such relationships: the crux of good schooling. A child reluctant to be educated—as many returners were—needs to be surrounded by the unanimous optimism of her teachers. Such unanimity is very powerful. But teachers are not encouraged to become powerful 'parents', but assessment technicians, penurious box-tickers.

This book seeks also to disclose what return can mean to those who risk it.

Roger joined an Access course as a washing-machine engineer, and will leave polytechnic with a degree in micro-electronics. But his education—of which he was cheated in the 1960s—has meant much more to him than this metamorphosis begins to suggest. Return has a rich variety of meaning for those concerned. This book sets out to discover that variety; to disclose some of the significance of an extraordinary experience. Its emphasis is more upon travel than arrival; more on the journey towards higher education than on what returners find when they get there. However, what returners—particularly in Part II—say about their learning in adulthood will be of interest to those who want to improve provision for mature students.

What returners say can refresh our sense of the importance of education; and of what it means for a civilized society to make education a right—the accessibility of which in adulthood is still in this country as random and inconsistent and inequitable as our system of schooling.[1]

The returners I have met widened the focus of this book to include much more than education. They showed me some of the mystery of biography: its odd latencies; the way intellect gets to work on difficult experience; the way a mind can take hold of a life and revise its deepest assumptions; the enigma of a mentor's arrival in the nick of time. These revelations were important: if our education system—especially our schools—does not take more account of the unruliness of biography, it will continue to fail too many people.

I carried out long taped interviews, sometimes meeting a returner on several occasions, and talking as well to other

---

[1] Note, for instance, the difference between accessibility for many city-dwellers, and for people living without means of transport in isolated villages.

members of his or her family. I quote at great length from transcripts in Part I; and thereafter more briefly. The five accounts in Part I offer the rich detail of return in five lives; the nine in Part II are snapshots of those on a recent Access course: increasingly the common means of return to unqualified adults. I have no reason to think those nine untypical. In Part III I look at two matters often associated with mature students: first, in what ways experience makes mature students' learning distinct; second, the strains return can put upon marriage. Gradually, throughout the book, I develop an argument about schools, which builds on the case I developed in my first book. This argument features most prominently in Chapters 5, 7, 10, and 13.

Though I hope it will be of interest to specialists, what follows is not a contribution to the academic literature of adult education. Those I write about here do not amount to a 'sample'. Their biographies I found of great intrinsic interest; but my main reason for choosing them is that they exemplify themes and patterns in the experience of the eighty returners I have talked to at length.

The important debate about education is a lay debate to which returners richly contribute. Their knowledge of education makes their arguments cogent, because they have two separate sorts of experience to compare: schooling that cheated them; and triumphant return. They know so much about what assists learning and what does not; about teaching that destroys and teaching that enables; why schooling fails so many working-class children and so many girls; what adults need from their teachers.

The currency of this book is what people say about themselves. Each account quoted here is a mixture of recollection and argument. Some memories are suddenly recalled, a fact jumping out of a brain cell as fresh as when it was stored. Others do duty in a uniformed polemic. Each account mixes the specific and the general: a handkerchief stuffed up a knicker-leg, and a grandiloquent claim such as 'you never learn anything at school, do you?' My interest has been in all that I have been told—in plump facts, polemical assertions, rhetorical flourishes, memories posed as if for a photograph, and others put up in the dock to bear witness against a school, a teacher, a parent; against patriarchy or another 'system'.

From time to time, another voice joins a returner: a daughter adds to her mother's testimony; a wife offers an ironic postscript to a particular memory offered by her husband. Occasionally, but not often, I recall my own experience, as pupil, student, teacher.

2

Peter: The Search for the Abbé

Peter had to wait until his late forties before beginning to satisfy his need to be properly educated. He is now a graduate of the Open University. He was born into a working-class family in a Midlands city in 1929.

At the time of our first meeting, Peter lived with his second wife in south London. He asked me in as if we had met before—as if he could easily accommodate novelty, new people, new experiences; and this first impression was accurate: he is restlessly curious.

There are physical clues to this vigour. He is strongly built, but agile: moves impulsively and quickly. To emphasize a point he will sometimes turn to look at you, very directly. He used to do judo at an advanced level.

We talked in a comfortable room upstairs. My notes say:

Bookshelves, full of all sorts. Penguins. Art—Russian Art, big book on Manet, one called the Impressionists . . . Peter talks quietly and then something catches fire—catches his mind or his humour—and his voice is louder, smile vivid.

His schooling began in 1934.

I can go back till I was about 3. I went to a little nursery school then—I remember wetting my pants there. My mum used to take me through these big iron gates—that was my introduction to schooling.

Then I went to an infants' school when we moved to another part of town, and we had to go to church, and it was high church—with incense—and everybody dressed up, and I remember going home and telling mum that I'd seen God and he was cooking his dinner.

I don't remember learning anything at that school.

I went to junior school when I was about 6. I was always chattering. The teacher would creep up behind me and try to catch me. I remember having a fight in the school playground.

I didn't learn anything—I can't remember learning anything: you don't in school, do you? No, there was never anything I could really say I learnt.

Then I went to Stenning School, junior school. I liked the head, Mrs Cawthorn, she was friendly, she always tucked her handkerchief up her knicker-leg. Very discreetly. Most of the teachers were friendly, except for Miss Gunn: she was too stern. They never used to push you—it was a nice relaxed sort of place.

But no, I can't remember learning anything—I think I went there for a good time: I used to chase the girls. I don't think there was any priority in learning.

Peter ended up in an elementary school, after taking a test to see if he could go to a technical school—which he failed. His memory of the test gives a foretaste of the frustrations of many who took the 11 plus after the war and were mystified by some of the general knowledge questions:

One question was, what is a lover's knot? And I didn't know what it was—nobody had ever told me. I wasn't really interested in anything like that.

You just sat down and they put a paper in front of you. They never explained what you had to do with this paper, you just saw this paper and then you filled it in with all your rubbish. Well, it was obvious you weren't going to pass anyway. Just two in the class got through, and they were teachers' pets. You know what your chances are when you're in a school like that and you're working class and your father works in a factory. Your chances are nil.

I asked him what was expected of him at his elementary school:

Nothing. They just went through the routine, so that we'd finish at 14 so they could chuck us out. It was just a routine. Nothing was expected of me. We were being processed, like sausages. All they had to do was pump the three Rs into us

and just a little bit of the arts, just a little bit. I look on it now
as a complete waste of time.

Meanwhile at school he was held within certain rigid social
constraints:

> You had to be one of the boys, there was this inverse
> snobbery, nobody liked clever sods, they were teachers' pets,
> those sort of people: they were despised.
>   But school taught me to read very well, spell very well.
> Simple things, your basic skills, we learnt very well. Tables,
> we learnt very well, you remember them all your life, and
> it's very important.

What he criticizes is the assumption that he was to be doled a
certain amount, but no more; a few skills, but no intellectual
development.[1]

Penny Spitfire, Aunt Liz, and the Count of Monte Cristo

But there were good things in Peter's last school. Penny
Spitfire was the best.

> We called her that because if you sat in the front row she
> sprayed you. She was marvellous for Shakespeare. We did
> *Macbeth*. We did the play and she also read a lot to us.

She was not the only one who read to him. There was also
Guts Gresham, one of the retired teachers brought back during
the war.

> He used to ride to work on a bike. He used to teach my
> mother: he was an old feller, and he used to have punctures
> nearly every day. He used to say to one of the boys, go and

---

[1] While working on this book I have often talked about its subject in
chance meetings. While I was working on the first draft of this chapter, we
were having some tiles put up in our bathroom. The tiler, Derek, was, I should
say, 29 or 30. We talked a lot—he told me about his schooling in the 1970s: 'In
maths every new teacher would start again at the beginning. When I was doing
my apprenticeship as a plasterer, I went to Birmingham, and we had to know
about logarithms. I hadn't heard about logarithms. English was a joke—all the
teacher did was read us stories. We didn't even have good stories, no
Shakespeare, we never did poetry.'

ask cook if there's anything to eat: the kids used to scrounge
grub for him: he was a complete scrounger.

His attitude to learning was beautiful. He used to sit back
and read to you if he could be bothered. If he couldn't be
bothered, he'd say, get your books out and read. But when
he did bother he used to read to you and he read beautifully.

This scholar's approach typifies the mixture of routine and
haphazard in Peter's early education. Mr Gresham's occasional
early readings and Penny Spitfire were both happy accidents:
they were not what Peter's schooling aspired to, but exceptions.

And Penny asked nothing in return. *Macbeth* was sprayed at
Peter from the front of the class. He listened—and was excited;
but he did not take part: there was no expressing of opinion.
Peter was not asked to say or write what he thought of the
play, except in the most perfunctory manner. Though at least
introduced, unlike in the tiler's day, Shakespeare was spectacle,
except for a little acting of a scene or two. But that was like
mumming on a float in a pageant.

I had no objective, no aim, no purpose.

I was never *taught*. Nobody really latched on to me, and
said, *you must learn this*. I never had one piece of homework
in all my schooldays, never one piece to go home with that I
had to do.

He looks with regret at the very different nature of modern
schools. What strikes him as most enviable is the chance to
express yourself. His words begin an argument that develops
through successive accounts in this book: about the difference
between education and something much more like *training*. A
dumb pupil is easier to instruct.

I think they have more freedom. They have access to
libraries. They can do individual study, freedom is greater,
we didn't have freedom. Freedom of expression. When you
go into schools now the first thing that impresses you is the
art on the walls.

I went into this junior school a little while ago to see a
play, and there was all this art on the walls—all free
expression. Everything's different, nothing's the same, and

everybody's got a different mind, a different way of looking at things.

After we had been talking about his schooling I asked him what he thought of it now. I had pressed him to talk more about his lessons; what they had been like; how his teachers had taught him the three Rs. But he could not or would not remember. I suspect a mixture of involuntary and willed oblivion. Much of his schooling was so dull it was unmemorable. Why should he give space in his brain to recalling the detail of an education that was so limited? He remembers Penny Spitfire instead. But that memory is sad. She was as constrained as he was. Gradgrind haunted her timetable. Poetry was inessential: sanctioned, perhaps, as a small subliminal addition to social control: you shall hear the words of the poets; be awed by what you hear, but be silent as you listen.

Penny Spitfire was in her own way a subversive. I suspect that she would have enjoyed teaching in a good comprehensive.

I see my schooling now as a complete waste of time. The only thing that really got me interested in education—you might not believe this but it's absolutely true—was my Aunt Liz. She was quite an intelligent person and she always used to buy me books. I was an avid reader. I remember reading the paper before I was 5. I used to read way into the middle of the night.

She was about five foot ten, and she had great big owl-like spectacles. Her eyes were very bad, she had thick lenses like mine. She was a spinster. She was going to marry this Scotsman, McTavish or somebody, and she was going to have me as a page with a kilt on. I wasn't very keen on that. Anyway something happened, and that plan flopped. I never actually saw him—he might have been a figment of her imagination.

She was nice, she was very strict, she wouldn't brook any nonsense. You'd go up with a cut finger—look, I've cut my finger, auntie—but she wouldn't take any notice. She wouldn't have anything to do with any old nonsense from kids. She told you you'd got to behave yourself.

She was an educationist, she was an intelligent woman.

She was a mental nurse—and reading was very important to her. She always used to buy me books and try to encourage me; always at Christmas there'd be books—and any other chance she could take. And though she probably sounds strict, she used to treat me as a person, and that was unusual: she explained things—she'd go out of her way to take me up Masons Lane to see the squirrels, to show me things.

That's what education is all about—to make people interested. They find out for themselves then.

It seemed as though Aunt Liz was either reading or working. She kept all my grandfather's books, the very old Victorian books. And she seemed to know all about the right books for me, the interesting kids' books that I should read.

She used to teach me the social graces too. She used to take me down town to the Cadena on Saturday morning. I used to have a glass of milk and some chocolate éclairs, and I used to have to sit up and behave myself properly. That was all part of the education process as far as she was concerned. It was good, I used to love it. She was the one who always talked to me as an equal.

She used to scatter around the country a lot because she was always getting fired. She always spoke her mind. She missed her opportunity too, I think. She was very ill as a child, she didn't get much of an education: she taught herself with books, and she was trying to pass it on to me.

It was probably Aunt Liz who put the *Count of Monte Cristo* under my feet. She had the knack of doing this to me. I had the knack of finding these books in the library, so I might have just picked it off the shelf.

I probably read it half a dozen times. You read them and re-read them: they impress themselves on you. I first read it in my early teens, maybe just before leaving school.

It was that book that made me realize that I was ignorant, and that I needn't be ignorant. That book changed my whole life.

It really kicked me off. This chap gets slung into prison, because someone else fancies his girlfriend, and he's in this island fortress, in a dungeon, and he digs a hole to the next place, and there's an old abbé there, he's an ancient man— very highly educated—he digs through to him.

And the old man teaches him all he knows.

Now this is a marvellous thing, a beautiful thing: he's getting a terrific education; just him. I always dreamed that perhaps I might meet one man who would tell me everything. It still fits—to me—now.

I left school at 14.

I went to work straightaway as an electrician's mate. That world was absolutely useless, it was nothing to do with real life.

But I tried evening classes pretty soon.

I started off all right. I was starting to feel I was getting more individual attention because there weren't many in the class. I was starting to learn mathematics. Then I was moved up a class, and it was too advanced for me and I stopped.

I went because I wanted to learn and I wanted a piece of paper. I didn't know what sort—I just wanted to learn.

I used to read books and I'd see a word, and I didn't understand what it meant. Quite often I missed the point because I didn't know what the words were. And I thought—I'm completely ignorant, I don't know anything.

The next stage was in the Navy. I was a boy seaman, on a heavy cruiser, and the days are long and the evenings are long on a ship like that. I grabbed hold of a book—a mathematics book, and I thought, this is good—a home instruction book about mathematics. So every evening I sat down and went through the exercises, and I thought—I'm getting to learn this terrific thing—mathematics! At last I'm learning mathematics.

And I got to the middle of the book.

Somebody had pulled out the middle of the book, hadn't they. So I lost it then.

I was in the navy 22 months.

The day I came out, I went down town and to W. H. Smith's and bought a poetry book. I've still got it now. It was Penny Spitfire who interested me in poetry, and it lasted. It was the pattern of words that interested me.

I've got a terrific urge within me to do these things. Years later for instance I took a job and somebody said you've got to use a typewriter, and I was making an awful fool of myself with two fingers, and this bloke said get out of the way, I'll do it, so I said—right mate; and I went to the boss and I said I want some money to learn to type. Right, he said, you can have some. So I signed on for typing, and I sat in among 20 girls and I learned to touch-type.

After the navy? I got married when I was 21. Then I went to Australia in the mid-fifties, doing the job I'm doing now. I didn't do any learning out there. We came back, and I worked in a car factory for a while, then we moved out of town, and I did the job where I learnt typing.

There was a man there who could speak German and tell just the one joke in it—so I thought, I'll learn some German. I went to evening classes and learnt German.

Then I got interested in a Swiss who was teaching mathematics based on 11s not 10s. It seemed a terrific idea and I went through all that and it seemed pretty good.

Then I saw an advert that still appears—Dr Bruno Furst, memory training—which interested me because I've got a terrible memory. I went through that course and did quite well—and then forgot all about it.

Next thing was the TUC were offering courses and I did one on economics and that was quite good, eventually I bought a book on it, I got fascinated by it.

Peter was 47 when a friend said to him when they were driving somewhere together in his car: 'why don't you join the Open University?'

Family life was demanding—one of his children, for instance, was handicapped; and his work was hard: long hours, a great deal of overtime, and none of the stimulation he craved and tried to find in his classes and courses. But what he was learning did not yet fit together; there was no sense of sequence; of being taken somewhere important.

Peter's aim was higher education. At the stage where I have left him he would probably not have been able to voice that aspiration though he seemed instinctively to have known that his intellect would be starved till he fulfilled it. But the door had slammed at 14 before he had learned anything deeply and thoroughly at that level. So he did not know how to force the early stages of German to take him quickly to the level he wanted. And economics was fascinating; but it was just

economics—there was not much individual attention, or
training in how to write, what sort of questions to ask, how to
formulate an argument.

Nor did he realize that learning sometimes has to be arduous;
disciplined.

> I didn't realize that learning's a discipline. It wasn't until I got
> to the OU that I realized that you'd really got to work. I
> didn't work at night school—I just thought you listened to
> someone, and you knew.
>
> There was no structure I could follow. Nobody told me
> how I could improve myself. I was groping, grasping all the
> time. I wanted to be educated, really, underneath it all—
> really. I wanted to know more. I felt so ignorant.

The abbé, though inspiring, was perhaps a bit misleading as
well.

It would be rash to suppose that Peter's search, before the
Open University, was sparked only by his aunt, Penny
Spitfire, and Alexandre Dumas. All the returners I have talked
to have been partly spurred by dissatisfaction. It is possible
that, for Peter, the Open University was not only the end of
his 'search'—the abbé embodied in an institution—it was also a
way of managing unhappiness at home. When he got home
from work, he had to study: he could fence himself off from
unhappiness. His first marriage was nearing its end. He has
chosen not to talk in detail about his predicament; but he and
his wife were becoming steadily more estranged.

But for Peter there was also the slog of boring work made
more intolerable by his mind's craving for stimulation. Books
and his aunt and the abbé had let him glimpse what he could
not yet attain. He was like Alice, at the garden gate, but unable
to get in. Class had locked out this seeker after truth. And he
knew that the world in which he had to toil was in some sense
false: 'that world was absolutely useless, that world was
nothing to do with real life'.

Pride too gave him dissatisfaction. For a while as a young
man he worked as an electrician on the staff of an Oxbridge
college.

> We worked in undergraduates' rooms and I saw what I had

missed. I saw that these people were different to me—there was no way I could be one of them. I was the under-privileged; I didn't like being one of the underprivileged, and I didn't think there ought to be that difference between us.

It really annoyed me to think that people had more of a chance in life than me. It was even more pronounced in those days. You know the college servants? You have a staircase and you have one servant looking after a few under-graduates. Well—it's not a very nice subject, but they used to have pots, and these undergraduates used to fill these pots, and sometimes they wouldn't even bother to go to the toilet for the other thing and they would leave it in the pot for the servant to empty.

That's real degradation isn't it—and I saw it. No wonder people turned Marxist. I'm not a Marxist but I have quite a lot of thoughts that way. It's just like rubbing a man's nose in the dirt, and a man could say nothing, it was his job and he was paid to do it.

Before the Open University, his search became more focused.

I wrote off for the Open University, and before I knew where I was, I was going for it.

Then I thought—oh dear, I don't know anything about learning, so I'd better go to night school and start learning something difficult—so I signed on for A level English—which was pretty ambitious, because I was ignorant, I'd learned nothing. I was an outcast.

So I got involved in English literature. He was a terrible teacher, he didn't teach me how to pass examinations. He told us a lot about different authors, and then he asked us to write essays, and I thought, this is good, I'm learning to write essays. But I didn't have a clue—though I did get interested in writing. In fact I wrote an essay explaining why Tess of the Durbervilles was seduced. I worked it all out—it's all written in allegory, the seduction in the garden. I got interested, very fascinated. He accepted it, but said no more.

I think it was back to the old process: we were sausages, he was getting his overtime, his perks. He sat there for two hours pumping literature into us. He talked a lot about the books. He did most of the talking. He did talk agreeably: he passed his enthusiasm on. But he didn't tell us how to pass exams. I sat in the examination room and made a complete fool of myself. I saw this paper—and it was completely foreign to me. I wrote a load of rubbish, I know now, and of course it was a flop.

I suspected—and Peter agreed—that he had wanted this teacher to become his abbé. His long essay on *Tess* was a ritual gift, for which he wanted acknowledgement that honoured his serious-ness.

But his teacher did not see the meaning of what was offered him. No doubt the essay was impulsive, disorganized; no doubt Peter did not manage to say what he wanted to say. But his essay was an offering—and it was not accepted.

He moved to another class. But this time he found a teacher who took an interest in him. She was almost an abbess:

She was a different kettle of fish altogether, a good teacher, a lovely woman, interested in me. She was interested in me as a person. When I was accepted by the OU and I said, I've got to stop, because I didn't see how I could do A level and the OU, with my limited capabilities, especially since I had a family—she wrote to me a couple of times and said the examinations are coming up, please take them.

She took the trouble to explain things.

That's what teaching's all about: you've got to get through to a person that you are personally interested in them—it was the first experience I'd had of that sort of interest.

Adult Learners: Peter's Experience

Distinguishing adults as learners from adolescents and children is their capacity to command and execute their own learning. I have mentioned the randomness of Peter's learning, which suggests that he was far from attaining such command before the OU. But Peter did by that time possess an immense capacity for 'self-directedness'[2] in learning which *had yet to be*

[2] See especially chs. 3 and 4 of Stephen D. Brookfield, *Understanding and Facilitating Adult Learning* (Open University Press, 1986), for a scholarly account of this concept of 'self-directedness'.

tapped for intellectual work, though it had been used in other parts of his life. He had 'directed' and carried out his responsibilities as a father, for instance, learning as he did so. He had monitored the complex electrics of the part of each industrial plant for which he'd been responsible. Presented with a new factory *he* would have 'directed' his own steadily developing command of his new responsibility. Experience had taught him that he could, unaided, achieve certain aims in those parts of his life in which he was independent.

But intellectual work was different. What he had learned he could do as an electrician and at home seemed, to begin with, to have no relevance to his higher education. His 'why' was clear: he burned with the zealous motivation teachers yearn to find in their pupils. But as far as means were concerned, he was far from confident, and lacked knowledge. He has admitted himself, as we have seen, that he 'thought you listened to someone and you knew . . .'.

His good experiences of 'learning' at school had been chiefly passive: Mr Gresham one day deciding to read to his class; Penny Spitfire indiscriminately spraying her love of poetry.

His dream of the abbé was prescient and accurate as a statement of what he needed *before* he could call on his capacity for 'self-directedness' in the fifteen hours of solitary labour he had to put in each week for the Open University. He needed one good experience of learning at the necessary level to acquire an approach he could transfer to all subsequent learning. But what the dream of the abbé suggests, above all, is that he needed a close relationship with a teacher as well.

Like many adults—nearly all of those I have interviewed—he had little confidence in his ability when he began.

> I never used to think I was intelligent. I never used to kid myself I was bright. I think I used to think quite the reverse, I used to think I was stupid at times.

In his need for intellectual confidence, he was 14. In my book *Invisible Children* I write about adolescents who never gain that confidence because they never gain the interest and what I call the 'acknowledgement' of their teachers. Peter now needed that acknowledgement. The abbé—above all—would take a special interest in him. The key to the dream is that the abbé would be teaching him and him only. This phantasy does not indicate solipsistic greed; it is a declaration of what Peter had never had: a relationship with a teacher who thought highly of him, who liked him, honoured his seriousness, and wanted the best for him. Thought unworthy of a life of the mind, he had been cheated of the intellectual apprenticeship an academic pupil enjoys, sooner or later, with one or more of his teachers.

But the accuracy of his dream goes further. Learning at school, and afterwards until the second A level teacher, had not provided such a relationship, nor the activity and energy that it generates. Learning had been passive. He was one of many listening; one of a class doing exercises in a repetitive way scarcely distinguishable from passivity. Nor did he talk, argue, discuss, ask questions.

The acknowledging teacher and her pupil—above all—talk to each other.

Peter, then, needed three things:

- To be given an approach to learning. Much of what he needed in this connection was technical: to do with note-taking, writing, ways of thinking.
- To be liked and honoured and taken seriously as a seeker after truth.
- To be energetically, actively engaged in learning: to talk to a teacher and to other learners.

When they take the first step to 'return', many adults feel on foreign ground. If the ground begins to feel familiar, it may be because it reminds them of school—an unhelpful memory, because school may well have failed them. Peter needed to feel that he belonged; this his claim to the right to a decent education was not a fraudulent one.

Once he had mastered a patch of his new territory, he would be able to explore the rest independently, and with growing confidence. He would still need to talk and to be encouraged; but he would no longer have the same deep need for acknowledgement.

That need was satisfied by an abbess: Sarah, Peter's first tutor-counsellor—an ex-student of the Open University herself.

There was excitement from the start:

The OU was another world. It was as if you suddenly stood on your feet; you had grown up, and you are treated as a person, a very individual person.

Sarah was my tutor and counsellor. It was marvellous to have an individual person knocking hell out of me, and then being nice to me, you know. Severe criticism, and boosting you up at the same time.

What was she criticizing? My sloppy methods, my bad grammar. And I had terrific problems initially because I couldn't write essays—I didn't know how to write essays, and the marking was pretty severe. There was my misuse of words; my inability to make a proper sentence at times, let alone a paragraph. She just kept my nose above water. I was a drowning man—I had a lot of learning to do. It required a lot of skill and determination on her part to keep me going.

Yes, she had a lot of sharpening up to do. There must have been improvements in standards throughout that year, but I despaired quite a lot of times. It wasn't easy for me at any time. I saw other people and they seemed to be able to manage it quite easily. Clever sods. They'd had a better education than me. They seemed to be coping quite well, and I was always struggling for hours on end trying to write these essays, and family life was tough. My wife was antagonistic—well, completely anti.

So I used to get stick from that, and stick from Sarah, and stick from the work itself.

She stuck with me, and pushed me through it, and I passed the first examination—the first examination I'd ever passed.

How did she do it? She offered me friendship. I would consider Sarah one of the best friends I ever had. She took a lot of interest in me—she was a very dear friend. Although she was very critical—she set high standards, and I accepted that.

She was a mentor, she gave me enthusiasm, she kept pushing me on, she willed me to get through. There were many times when I wanted to drop out, and I thought—I can't do this! I'll chuck it. But there was her driving force, and also a bit of stubbornness that kept me going.

It was very hard. I had to do a day's work and then fit in the study in the evenings. Sometimes when I was very tired.

I was working in the car factory. Well: very, very tired. Sometimes exhausted. I was doing the night shift too sometimes. Very difficult. Very, very difficult. I would try and shut myself up in a room or in the kitchen, and try to study. There'd be the television blaring out, and the family coming in and out, and my wife, who saw it as a threat to the marriage. I don't know how I did it really.

But Sarah's coaching helped me. Her comments were always on the margin: you should have done this, you should have said that—or: I don't agree with you;—and the marking of misspellings. She was very forthright, but she praised me, she gave me encouragement too. That's a fine balance—you can mark somebody into the ground if you want to; but what she had to do was elevate my nose above the water as well!

So Sarah 'acknowledged' Peter. She offered him a rich, complex partnership: encouragement and criticism; praise and hectoring; excitement and disappointment.

Peter's reactions had a similarly wide range:

I sometimes resented her critical comments like mad! I used to hate it, and say some awful things about her. When you get your stuff back, after you've spent hours of work, and you think this is the real stuff now, and you come back with a terrible C and a D—Christ, you can kill them. But you get inspiration—a word comes from somewhere else, don't give up, give it another whirl. And that's how you go—from high to low, low to high.

But yes, she'd praise me, she was a lovely teacher.

She always used to say to me, remember the swallows— this was one of the things between us. I had to explain something in inductive logic, and I thought of swallows, and came up with a statement like: 'If the swallows are flying high in the sky it's going to be a fine day tomorrow.' It seemed to tickle her fancy—she liked it. She seemed to use it quite a lot; in fact if she wrote to me tomorrow she would probably mention swallows. It was sort of a bridge between us.

But the thing about the OU is that for the first time you're able to say something. You see, I'd always been taught didactically: the teacher sits behind a desk and you can never really tell him what you think. But in the OU you can contribute. We used to meet Sarah once a week and she would iron out any particular problems we had to go through, and she would also talk individually to you. And I talked to her over the phone—if I had problems I could ring her up. I had lots—loads.

You talk—she talks—everyone talks, everyone can say. You have general discussions, you make a fool of yourself. To start with I wasn't one of the persons who talk in groups, or argue—I was one of your silent pupils. But gradually I got very forthright, very involved in arguments. It brought me out. And when you go to summer school! You have a week of intense learning, and everybody's full to the brim with it, we're all chatting till about three o'clock in the morning, and boozing up in the kitchen. Marvellous stuff. And you're over the top with all this knowledge.

What things interested me most in the foundation year? Oh, everything—art, literature, architecture, poetry—oh, goodness me, science, everything. It's like Aladdin's cave—complete enlightenment. It's like a world that's opened up to you. This is what I wanted. It goes back to the *Count of Monte Cristo*. Eventually you get your old abbé, and he's giving you all his knowledge. It's a marvellous experience.

Not only does Peter find 'acknowledgement', but his silence is broken as well. From his late teens to his late forties, he had been walking into class after class looking for his abbé. He sat, and he listened—because that is how he thought he should learn; that was the idea of learning his school had bequeathed him. Until he discovered that speaking[3] was just as important, he was unenfranchised. To speak was to begin to enjoy the

---

[3] For further discussion of the importance of talk in learning, I would suggest M. J. Abercrombie, *The Anatomy of Judgement* (Pelican, 1969). It is a fascinating account of an experimental use of discussion-learning to improve the ability of medical students to diagnose. An enduring classic. And in M. J. Abercrombie and P. M. Terry, *Talking to Learn* (SRHE, 1978), the implication is that speech, particularly in small 'syndicate' groups, assists autonomy. When the student learns to utter, she claims validity for her own thoughts; learns to trust them; to rely on her own intellectual fertility.

right to make ideas and knowledge his own: was to belong, to be an insider.

His commentary offers a gloss on his earlier emphasis on the importance of 'self-expression'. He emphasizes his tutor's strict standards, her rigorous expectations. He wanted—yes—to express himself. He wanted the freedom to state what he thought; but not uncritically and uncriticized. He implies a notion of the learner as initiate. So that when he looks with regret at the possibilities of self-expression in modern schools, I take him to mean freedom within the liberating constraint of a close relationship between learner and teacher. But the teacher's authority breaks down if he does not allow his student to speak, and fails to acknowledge what he has to say. The teacher's authority must be founded in reciprocal respect.

In his first year, then, all three of Peter's needs were met, and he could 'direct himself' through the next five years—coping even with the 'swine of a tutor' he had in the third year:

He was vicious, he was really tough: he gave me fails. He would make very abrupt severe comments. No tact, no encouraging comments. Sometimes he'd say—good. Then he'd really hammer you. I don't think he realizes how fine a line you walk on when you do the OU: it's a tightrope; all the time you're walking gingerly along.

But when we met on summer school, he turned out to be quite a decent fellow: we spent all one night in a kitchen boozing it up—he was sitting on the floor, he was quite a decent chap really.

In his sixth year, he graduated. There are photographs in their sitting room of him and his second wife on graduation day.

We shall hear more from Peter. But now I want to compare his account with Eleanor's.

3

Eleanor: A Place at the Feast

Eleanor lives in a terraced house in a town in the south-east which I shall call Stembury.

As soon as I had met her I felt as if I were talking to someone who was used to running things; who would be able to make a quick, clear decision. She seemed charged with energy; confident that her intelligence would lead her smartly to the essentials of anything we might discuss. Her company was invigorating. It was impossible to imagine that this authoritative and gifted woman had been cheated of higher education until her forties.

She led me into her work-room on the ground floor, where we sat at a table on which stood a typewriter and a scatter of papers. She was writing a report on a year's research she had carried out for a well-known charity.

My notes say:

> She has a vociferous midget dog: a canine burglar alarm. Just ignore him, said Eleanor.
> When she talks her face is very expressive; shows her conviction—and contentment: I felt that recent developments in her life had given her enormous pleasure.

I found our first meeting exhilarating. I had been excited by what she had told me about her return; and made welcome. Her house seemed furnished with affection and strong feeling.

She shared her house with three of her four children.

> I get enormous joy out of my children and my relationship with them. I loved having them, and absolutely loving them to smithereens.

She had gained her university degree—a 2:1 in psychology—a year before we met. She and her husband had parted during the time of her return. Their estrangement, and the agony of it, she chose not to discuss in detail—except to admit its importance, to offer it as an unelaborated accompaniment to her account.

Her life, when she began her return, was in crisis. With four children, she was working at several ill-paid part-time jobs, and in a predicament shared by many returners before they take the first step. She felt trapped, desperate, depressed, frustrated. But despite the loud and treacherous voices of doubts and fears, she also sensed that she had the solution to her predicament within herself, if she could but find it. We will see what prompted her to choose education.

The Feast

Before going back to an earlier phase of her life, I want to compare Eleanor's first reactions to what she studied with Peter's experience of the OU. Like Peter, she quickly became absorbed—despite money difficulties, her work at home, the need to stitch together an income from poorly paid bits and pieces: a job as a playground attendant, for instance; and despite the familiar problem of finding time in a day without any to spare. Hardest of all was to speak up against the voices that insisted that a mother should be dedicating herself to her children's education, not her own; that her bid for fulfilment was selfish. Though:

> The hunger for personal identification, to be admitted to some region where I could just be myself, had got so strong that I was prepared to stand up and say, this I need and I must have.

A tutor at the college of education she attended met her guilt on its own ground the first time they talked about what Eleanor should study:

> He said why don't you come here and study maths and English at O level, because that will give you a basis to go on, and then you can do A levels, then you can go to university. And I sat there and chuckled—but I can remember saying to him, and meaning it most sincerely— thank you, Mr Pritchard, for not making me feel ridiculous!

That was the feeling I had to overcome: I was over 40 with four children—and really! How ridiculous!

You feel you should be helping your children, sitting at home and helping them; but he said, how far are you able to help your daughter in the sixth form with her physics?

And of course I couldn't! Her maths—a mystery!

But her guilt could not be trounced quite so smartly. A recurring theme in the accounts of the women I have talked to is the pain of what feels like disobedience when they try to dust off gifts and hopes they have forgotten for so long, or never knew they possessed. Eleanor went on feeling guilty.

But I tackled English and maths at O level as he suggested.

Getting back to studying maths was so absorbing. There were old friends—but whole new concepts: set theory, matrices, trigonometry! Just the word was enough to scare the ears off me—but once it was demystified, it was marvellous! You could plot the course of a vessel at sea when you got down to the application of it.

It is stirring to listen again to the tape of Eleanor talking about this stage of her story, because her voice sounds excited as she describes her excitement. Writing about her, I constantly feel the need for strong words: perhaps exaltation would be a better one than excitement: she sounds as if all her life she had wanted to be able to plot the course of a vessel at sea.

There was calculus. The teacher was wonderful: I said, this is interesting, but I don't know that I really understand it; and he said, I'm never sure whether I do either—and he gave me this book to read—and the writer's English was so beautiful: he used language perfectly to write about calculus.[1]

There were tears—nearly all to do with algebra. My husband had had a very good education and he helped me with that. The problems came when I started to do well in areas he knew nothing about.

I think I've had enormous problems about pleasing people. My parents would never have been able to see the value of

[1] Sylvanus P. Thompson, *Calculus Made Easy* (Macmillan, 1978).

learning about things like vectors and algebra, because what use would they be to you? So I've had to find my own path to the sheer joy of apparently useless things, and not feel dead guilty about it.

The maths teacher was wonderful. He found me quite threatening at first; but as with most teachers, I found that once he had realized that I wasn't a smart-arse, but was hungering and thirsting for what he had to offer, he was wonderful.

On one occasion I said I didn't know whether I could go on—I was having a very bad day—and he said in such a matter of fact and undramatic way, well, if you give up, we might as well all go home.

I had enormous self-doubt, about my right to be doing it. And I had consciously to resist attributing everything that went wrong at home to what I was doing. It was actually consciously having to resist being undermined; especially by ideas of what a woman with four children should be doing with her life.

Her English teacher quickly decided that it was absurd for Eleanor to do English O level; and she was persuaded to go straight into an A level course.

That course was just mind-expanding and marvellous, and the two teachers were so good. I had Jenny for poets, Shakespeare, and some novels, and David for Chaucer.

The first lesson I walked into of Jenny's was a bit of a hubbub. The building itself is pretty unattractive, no velvet, or wood, or lovely things to stroke: it's all plastic and concrete.

And it was an ugly room with formica-topped tables. The people were of mixed ages, with a couple of older women. The very first thing Jenny did was hand round photocopies of a poem, and she said read that and put down whatever comes into your mind.

And it just blasted me completely—it was one of Wilfred Owen's poems. Will it embarrass you if I get emotional? I can't remember which one it was—there was mud and a church—I can't remember. And I was so keyed up—and I just read this thing and I was blasted. I'm not so bad now, but I used to be pathologically self-conscious, and I sat there just streaming with tears, and wrote.

To my absolute horror she came round and said what have you written? I started to read it out—but I just had to stop, and I looked up at her, and there was a sort of meeting, and it was all right, all right!

And for me that was a turning-point, because someone was saying to me, it's okay to feel strongly; but what she was soon saying to me was you've got to learn how to use it. And she did. She taught me—discipline, I suppose is the word. I think my essays over the two years did develop into being controlled. I learnt that you can actually feel intensely about something, but if you want to share it with anyone, you can do it in disciplined ways. You can operate at different levels, and be intellectually organized as well as reacting emotionally.

And then Chaucer with David! I'll always thank him—it was a beautiful experience. His approach was to get you to relax and just let the text work upon you, and then start to think about what it's doing to you and how it's doing it. It was completely different from university which was—you know—seek the reference, rush to the library; which was anathema to me. It was such a rich way of doing it. And of course—with Chaucer—you could go out and SMELL England at the weekend; take it all in, touch it, feel it.

And on the first essay I wrote for him, he wrote, 'you obviously enjoyed writing this as much as I enjoyed reading it . . .'

I was desperately worried that I was enjoying it all so much that I could be spoiling it for other people: it worried me a lot, the feeling that I was taking it over. But I had good relations with the other students; and the teachers said no, it's all right—we know what you're talking about, but it's all right. And in fact there were two occasions when I was under a lot of stress and I just wanted to sit quietly and absorb—and it completely threw everybody!

At the beginning of her second year, Eleanor took on geography as well, so that she could take two A levels and be qualified to apply to university. She had by then rejected sociology. She was lent two textbooks to help her make a decision, and she thought they were

> so weak! I'll never forget one of them, because I thought—it CAN'T be as awful as this, so I'll put it away and look at it later, but when I did, it still said—these were the immortal words—'as anyone who has been married will tell you, married life is not a bowl of cherries . . .'.
>
> I really couldn't hack that for a year.
>
> But geography—I'd never considered it. It had been awfully badly taught at school. I always got top marks—you did if you could draw an even blue line around the map.
>
> There was a terrific volume of work, but it was absolutely fascinating—I mean—glaciation! It was absolutely riveting! And river formation! It just opened a different world.

She said that her children still tease her about her enthusiasm for geography—remembering that she used to shout when she identified cloud-formation.

Then we talked about knowledge—itself, for itself; why it can be so—in her word—'riveting'.

> With physical geography, it's the sheer beauty of it, the whole process. It ties in also with mathematics. If you really want to get right down to it, it's all part of the quest for meaning. I still find it overwhelming.
>
> I think it does tap into something that's very deeply part of being human. And it predates human life!
>
> Anna was a dynamic, authoritative, interested teacher. She knew her stuff, she knew what the task was. She was absolutely marvellous on the developmental geography.

She talked some more about the teacher with whom she studied Chaucer.

> I'd started reading Lawrence off my own bat, and I referred to that in something I wrote, and David just ignited—it just happened to be his real love.
>
> And we read a poem about the birth of a Down's baby—and there again was an example of how you can harness intensity and by using everyday imagery not lose the force that makes it accessible. He was talking about things like

traffic lights and the hospital building and a bridge—things you can see—and yet he didn't lose any of the intensity.

Eleanor and Peter: Their Similarities

Both were unhappy; both were unfulfilled; and both had the frustration of unsatisfactory working lives. Eleanor seems to have reached instinctively for the sort of life her gifts had prepared for her. In an interesting phrase she says that at first she was trying to 'take responsibility for her endowments'. It is almost as if the person she could become had already been cut out; and all she had now to do was to become her own tailor and finish the job. There is a sense in her account of compulsion to become this person—that the only way to transcend emotional pain, frustration at work, and her money troubles would be to find out, first, what sort of person she could be. That at least would then be clear; and clarity might spread.

For Peter, too, answering a call first spoken by Aunt Liz, was to bid for clarity in his life. In both their accounts, there is a sense of relief when return begins: at last they find themselves where they belong. Both, too, are quickly aware of the need to learn control; to learn technical mastery.[2]

But Eleanor's need for control was different from his. Peter became absorbed in learning how to write, how to drill his undisciplined thoughts. But Eleanor talks about feelings. As climbers, Peter had to learn rope and belays and pitons; Eleanor, a little more familiar with the mechanics, had to learn not to be overwhelmed by her excitement at what she could at last see.

The first part of her ascent was steep and fast. Her memory of the first A level class is of transcendence. The poem lifted

[2] Readers knowledgeable about theories of adult learning will note that Peter's learning until now had largely been 'instrumental' (see J. Mezirow, 'A Critical Theory of Adult Learning and Education', *Adult Education*, 32/1 (autumn 1981), 3–24), and needed to become sophisticated in the handling of multiple interpretations. Both were engaged in 'emancipatory' work: learning about themselves; freeing their lives from old premises. (J. Habermas, *Knowledge and Human Interests* (Beacon Press, 1971)). 'Perspective Transformation' was certainly (Mezirow, 'A Critical Theory') their experience.

her clear of guilt, financial worries, emotional pain. Many of the women I have talked to, confined in the traditional role at home, have had to devise an economy not only of time and money, but also of painful feelings, fearing to express them too freely. The poem may also have been an occasion for Eleanor to see some of her own pain transposed, so that she could express it indirectly.

She was deeply worried that what she was doing was a flight from reality, and that she was cutting herself off from her responsibilities: 'it was an enormous escape, you know', she said at one point in our first meeting. But in that first English class—despite her guilt—she realized also that her flight was towards a reality that felt more important to her than anything except her children. While she responded to the poem, she knew—with intensity—that she was where she needed to be. She was made welcome by her teacher. The key to the moment of what she calls 'a meeting' between them is that she felt understood: her teacher's hospitality was unconditional. One woman was saying to another: 'You don't need to keep the purse-strings tight here: you can spend whatever feelings you like, however expensively painful they are.'

Eleanor's life was in crisis. She says—self-deprecatingly—'It's only when I'm pushed to the extreme that I get going.' Later she made this point rather differently; explaining that she sees herself as typical of many women in thinking of her own needs only when *in extremis*:

> I can only speak as a woman and I understand that this is the way it works for a lot of women. Well, this is the way it worked for me, anyway: I had to be under such enormous pressure that I got to the stage where I had to say, either I survive or I perish. That is the sort of pressure I had to be under before I could say yes, I am going to move forward. You just reach a point where you have to stand up and say, this is the direction I want to go in, it would be wonderful if others could go with me or at least give me their blessing. Taking on the risk that not only may you *not* receive the blessing but you may also be cursed.

Once learning begins, it often leads change, becomes its guide. The relationship between learning and integration in returners' lives is subtle. A poem can objectify, transpose pain. Glaciation and cloud-formation could help Eleanor to map her own life as well as in themselves, for themselves, being 'riveting'. Glaciers were before human life. She drew sustenance from their contemplation:

The world—one lapses into clichés—is just such a beautiful and intricate place.

Her life had become too small. Within its scope doubts and fears seemed big and powerful; but their power dwindled at college because Chaucer and glaciers did not recognize their authority. A woman whose life has been chopped too little is often strengthened when she returns by the official invitation to take huge matters seriously. Given a glacier to contemplate, dignity is implicit: she is being acknowledged as sentient, observant, philosophical, not somebody poked away in a kitchen, darting out for ill-paid drudgery, and coming back to the washing-up. And the threat to a partner may be not so much from definable changes—new vocabulary, new liveli- ness—but from the vague and frightening sense that the person you have been living with is larger. Eleanor, like Peter, broke silence as well: to voice delight, hope, intellectual excitement.

Being a student studying on a proper course made new dignity official; it was to have her right to interest in great things constantly made valid. Following interests on your own can feel like being somewhere you should not be, like getting in without paying; yearning in a corner. Eleanor's daughter remembers, too, that her mother loved the fellowship of other students.

It is no accident that at the same time as her return, she was making a sequence of discoveries and decisions about religion as well. I sensed that spiritual and intellectual sustained each other.

But she was presented with a new dilemma: she had to find ways of reconciling her old and new lives. The more acute the pleasure she felt in her new life, the more urgent the need for the new to make sense of the old. She must have felt pulled apart. To begin with, the purity of her studies was what sustained her. Her descriptions suggest the absoluteness of her response to what she was offered. Her mind became fervent, impassioned—glaciation could exalt her, could disarm financial irritations, make bearable her maze of part-time jobs.

But she stresses that what she needed to learn—and what indeed she did learn in her A level courses—was a way of managing the intensity of her response. She did not need to diminish her impassioned feelings, but to discipline them. Her teacher acknowledged those responses and acclaimed them— but taught her that she could think, organize, and feel simultaneously; that she could be impassioned and dispassionate at the same time. It is my guess that recent frustrations in her life had made her feel such a congested intensity of feeling that she feared that if she sanctioned one small escape— like a gas leak—there would be an explosion. But she found she could safely express some of that intensity after all. The art of writing a judicious essay which nevertheless said what she felt, was a model for what she now needed: to reconcile banality and exaltation; muddle and fervour. She needed to learn how to be an intellectual while at the same time being the mother of four children and running a household and coping with financial constraints. The poem about the Down's baby—set in its context of banal detail—seems to have been a poem in which emotion was well earthed. Her emphasis on the importance of its combination of fact and emotion is no accident. When I saw her at her desk in her own room, I was with a woman who had achieved just what she needed to achieve: home and mind in harmony.

To begin with, her need for purity in her studies—to set against muddles and confusions and frustrations—required a similar purity of approach from her teachers. Her standards were very high. She would not put up with intellectual dishonesty: she spoke loudly and eloquently against her English teacher's attempts—by praising the beauty of the language in the *Merchant of Venice*—to justify what Eleanor saw as Shakespeare's anti-Semitism. When her geography teacher had the temerity to be late for a class, Eleanor stormed round the college until she found her, and then berated her for not being where she should.

But by the time she reached university, her desperate need for absolutes had moderated.

She talks of an early and potentially very harmful experience in her first-year English course.

We had a most peculiar man as a tutor for work on medieval poetry. The Monk we used to call him because he had this medieval hair-do. I was very annoyed at having at last got to university at the limited scope there was, I couldn't spread myself and explore the way I had at A level, you see. And I thought—this is ridiculous, to come all this way just to sit down and hand in a standard essay. So I had a bit of fun with an analysis of a medieval poem; and when we got back into the seminar room I'd already done all this rehearsal of what he might say and how I would be tempted to feel if I didn't anticipate. And I thought the Monk is going to absolutely have to focus on me and put me down—because I'm enthusiastic, you see. And I'd rehearsed all the ghastly things he might say—but I couldn't possibly have anticipated how awful it was.

I spent about one line saying, yes, the received interpretation of this poem is such and such; however, if we stand back and look at it through non-Christian eyes and a different perspective, it could actually read—and then I wrote my different interpretation.

He sat down, and was flicking through the marked essays and when everyone was sitting down, he said—I can't remember the exact words but it was delivered from a great height—

'There are ways and ways of interpreting poetry, there are variations within what is allowed; and I shall now give you the most outrageous example of what is totally unacceptable at undergraduate level under any circumstances.'

And he proceeded to read it out!

I was well rehearsed, but I was still shocked—and I glanced round at the other students; and they were so mortified on my behalf. They were just on the floor.

Oh yes, I assumed that he wanted to damage me, that he wanted to threaten my development. I don't have any problem about acknowledging evil when I see it. He was a person too who hadn't found the courage to address his problems instead of projecting them on to other people. And that sort of behaviour can finish people.

Her reaction was not that of the absolutist she had once been.

She dealt,—albeit painfully—with this experience, and put it behind her, making sure that she would not choose a course that would lead to a further encounter with the Monk. And though she agreed with me that the Monk's behaviour was regrettable, to say the least, she said too that she thought it unreasonable to expect all university teachers to be sensitive and decent; that cosseting by kindly dons would be a poor preparation for the world. Encounters with evil medievalists can be useful. But nevertheless, the Monk's approach exemplifies university teaching at its unregenerate worst.

Two years later the third of nine children of a working-class East End family evacuated to a country town in the war gained her degree.

Class

I want now to return to Peter by way of an account of Eleanor's origins and her schooling.

When her family was evacuated, teachers at the school she went to were not all hospitable. But she did well. Used to the responsibility for her younger brothers and sisters, she was often put in charge of groups of the young children at school:

> Being about a yard taller than anyone else, I was expected to have responsibilities way beyond my years, and I responded to that.

She passed the 11 plus, and went to the girls' grammar school.

> There were definitely teachers there who thought we had no place in that school. The worst occasion I recall was in domestic science. I still had a London accent then. We were being taught how to make a purée—we were always being taught really useful things like that—and this teacher was going on about nutritional value and no waste—and then tipped the water that the vegetables had been cooked in down the sink. And I said—oh, my mum would never do that. And she made a really cutting put-down remark, to the effect that with my background we were probably lucky to eat dirt.
>
> I also remember an incident in the lower third. It was my

turn to read from some book we were reading round the
class—and I loved it, because it was like being in the air-raid
shelter when everybody got up to do a turn and when it was
your turn you got up to do your thing and everybody
thought you were marvellous. And this was my chance!

So I was reading, and I was suddenly stopped, and I didn't
know why. And I was asked to repeat what I'd said, and I
repeated it—wa'er. It took me a second to realize what was
wrong, but it felt like a lifetime. It wasn't that I was reading
incorrectly. I still to this day am never sure how you say it,
but I think it's water, yes?

But my mother, who I absolutely adored, said wa'er!

These things made me deeply, hotly resentful, because I
didn't know how to fight back. What did I do? I wept. I
would deliberately—in a typically female form of self-
punishment—not perform well for that teacher, because I did
not want to please her. My achievement record was almost a
barometer of how I felt towards a teacher.

I had my own class-prejudice. I assumed for a long while
that anyone who was a teacher at a grammar school was
posh. I've realized since that I've done a grave injustice to a
lot of those teachers. Ancient history and English literature
were both taught by a doughty little Welsh woman who
ruled us with a rod of iron. When I came back to Stembury I
lived opposite her. And she turned out to be the bright one
of a very impoverished family, a socialist born and bred,
champion of the underdog. All I knew was I found her very
fair.

But on the whole I didn't see teachers as the same flesh as
my lot. Londoners evacuated to Stembury: a Martian would
have been more understandable.

All the same, with the teachers I did like, I couldn't get
enough. Their problem was in keeping me down enough to
let others have a chance. I would have hogged all their time
and energy.

But she had to leave at 15.

There was this extraordinary group of beings who stayed on
after the statutory leaving age. That was a mystery. I was at
school long enough to realize that some of them—prefects

and people like that—weren't too bright. It was the arrogance of the cockney! We had it instilled in us from the word go: they think they're better—but you're better than anyone else. You could run rings round them.

But the thing that school gave me that meant I never lost faith in my ability—I have always known I am bright—was that I knew I was capable of always getting the top grade. It was the school that gave me that feeling: it wasn't cultural, it wasn't from cockney cockiness. That was different. This feeling was, as far as anything is, objective. I had plenty of evidence of it. And somewhere inside me I always knew I had that to draw on.

I always knew that the day I hit 15 I had to go out and earn my living. But when I took the inevitable note to the head—as Eleanor is going to be 15 in October, we expect her to be gainfully employed—she was very angry and insisted that I stay until the end of that term.

She did something I shall always thank her for. She had me in her office again. I didn't quite take in what she was saying at the time, but she put it in such terms that I couldn't forget it. She said, you have got something which all these others you may feel intimidated by would pay millions to have: ability. I thank her dearly for that.

I can see her very clearly in my mind's eye. And I remember the smell of tobacco: she smoked cigarettes on the sly. It would be nice to think that it reassured me to know she'd been nervous enough to need a cigarette, but I don't think I had the sophistication to think like that.

I felt her warmth; and to be honest with you I think it was something I enshrined. I knew she had told me something terribly important, even though I didn't understand it fully at the time. I wouldn't risk breaking it by sharing the secret with anyone else.

The other thing was, it was probably my first experience of someone cutting through everything to me; to a me I hardly recognized myself, the person that had to wait another thirty years.

The similarity with Peter's history is considerable. In his case, it was not his school that kept his hope of learning alive, but his aunt, though Penny Spitfire helped by giving him a nagging need for poetry. Eleanor was cheated of a successful university career at the conventional time; but her school in one sense served her well. She never seriously doubted her ability—even though she feared she might fail when she returned, and felt guilty about doing something for herself, and thought she must seem ridiculous to others. Despite these fears she knew she was bright.

After school, she trained as a nursery nurse. She read books. She played chess. Like Peter's, her mind was irrepressible, and went on a thirty-year prowl, finding more than scraps. But it prowled in circles. The difference between the reader and occasional autodidact, and the student on a course, is progression. We have seen how difficult it was for Peter to go forward on his own without an abbé or an institution to help him. Eleanor's education left her far better equipped at 15 than Peter had been at 14. But her intellect did not develop until she returned.

She went to Australia at 22, after working since leaving school as a nursery nurse.

By the time I was 25 I was married with a child and running a 60-place kindergarten. We were living in a little country town, and they had a pretty moribund little playgroup that parents had organized, and it was really at a stage when it was going to close down because it was falling to pieces. I had befriended an American academic and her husband who wanted to send their children to this kindergarten, and they said how absolutely awful it was. I told them what I'd been doing, and they said—write to them, tell them what you can do, take it over!

So I did. And I worked there for 5 years.

When it started out we hired two rooms in the scout hut— filthy, it was ghastly. The assistant was an Indonesian lady and we got on very well, and I said what I wanted was a place where the children were actually doing something, where they had a structured programme, where they could expand their minds and learn to express themselves. She entered into this vision, and so first of all for a small outlay I acquired the basic materials—sand, water, paints. Yes, I had a complete idea of what I wanted—a vision of what I could provide in the way of an environment for those children, to get them responding. I didn't have a vision at all from a managerial level because I had no idea how things worked— money, things like that—no idea at all. But I had an idea, and I conveyed it to the management committee. They were fired up by this and got all sorts of fund-raising things going and it culminated in them borrowing money and putting up a purpose-built building.

No, I didn't feel anxious. I'm divorced now; but when I look back I didn't need to have anxieties because my husband carried them all for me, and expressed them. I didn't read it that way. I might still be married now if I had.

I just saw what had to be done, the children were responsive, most of the parents were responsive. And once you get something creative like that going—the feedback makes a sort of current, and it's self-feeding.

Yes, it was to do with what I gave it as well. The bad side about being an outsider is being paranoid about your own identity and background. But the good side is that if you suddenly land on a foreign planet and say: here's your problem, this is how you can solve it, this is what you do . . . they just think—well, she must know, let her get on with it.

A saviour coming in by parachute, I said, and Eleanor liked the image. I also suggested that this enterprise was a beautiful example of the irrepressibility of intellect. Eleanor took on her town's problem, and came up with a solution. She did so with fierce intelligence; and her energy—what she calls her 'drive'— then put her solution into practice. She accepted my suggestion, but added:

But you also carry forward an awful lot of junk. When we got our new building and were becoming part of the establishment—of the pre-school kindergarten movement— that's when things started to go wrong for me, because we had a different committee and people safeguarding a big financial investment. We had people who wanted to be on the right side of the establishment, and we hit a problem because people started asking questions about my formal

qualifications. My NNEB wasn't regarded as on a par with
the Australian nursery teacher's training. Looking back now,
the committee very sensibly approached the pre-school
kindergarten movement to have a look at me, and they were
impressed with what they saw, but said, we would like you
to go through a course with us so we can make you one of
us. Perfectly sensible.

It sounds awful but my gut reaction was to go back to a
self-destructive strategy and just give them two fingers!

It was, I'm a Londoner, and if to be accepted by
Stemburyites I've got to be like that dumb schmucky lot,
then up yours mate!

I can see now what was happening, I'm 50 years old. I
couldn't at the time. All I knew was I was under attack yet
again, thousands of miles away in bloody Australia. I might
just as well have stayed in Stembury, because the establishment will never ever accept me.

How did they put it to me? I think they stayed up all the
night before trying to think of a way of approaching me! I
was so wrapped in protecting myself, I didn't appreciate it
was difficult for them too. I think they did it quite nicely.
They were at great pains to say in no way was my position
under threat, and I was a popular figure in the town, and by
then I had four or five years of parents behind me. But for
me it would have been going over to the enemy, that's how I
saw it at the time. And all I knew was that my marriage was
very stressed. I think I was right—if I'd succeeded to that
extent it would have been altogether too much for my ex-
husband. In the light of what's happened since.

And then my husband had the opportunity to do what
he'd always wanted to do which was farm. It meant moving
further out; it was his big chance so we packed up and
moved out. I was pregnant again then—and I don't think I
regretted leaving the nursery because I was so thrilled that
this was something I could do for him. It would relieve all
the tension. Now I could do something for his ambitions.

She did not enjoy her new life. She recalls:

The worst sort of male domination because everything was
measured by brute force. And I couldn't operate creatively at

all, I couldn't write, couldn't draw. And these were things I'd been doing. If I had ten minutes to spare I might think— let's write an article, let's draw the cat. Before I left England I'd done little articles for newsletters for clubs and things like that.

But when my second child was ready to go to kindergarten in the nearest town I started to come to life again, became very involved in the management committee. That was a big deal because you had to raise $3,000 a year, and I'd never dreamt of such money before. That gave me an idea of how things worked from that point of view: if you're responsible for that sort of money you do have to take into consideration things like the qualifications of your staff, what scale you pay them, who's going to pay for the maintenance of the building. Then it got very exciting because we went for one big blockbuster fund-raiser which was an Art Weekend, and I found myself going round interviewing local artists, and writing again, submitting articles to the paper, interviewing politicians, rabble-rousing: what about our kindergarten! All that sort of thing.

That phase lasted for three years. Then we sold our bit of land. We would have had to leave our farm anyway: changes of company policy meant it was sold up a year later.

For the first time ever we had a lump sum. The marriage was in difficulties. My mother was very ill, and I could see what I had to do was get myself and the children back to England. We came back after thirteen years.

We took out a lease on a village shop. I took on the newsagent side and my husband ran the grocery.

This story, cut short, was the same as before. Eleanor was a success: she made it her business to satisfy every possible order, however obscure. She stocked what people needed; she organized the newspaper boys and girls efficiently; she built up a reputation. She doubled the turnover of her side of the business. But the grocery side did not succeed. Her husband had very bad luck: new supermarkets were springing up in the nearest town, and the rise in inflation was devastating.

After five years they had to sell up. Back at Stembury, they put a deposit on a house, her husband took a selling job which he hated; and Eleanor resorted to bits and pieces—dinner lady, volunteer in a primary school, playground supervisor.

We have nearly come full circle. A year later Eleanor began her return. But her cockney prejudice against the instituted powers, against *them* and all their powers and emplacements, made one last attempt to put the kybosh on her progress. Her prejudice against the official way was still strong, and had to be diminished before she would consider a return.

I think what did it was watching my oldest daughter go through grammar school. Watching someone, still being themselves, going through the due processes, and absorbing from her that you don't then necessarily become a creature of the system, you do take on a lot of value in terms of approach, self-discipline, and all the rest of it. You can still remain yourself.

She recalled again how her speech was constantly corrected when she went to grammar school herself; she recalled her resentment. That resentment still burned. But:

Catherine demystified the system for me, and in a big way. I nearly collapsed the day she came home and said, I'm going to try for Oxbridge and I'm going to do it a year early because I know you couldn't support me for another year— we were living hand to mouth then by this time, she was doing holiday jobs to keep going. I asked her if the headmaster knew, and she said yes—and her eyes filled. She said his response was, don't come to me in tears when it all falls to pieces. And she had the guts to go on to arrange her own tutor to prepare herself, with no help. And she got in; she went to Oxford and she graduated.

All I'm doing is stating facts: I would not have done what I did without her.

Her daughter, then, was exemplar and inspiration.[3] But it is

---

[3] Catherine has read this section of the book, and I altered certain details at her suggestion. She noted in this connection the possibility of Eleanor's competitiveness—with her. This certainly seems an implicit part of her daughter's 'inspiration': following suit, emboldened, Eleanor also wished to emulate Catherine, to show that she could do it too.

significant that Eleanor may have been most keenly inspired by
Catherine's fight against *them*, the established powers of her
school. The story is unusual. Catherine has explained to me
that she decided to try for Oxbridge, but that her teachers—
with one exception—did not support her. Her own view now
is that there was an element of class snobbery in this; and a
subtler sort of preference for what she calls the 'stars'—a certain
sort of pupil the school favoured, gaudy high-flyers. She was
not like that. She was undemonstrative—though she attracted
the interest and acknowledgement of some members of staff,
especially her biology teacher, who supported her bid. But her
maths teacher joined the head in advising her not to try for
Oxbridge. When she refused his advice, he stopped talking to
her; sent her to Coventry, communicating only in curt notes
about homework and such matters.

Her refusal to be put off by this extraordinary behaviour
appealed to her mother; completed the inspiration. Catherine
agrees that other aspects of what she did were also attractive:
her diligence, for instance. She would get up very early to
study; and she agrees that her hard work appealed to her
mother's love of challenges, her energy, her own willingness to
work very hard as she had in Australia. Catherine mentioned
the art exhibition as an example, saying how hard her mother
had worked to make it succeed.

Catherine also mentioned the group of friends she had at O
level who all helped and supported each other, constantly
visiting each other at home. She sees her mother at that stage as
being very lonely, so that the idea of college suggested in the
end the possibility of similar friendship. She recalls a particular
friend, a boy who had started his schooling at a secondary
modern, and who won his way into the grammar school sixth
form. Eleanor liked him, thought him special, spoke often of
her admiration. He too had been forced to struggle against 'the
system'.

Catherine says too that Eleanor helped her a great deal at O
level, especially with English literature. Eleanor enjoyed doing
so; and Catherine feels that her mother was very conscious of
the fact that at A level she could no longer help, except with
loyalty and encouragement.

Her daughter's contribution to her return was complex. But

I am sure that the key is Eleanor's word 'demystification'. Catherine's[4] example told her mother that higher education is not a route to a club of snobs; a club whose members preside over all institutions, running the show for themselves and keeping the rest of the world out. Her fear of the club ran deep. She suspected that applying for admission would be disloyal to her own club, the cockneys armed to the teeth with different pride. Her club—or her 'lot' as she called them—scorned the snobs, believing that what they valued was valueless and what they did was easy, lazy, and effete. They were not real; and they were stupid—deeply stupid and easily gulled.

Such was her prejudice. But of course it was not her only idea of education. She valued some intellectual things very highly as a young adult; she had been secretly disobeying the rules of her club ever since leaving school with her head-mistress's sad accolade safely locked away for future use. It was her choice to read books, to play chess, to write articles for newsletters—to cry over *Tess of the Durbervilles* which she read three times while she was in Australia; to interview artists for her fund-raising Art Weekend and be very interested in what they did. But as long as she did NOT choose to join the artists and the teachers and the chairwomen of management committees and aspire to accredited advancement in their world, she was safe. She could be better than them by knowing their game; by talking their talk in her middle-class voice; by reading their books and genuflecting to their icons. She could pretend to be one of them and enjoy the disguise, perhaps enjoy her masked life much more than her Real Life. But as long as she never made the mistake of actually joining them, she would be safe.

The accreditation crisis was very significant. While she was a maverick manager, her intelligence and instinctive authority burning bright, she could feel that she had not been disloyal. In fact, her achievement with the nursery was cocking a snook at

[4] Catherine adds that her refusal to be browbeaten out of competing for Oxbridge 'was typical of the non-conformist character my parents had fostered in me'. A version perhaps of what she describes—in a felicitous phrase that pleases Eleanor too—as her mother's 'cockney hauteur'. The gritty worker, she notes, was for Eleanor 'a familiar and comfortable self-image'.

the club back home. She was saying—'Look how easy it is! And yet *your lot* invent those stodgy old rules for setting up places like this, and I've proved they're all unnecessary.' So long as the organization and managing and bossing and publicizing and fund-raising were *unofficial*—were her own, her singular achievement—she was safe; she could be a reckless pioneer free of the constraints of the Old Country. And of course the true work was real—what more so for a young woman than looking after children, a job sanctioned by her lot as important. Hadn't she looked after her younger brothers and sisters when she was a child, her mother gratefully approving? The work itself was perfectly loyal. The rest—the sort of stuff done as a job back home by people who thought themselves important and had all sorts of bits of paper to their name—she could do as a pleasurable extra; an act—a chance to do lots of turns like she did in the air-raid shelter.

No wonder she was so angry when it seemed to her that THEY thought what she had been doing all the time was preparing a sort of backhand admission to the club. She'd be damned if she'd learn the handshake! If they couldn't accept her just as she was, without the right bits of paper, then to hell with them. She took their formal scruples as snobbish disapprobation. So our heroic cockney went her own way. It is no accident that she went up country, where she could still be a pioneer—and be safe from the rules; the world of Stembury which had suddenly established itself where she thought it would never encroach.

But Catherine showed her that instead of losing what Eleanor called 'value' by working for university, you took 'value' on. If the route to that world meant persistence and courage and bloody hard work perhaps she had been wrong all along to think of that world as valueless. She had, too, perhaps believed that she could enjoy its riches to the full while leading a real life; just as she had read *Tess* while bringing up her children. But when Catherine, studying for A level, left her far behind intellectually, she could no longer deceive herself that this was true. It was clear that you could not go where Catherine was going in the odd half-hour, doing some cooking with your other hand. It is interesting that Peter too had to realize that education meant hard work.

And Catherine did not become unrecognizable. The 'value' she gained was the sort that belonged in the real world. What more real than hard work? Though, as I have already suggested, it may have been Catherine's refusal to be browbeaten by the head and his maths teacher henchman that completed the inspiration.

Class moves in a mysterious way.

Peter Again

When Eleanor realized that the club was a phantasy—or, at any rate, that her fears were groundless—she could become the person she now is. The decision to educate herself was made possible by her escape from myths and confusions she had acquired in childhood.

Peter's experience has been very different. He learnt more about those confusions after his return than before. When his dream did begin to become reality, he wanted to talk about his excitement, and wanted—because he is that sort of man—to encourage other people to make the same attempt.

He sometimes met derision when he talked. I can imagine him doing so in a mixture of pride and excitement, and in an almost evangelical spirit. It is not romantic hyperbole to say—as of Eleanor—that his life took on meaning when he returned. It is hardly surprising that he was moved to talk to other people about what was happening to him.

I talked to him first just before he retired. Bosses thought he was getting above his station:

My boss is a terrible dunderhead, he's terribly muddly, he says strange things. A lot of people agree with him, you're supposed to agree with your boss. I say to him, no, it's not like that, it's like this: because of this, and this, and this. I disagree with him and create an argument. I usually speak with an air of authority, and he hates me for it. But he could argue if he wanted to, and he could say, well, I don't agree with you, because of *a*, and *b*, and *c*. And we could come to some sort of agreement and synthesis. But he doesn't know how to do that.

There was another time earlier on when I was at night

Lives

school before the OU, I had a supervisory job then, and I was going to Newark in a car with one of the managers. We were doing Chaucer at the time, and I was very enthused with one of the tales, and so I told this man all about it—I was really enthusiastic, I thought it was lovely stuff.

He looked at me, and he said, I don't like clever people.

All I was doing was lifting the conversation a bit above the mundane, talking about Chauntecleer and Pertelote, the cockerel and the hen. Yes, it was because I was jumping out of rank—and I was only talking about a bloody cockerel. I shut up then.

It's because you're stepping out of your station. D'you know, my brother didn't even say well done when I got my degree. And the family don't mention it. I remember one day I was in the garden with my father, and we were talking about art—he does a bit of painting himself. There is something in me of the teacher at times—they always say I lecture. And I gave him a lecture on art history. I went right through from Byzantine times to modern art. I explained how it all happened—the evolution of art. But he wasn't interested; he'd just say I talk out of the top of my head. He tells other people that. He's not interested in what I know.

There is an implied self-criticism here, as if he blames himself for his reckless lack of reticence; for a dereliction of humility. And yet, his memories of coming home from summer school and being 'over the top with all this knowledge' do not suggest bragging but irrepressibility, like Willy Russell talking about *Animal Farm* in the hairdresser's. And they are sad memories:

You start talking about all this knowledge, and oh! you get a flattening. They're not even interested. You're back to sheer domesticity, and oh—it's terrible.

Perhaps it was impossible for Peter's wife not to envy such excitement, and to be ill-tempered at the thought of his sudden acquisition of a new world, new friends. But Peter's post-summer-school flattening suggests the gulf of class more than anything else. Peter had gone wrong. He had moved away from his rightful place. 'My mother thought I was mad, my father thought I was mad.'

At school, the less you knew the better you were. We had a new bloke who started at work, and he must have heard that I had some sort of qualification, even though I'd never mentioned it to him. He made this remark that was obviously directed towards me, about spelling: I don't know anything, he said, I don't know how to spell that—whatever it was. It was as if NOT knowing anything was much more important than knowing something.

Oh, I got in a terrible fix. I was hated at work and at home. My mother thought I was going way above my station, and she thought that I'd do my brains a severe injury, that it was too much work for me. Most of the family gave me up for lost, they thought I was going crackers.

I remember my mother saying it was too much work for me. I used to go down and see her and talk. But she wasn't interested at all, she would say, it's too much work, she'd push it aside. She wasn't pleased to know that I was doing the OU, and my father was never that interested. We're a rare breed. Got to be a bit mad.

So Peter was evidently forced to accept, with irony, that he was 'crackers'. There was pride to be salvaged in being 'a bit mad'. But the way he talked about these memories suggests that he was hurt by the realization that what he was doing at the OU was incomprehensible—while to him it seemed so clear. What he found so hard was his family and friends failing to accept that his excitement should be theirs as well. He did not see himself as cleverer than his workmates or his family. If he could cope with the demands of the OU and find such fulfilment, then so could they. He was demonstrating to them their own unspent riches, their unemployed powers. In a sense, what he was doing was for them as much as for himself. He offered to be representative; but his offer was rejected.

What perhaps he did not see was that the fervent convert is always a threat. It is safe and comforting to accept that you are where you are because you could not be anywhere else. Unintelligence is a good alibi. Ignorance is a proud defence. It is disruptive to admit that you have been deprived of an education; to begin to wonder what might have happened if

you had been more fortunate, or what still might happen if you
could be as reckless and crazy as Peter and have another go.

> I'd talk about anything I was learning. There were so many
> subjects: it was so diverse, there must have been about fifty
> subjects altogether that you study. But when you talked
> you'd get a glaze; they'd die on you.
>
> I remember once in the pub when I was doing musicol-
> ogy, and I was getting deeply involved in all this music. I
> went to the bar and this bloke I knew was standing there,
> and there was a juke-box beside him. He put his money in,
> and this music came out.
>
> I said to him, why d'you like that music?
>
> He said, because I bloody do, don't I? and it sort of
> flattened me. The people I was beginning to know would
> say, I like it because . . .
>
> And I'd been all on my own in the kitchen, getting
> enthused, listening to tapes of music—and it was a natural
> thing for me to say. But it was completely unnatural to him:
> he thought I was an idiot.
>
> It flattens you.[5]

Peter had acquired the skill to *look again* at the world from a
fresh proposition; to play with explanations and questions. The
incident shows us a cheated man and an intellectually
enfranchised man staring at each other across a fence of
incomprehension.

I asked him what it was like to experience all this flattening—
and when he decided to divide his two worlds.

> It's a very slow process. I haven't completely learned it yet. I
> don't know whether I ought to. I keep arguing with
> myself—should I push it, or should I keep quiet, and act like

[5] After working with Nigel Evans on his film *Catching Alight* (Channel 4,
1989), *Roots* has become one of the texts haunting this book. See Beattie's last
speech: ' "Blust," they say [the writers, composers etc.], "the masses is too
stupid for us to come down to them. "Blust", they say, "if they don't make no
effort why should we bother?" So you know who come along? The slop
singers and the pop writers and the film makers and the women's magazines
and the Sunday papers and the picture strip love stories: that's who come
along, and you don't have to make no effort for them: it come easy . . .'
(Arnold Wesker, *Roots*, *The Wesker Trilogy* (Longman, 1984), 140).

a cretin, use the old jargon, use the old slang and be one of the boys. It's easier for me to do the latter, because it only creates antagonism not to.

I feel sorry for the people I worked with, the ones who read the *Star* and the *Sun*, and the sum total of their conversation is crumpet or winning money or going on holiday. Nothing else. Going on the booze at weekends. Consuming vast quantities of lager. Having terrific head-aches. Talking and laughing about it.

At odd times I try to encourage them, grab a youngster who's got some intellect: they're intelligent, a lot of them. And I would try to fire them with my enthusiasm for education. But it just falls on stony ground. I tried hard with my son, too, to get him to do the Open University.

His son, leaving school at 16, is successful in his work with computers. But the rules he has made for his life do not include more education.

It was a tall order for Peter to try to change the rules in the lives of all the people he talked to about the OU. But the evangelical spirit was strong in him; and I sense that he is disappointed now at the way his adventure has been received by those around him, at work and at home. He is not embittered, because he has gained so much from his return. After graduating he chose to continue to work as an electrician until retirement; but despite doing the same job, his life had changed.

Absolutes and Escapes: Circles and Straight Lines

Class-rules can still dictate the chances of pupils in schools today, though opportunities look more generous than Peter's were when he went to school. But no adult of Eleanor's age in the 1930s had the automatic right to a full grant for higher education. At least when a child enters a good comprehensive now, no doors are fully shut. Peter's eloquent polemic about his own schooling argues persuasively that from the start he was on the short commons deliberately allotted his class. He does not mean that he learnt literally nothing when he says three times in the first long quotation from our first talk that he cannot remember ever learning anything. He stresses that his school equipped him efficiently enough with the three Rs. But he wanted to contrast his school with the feast of the OU: at school he was drilled not taught; instructed, not excited.

Even the good things were casual, leading nowhere. Penny Spitfire was like a lecturer parachuting into the jungle in Burma in the Second World War and giving the troops a rousing talk about Michelangelo. Only a struggle after the war—if he was lucky enough to survive it—would have brought great art back into the life of a private who had been inspired by the talk, when he returned to his job in a factory. But to an ex-undergraduate such as Peter saw when he worked as an electrician in a college, such a talk would have found its place amongst rich possibilities—galleries already known; books later sought; friends who would go with him to Florence.

But Peter and Eleanor both tell us about the enduring strength of myths and mysteries and fears about education. It has been so bound up with social standing that its possession can be a threat to those who have been cheated of it. Education still feels exclusive. For many returners, a crucial revelation is that they are not turned back at the first reception desk. We will see later in this book how overawed and terrified many returners are to begin with; how memories of school can paralyse if a returner meets a teacher whose manner and method reminds her of some terrorist pedagogue who froze her mind in a classroom years before. Worse can be the enduring conviction that none of this is really for you: that you have no right to be striding the corridors of a polytechnic; and that sooner or later you will be rumbled, and the administrative error that let you in will be corrected.

Eleanor's story reminds that while bodies of people still need to scorn education as valueless—rejecting it proudly—the attempt to create a just system of education will still have failed.

It is no accident that, for somebody born into the working class like Peter, a dream of education is for years just that: a secret to be polished in solitude; a phantasy he dare not mention to his peers for fear of their derision. The dream did not belong to the essentials of his life; it was bestowed by Dumas and his wonderful Aunt Liz. The key to Peter's memory of life at a college is that what undergraduates were being offered was out of his reach. Education was not for the likes of him. It is interesting that his particular dream, lent by Dumas, is so fraught with imagery of imprisonment, conspiracy, tunneling to freedom against the odds.

Their accounts tell us more than about class; beginning, for instance, an argument about what adults need in order to learn.

At the beginning of their return Peter and Eleanor were vulnerable and uncertain—as well as possessed of huge strength of will; determination born of their experience. Experience focused, charged, and heightened their learning—in ways I consider in more detail in Chapter 12. But until a detonation of confidence, their experience, like the main fuel in a rocket, could not ignite.

They needed the 'acknowledgement' of their teachers; needed the intuitive understanding of another adult already familiar with what they had decided to enjoy for themselves. Both needed at the outset someone to reflect emphatically and vividly their strengths and their progress and whose arduous standards they could trust; so that criticism could be stitched into affection and optimism. This need diminished. As they progressed, their learning did become much more 'self-directed', though they continued to want and to benefit from the respect of their teachers.

The stories of how Eleanor and Peter became students also say much about the quirkiness of biography—its ironic reversals; its prolonged fallows and sudden accelerations. After working on this book, biography seems to me mysterious. Why should Peter's dream have been so durable; why should Eleanor's daughter have been so accurately, so precisely illuminating to her mother just at the right time? Their stories introduce a key paradox of the subject of this book: though their 'first' education should have done them much more justice, the intensity of their learning in adult life may be partly a function of its long delay.

Both Peter and Eleanor needed change. Education was a means of change; of moving on. Return to learning begins a sequence that has no necessary end; and if a life craves change it needs the promise of sequence, of progression along a visible route.

Peter and Eleanor had been going round in circles. Circular movement wears you out; sequential movement does not. The OU began a sequence of renewals in Peter's life; Eleanor's return prompted general change in her life. She sees herself, for instance, as having been 'pathologically self-conscious' in her early forties; but aged 50, with her degree, she is no longer so. She knows that, a few years before she was taught by him, she would not have been able to deal so well with the medievalist's scorn.

But I am not just offering a therapeutic–utilitarian argument about learning. I am talking as much about spiritual needs as about psychic hygiene. Both Peter and Eleanor were rescued by ideas and knowledge as well as people and institutions: by glaciation, the history of art, calculus, inductive logic. Not all of what their learning did to them and for them is definable. Their excitement cannot be reduced to its salutary results. The meaning of their return was for each unique, and richly complex. That is why their testimony is important, at a time when the debate about education tends to be reductive, technical, inimically specialized.

But the taking up of a right should not be so difficult.

Social iniquity cheated them, fenced them in. Other influences can be inimical despite luckier circumstances.

4

Vanessa: The Fishbone and the Pea

People born into a different class may also have to wait a long time before educating themselves.

Vanessa sat opposite me on a Victorian armchair with carved wooden arms. We were in one of the many rooms in her house: a big untidy sitting room, full of things to look at: rugs on the floor, pictures, interesting furniture.

I was at a Convent of the Sacred Heart till 15. If you've read Antonia White's books, it was exactly like that. Because I thought myself not very good academically, I excelled in sport. At the end of my time at my first school, which I loved, it appeared that I would only be getting O levels in things like knitting and art, so I was sent to a more humble convent where I did get six O levels. I left at 16 presuming I would get married, and that was the expectation of most of my friends too.

I then went to school in France for a year; to Germany for nine months to be an au pair and ski; then back to England— by which time I was fluent in two languages—to start a secretarial course. During that time I met my husband. I was 19, he was ten years older, and we were married.

He was a tea-planter in India, and had come home, as it turned out, expressly to find a wife.

I was in India for two years. My first son was born there. It was not at all the life my husband had described, both to me and to my parents. Tea-prices didn't fetch the great sums that they had: it was the very tail-end of the raj. I found it just dreadful, part of it. There was no please or thank-you in the Hindi I was taught for my servants. In one way it sounds wonderful. I was 19, I had ten servants. I've actually seen

Everest. A leopard was shot for me on my 21st birthday—
these things now make me cringe. But I have seen Everest;
and I have a wonderful son too.

I wouldn't play bridge, because of the terrible post-
mortems afterwards. So I played a lot of tennis, and I was
ladies' champion. But we led a very subsistence life, it wasn't
like pictures of the raj. When I came back, my parents met
me in France, and I couldn't eat the food, it was too rich—
we'd been living on a very impoverished diet.

I came back and lived with my parents.

Now, looking back on it, it strikes me as extraordinary
that I didn't do anything with my life then. I was just living
day to day with no particular plans. I was just going to find
another husband. It was the only thing that I thought of,
apart from caring beautifully for my small son. Getting
through the divorce first.

Yes, of course the choices open to me were very limited. I
was born in 1940. I have a sister who is three years younger,
and it almost happened between the end of my education and
hers, in that all of her friends presumed that they would
work; they thought of how they were going to live, how
they were going to earn their money. Whereas almost all of
my friends didn't. By the seventies, I began to feel very
dissatisfied; although by then I had a second, wonderful,
husband, and a beautiful home, and four excellent children.
But everyone said to me, do you work?

At first I said, no, I'm only a housewife. I then changed it
to, yes, I'm a housewife. I then changed it to, yes, 24 hours a
day, yes, very hard. But it all sounded very apologetic—oh,
only at home.

When I think of the richer choices available to young
women nowadays, I just feel I missed a splendid opportunity. I was living in my parents' house; they had daily help
because I was so young—my mother thought that because I
was so young we should have extra help with my son, so we
had a Danish au pair girl. Here were all these women milling
around my small son; I could easily have trained to be a
nurse—that's about all I might have imagined doing then. I
certainly wouldn't have thought of going back into education. Doing a degree then wasn't possible as a thought at all.

What interests did I have? My husband says we have
more books than any bookshop. I think I have a very wide
open mind, I'm interested in nearly everything. When the
children asked questions—certainly I didn't know most of it,
but I always had a book that I could turn to. I didn't read
very much as a child. It was in my early twenties when I
seemed to have a need to have all these books with me. But I
didn't think of going back into education. I didn't know it
was possible.

My husband's job moved about a lot in the seventies. I
think it was about 1978 when I began to feel uneasy,
unsettled. By then my youngest child was 4, and it was
maybe when he was 5 and going to school that I really began
to feel—is this it? Extremely uneasy, not very content, not
very certain why I wasn't.

In 1983 we moved here, and we had tenants at a nearby
poly, and one of them said, do come to a lecture with me,
and I thought it was one of the most exciting things I'd ever
done. It was a lecture on the law of tort, and it was
fascinating, because most of the examples were about the
thalidomide babies, and it so happened that I took thalidomide
with my eldest son James, but thank God it wasn't at a
dangerous stage.

We went in by the back door of the lecture theatre, and we
looked down on all these heads. It just was wonderfully
exciting, I was on the edge of my chair: it just was a
completely new experience that I hadn't realized I was
allowed to have. I was caught up in how exciting it was to be
there, and half of it could have applied to James.

I also had a very, very good American friend in 1984. Her
husband was here on a year's sabbatical. She was a very
talented and educated woman; she regarded this year as a
gift, she raced round doing a million things, and I trotted
round behind her doing a third of the things and loving it all.

She was the person who said, why don't you go for it! To
a certain extent I do have her to thank for my being at the
poly.

I heard about the Access course, but I stupidly didn't find
out about it, I thought it would be flower-arranging and so
on, and I wasn't interested in that. I'd had thirty years of

coffee mornings, and chat about entertaining arrangements, and I wanted something serious, and more worthwhile.

We went to the lectures at the BM about all sorts of subjects; and then we'd have lunch in a pub. We went to concerts—she has an enormous knowledge of music. I suppose I've always enjoyed learning, without realizing that I did.

She had such a wonderful sense of 'Wouldn't it be fun if . . .'. And she didn't seem to have the guilt which so many English women suffer from, at doing something that was actually enjoyable.

My bright, shiny American friend was very generous in a way that I suppose I hadn't found before, and if we had half an hour to spend over a cup of coffee, she'd say, tell me your hopes and fears. I'd talk of myself for a quarter of an hour, and then it was my turn to ask her—and it was just a very rich and useful friendship. At exactly the right time.

I enrolled at the poly, and did an English module first of all. I even passed the exam. I started doing history the next term, but my younger son was only 5 by then, and there were problems at school. I'd always said I was a mother first, this was for MY pleasure, so I decided that the children were too young, and I'd give it up until they were a bit older.

The first module was absolutely fascinating. I was asked to read eight books I'd never read before, ranging from the 'Wife of Bath' to *The Rainbow*.

I found it really wonderful; but I also found it very, very lonely. Now having gone through the Access course it feels quite different—there's enormous support from a range of people. And I'm for ever giving new mature students the benefit of my experience and telling them not to worry.

The books? One that meant an awful lot was the *Doll's House*, because I'd seen it on the stage. That jumps out as a highlight. And also *The Rainbow* was wonderful. I think I have a very visual imagination, and there were wonderful bits in it that I could absolutely see.

But at the seminars, I was just terrified, my heart would pound even when you had to say your name—when it got round to my turn, I'm sure I blushed; I felt almost physically sick. Also, that first exam, having left school at 16, it was awful at 44 to be back in this enormous room with desks, having to find my place. I found myself in a panic. It was a dreadful experience. I struggled through the two hours somehow, and I was amazed that I'd passed.

It was very exciting—and there was my mentor, who kept saying, go for it, well done, go on to the next.

Then I decided to do the Access course. But I had to do one more module as well in order to be admitted the next September. It was very difficult: twentieth-century approaches to literary criticism, including feminist criticism. I was delighted to pass with a B.

The feminist stuff was fascinating. I hadn't read very much feminist literature. I spoke more in seminars, because of my excitement! That was a great change. What I read explained why I had been feeling restless, and a second-class citizen, and *only a housewife*. Because I had been living through these feelings, they had just crept up on me. Like the wrinkles in the mirror, you don't notice them.

I was able to stand back and say, that's exactly what I think and feel and felt and thought! It was magic.

Yes, it certainly led to changes—I suppose I felt more confident in saying things that I had thought but not been confident enough to voice; and in not accepting some of the things that people said: colleagues of my husband's joking about how wives' company cars should be fitted with a car seat for the child: these continual put-downs for the *little woman*—pat her on the head—I grew in confidence enough not to accept; to fight against things that had felt dodgy and uncomfortable, but I hadn't been sure enough to speak against.

For what it's worth, my husband thinks I'm the most feminist woman he knows. I don't regard myself as that. He isn't comfortable that I should be so, but he is proud of me.

Has it changed conversation here? Well, it does mean now that I have things to talk about, if he'll listen, that are as exciting to me as the things he talks about which excite him.

My older daughter Emma, now in her second year at another poly, is very, very supportive, and I find her a real ally—it sounds a bit wet for a mother to want her children to be friends, but I do find her a wonderful person, we can talk together about all sorts of things. She's doing history of art and design. I'm doing English literature and art history, so we have all sorts of things we can talk about.

I talked to Emma and to her younger sister Elizabeth shortly after meeting their mother. Before meeting them, I had talked to Vanessa about the value people put on motherhood; about her own feeling that she should prize, and others should honour, her thirty years' work for her children. She had been to a meeting at her poly about how to write a c.v. All wrote theirs. She put down her thirty years' parenthood—with names and dates of birth—where she would have put paid work if she had done it. The young woman running the meeting shrieked, and said, 'You mustn't mention your kids; it's bad enough being married.'

Elizabeth (daughter, aged 19): The first thing I remember is hundreds and hundreds of books appearing in the kitchen, on the bench and all over every table possible.

Emma: I thought it was absolutely brilliant when she got into the poly. Dad's got his degree from Cambridge. I was at poly—

Elizabeth: Mum's been searching around for something—

Emma: She's felt inadequate because she hasn't got a job—

Elizabeth: It was just incredibly exciting.

Emma: I remember this occasion when three friends of mine and me had all come in from the pub or somewhere and were sitting round the kitchen table and mum was there and she was trying to decide whether to do anthropology or English next term, and one of my friends had read anthropology at university, and one of them's reading English, and they had this huge argument, mum and these friends, and I was just sitting there not knowing anything about it really, fascinated to hear mum arguing, and it was real student talk, and I know mum enjoyed that incredibly.

Elizabeth: That's what the poly's done for her, it's given her so much more confidence in herself, in her own mind.

Emma: Which is why it was so exciting and really lovely to hear her having an argument with my friends. There are negative aspects to it, she gets incredibly het up sometimes over essays and she'll stay up till three o'clock in the morning and dad gets cross. And because we're younger we approach college life the normal way, we realize it doesn't matter that much. But she still doesn't have faith in herself.

Elizabeth: I think it's because she feels so lucky to be there she has to make absolutely the best of it she can.

Emma: D'you think? I think it's because she doesn't believe in herself enough. Her essay marks are better than mine, far better than mine—she doesn't believe that she could rush an essay if she had to. She went to a convent school, she was always told to put other people before yourself.

Elizabeth: And daddy's a very—

Emma: A very confident man, he's always achieved what he's wanted to achieve.

Elizabeth: And mum's been in the background and felt that she should keep quiet—and now she's doing something totally on her own and it's up to her only to do it.

Vanessa agrees about confidence:

I nearly abandoned Access. I went into this room packed round the edge with women, about twenty in all, and the first thing we were asked to do was say our names, and my heart thumped as it came to me as usual, and we also had to say the name of some important historical figure, someone important, and I just felt physically sick, physically ill, and in fact the name I mentioned was Luther—and there was a little titter from a rather confident and well-spoken American woman in the corner, and I just nearly died. I didn't know if she was laughing at some private joke, or whether she was laughing at me. It's hard to imagine that people can be so terrified of revealing their ignorance.

But that didn't last. The English was wonderful, and the art history in particular: it was the first time I'd seen reproductions of paintings projected on a white screen, and it gives the most amazing luminosity, and although we whizzed through 2,000 years of art history in four hours, it was the jewel of the course.

The philosophy was exciting, and the politics tutor was very nice. He ran an essay-writing skills day and really I think all of us keep those notes. He gave us a vivid image of writing essays being like making pastry, and you have to let an essay know who's boss.

The poly feels like a gift and a treat and a privilege when it's not most dreadfully difficult. It's such hard work. They say the advantage of being a mature student is that you have life skills; but the disadvantage, for me at any rate, is that you are so slow, by comparison with these 18-year-olds. Slow to do the reading, but not necessarily in thinking. Sometimes we make bigger, better, deeper, different connections. But most of them are so quick, so bright—so shiny. And they appear at times to find it less hard. I have a friend who appears to do very little reading, to think of wonderful ideas, and to produce wonderful essays very quickly. In many ways I fall into that middle-aged perfection trap: when I do a bit of work I never feel I've read enough: if only I'd just done that—I just never know where to stop.

But it just is lovely, it feels like a whole new life, a life of my own. It gives me self-respect, it gives me confidence. I long for people to say, d'you work? now; but of course they never do. For a while I kept it as a wonderful secret all to myself from colleagues' wives; but now I share it with anyone who'll listen.

For what it's worth also, when I was so tremendously excited at the beginning of the year, I found the most enormous support and encouragement and interest from women throughout—I'd be buying a pair of shoes and the 16-year-old salesgirl would say, oh, you're at the poly—and be interested. Oh, are you really? And from other women my age sometimes, oh you're clever, I couldn't do that.

The only really adverse comment I've had has been from an old friend, an extremely eminent lawyer, who literally—practically—patted me on the head, and said, what d'you want a degree for, my dear, I've got plenty, I'll give you one of mine.

Devastating, yes.

Several friends of my 19-year-old daughter Elizabeth have said, I've told my mother what you're doing, I wish she'd start something like that. A lot of interest, all over the place. But always, I'm afraid to say, female interest and support.

Life is very different from when I said to a woman friend at the end of a long summer holiday, oh, my goodness, I feel just like a fishbone, and she said, it's surprising you should say that, I feel just like a surprise pea—you know, one of those dehydrated peas. From then on I thought of both of us sitting on a plate, her the surprise pea and me the fishbone.

Vanessa's account both echoes and anticipates. Like Peter's, but in a different way, her schooling generalized her. She was a girl. Her purpose was marriage. Her first convent offered training: it provided her with accomplishments. Hers was much the kind of schooling for girls that George Eliot despised.

She was provided for; not discovered. She was trained to take her place in the regiment of wives. The danger of education-as-training is in its generality; in its assumption that all pupils are the same receptacle to be filled the same way. Many returners meet this sort of generality in their first education. It is evident in the stories of both Andrew and Sally, as we shall see. Vanessa was cheated of the chance to be seen as a surprising individual; with gifts that might not be easy to find—that might need subtle coaxing. Her first convent offered a different version of what Andrew in the next chapter calls 'factory farming'.

She also reflects a theme which appears again in several accounts. One of the accomplishments with which she was provided was ignorance: a pleasant lack of learning to set off her husband. But her first day in her Access course reveals how frightening ignorance can come to be. She felt ignorance as shaming—as did Peter. Many returners come to feel ignorance as profoundly inimical. Liz, in Chapter 11, talks of revulsion at ignorance—all at once, in an almost visionary moment. She was not so much talking of not knowing things, but of being fenced off from knowledge; of leading a life in which learning played no part. Afterwards, her return was inevitable, her desire to learn irrepressible.

Like Peter, Vanessa shows us the army of those who have not returned; the army of the generalized. Other women in that army sense her excitement, applaud her courage. She suggests a generous response: that women see her as admirable. But Peter meets rebuff from other men when he tells them about the Open University; much as Vanessa met rebuff from her lawyer friend: a man who did not like to see her moving from her proper station. Men and women seem primed to react differently to the idea of return—a distinction explored in more detail in Chapter 11.

Vanessa also anticipates later discussion, in Chapter 12, of the benefit of experience. Her daughter says that she—being younger—realizes that college 'doesn't matter that much'. She suggests the student insouciance that returners come to envy or strongly dislike. But for Vanessa, everything she studies bursts with implication, overwhelms with importance, ramifies uncontrollably. There is danger in seeing too much; in being too eager to make up for lost time. But mature students, she says, 'sometimes make . . . deeper connections'.

Learning for the mature student works well when her own life connects to what she studies. Peter's stress on the importance of self-expression, is this point made another way. He is saying that he needs to speak to think; he needs to use images and analogies from his own life, when asked to explain, when trying to understand. His own experience illuminates what he studies, as well as being constantly reinterpreted as he continues to learn.

The importance of recognition—acknowledgement—of the student as an individual is the same point made yet differently. With the same result as the attentiveness of Peter's first tutor or Eleanor's English teacher, the law lecturer who used thalidomide as an example was offering Vanessa an escape from generality. She was told: 'This is you: this lecture is you; this business is you; you belong here; your life belongs here.' I can imagine her longing to be able to reciprocate: to say, 'I know about this. Let me tell you how it was!'

It is this reciprocity—between learner and teacher, learner and subject—that adults crave, and on which their learning thrives.

5

Andrew: Learning to Fry

I had known from talking to Andrew just before he was due to take his finals that his sister had played an important part in his life. I decided to try to meet her.

She lives with her husband—twenty-five years a railway worker, now working for the council—in a small house on an estate on the edge of a large town in the south-west. She welcomed me, inviting me into the kitchen, where she was making rock-cakes for her grandfather, who was in hospital. Andrew teased her about them—'When she says rock she means rock; real geology.' But when we were on our own in the sitting room while June went back to the kitchen, he told me she's a very good cook, but that I mustn't tell her he said so—and did a mime of a swelling head.

Their affection is obvious, and is played in quick sketches in which one pretends to insult the other. 'Are you good at lifting?' he asked, casting me as the straight man. 'What do you mean?' 'Well,' he said, 'when they're done you'll need to come through and help me take them out, you take one side of the shelf and I'll take the other.'

We had a rock-cake. They were very good—spicy. Asked, I said, 'They're great, really good.' 'Don't overdo it', she said, 'I can't stand creeps', and laughed. But she forgave me, I think. Perhaps she sensed a shady implication of my praise: 'Here he is, trying to get me to talk into his tape-recorder, and he thinks he's got to butter me up about my cooking.'

I had another.

Some times I have the possibly deluded feeling that I can pick up the power of someone's mind like a radio signal. I was sure that June is as clever as her brother—who got two As and a C at A level in one year in his late twenties, and is fresh from Oxbridge with a history degree.

June works in a shop, and enjoys it, because she can be with people: she likes meeting them; likes working them out—understanding and assessing them.

'She can talk to anyone,' Andrew said, 'but I can't.'

His brother, he says, can make anything: 'He can build a house for you, he can brick, plumb, carpent, wire . . . all three of us are clever—I suppose that sounds big-headed.'

Then he thought, paused, and decided to be honest: 'Okay, I am clever. But I'm the only one who ended up going seriously into education and doing it there. I think David could have if he'd chosen to; I think you could have if you'd chosen to: still could. I just happen to be the one who did.'

'But I can't remember anything!' June said.

'I've been on to her to go, more than once!' said her brother.

'I can't remember anything when I read, that's honest, I can't.'

Andrew and I then demolished this argument.

'Once you're in it, and it's rolling, then—' and Andrew mimed a plane taking off and gathering speed, 'but it's getting in there.'

I then spoke about the excitement people feel when they return.

'It's damned hard when you start, that's the problem,' said Andrew.

'I don't think there's anything particular I would want to do. I quite like my life the way it is,' said June.

Then I admitted the cheek of evangelism.

All the way through the conversation I taped, June's dog padded about. It is a small black-and-white dog: with a body like a dachshund, and a high yapping conversational sort of bark. From time to time, its curiosity grew too strong and it approached the mike on the floor and nosed it, pushing it over. Deciding to accept me, it brought me one and then the other of a pair of furry pink slippers. It begged for rock-cake but was given none.

Their mother left home when Andrew was 5 and June was 14. Now, it seems, June is Andrew's champion. She is proud of him. Just before I left, she found the tape she'd made of Andrew's appearance on a radio programme. He went out of the kitchen and into the garden while we played the tape. 'He won't listen to it,' she said, but listened herself, mentioning the names of the people who made the programme, all of whom she'd met.

Meanwhile he was with the dog in the garden, tussling with it at dog level. Then he got to his feet and rolled another cigarette and began to stride about.

The loss of June's right to higher education is outrageous. But I wish to record her championship of her blind brother.

He revels in her company—as if her energy and affection feed his own. She believes in him:

> I've always said that, one day, Andrew will be famous, either in writing, or in something. I've said that for years, he will be. I know he'll do it. I know our Andrew will be somebody one day.

But whenever their true feeling showed itself, while we talked, the routine demanded a quick deflation:

> *Andrew*: Not entirely a nice somebody, but—

> *June*: He might be more of a ratbag than he is at the moment—but I think he will succeed, because he just keeps going, he will do it, because he won't let them get him down, he won't let them win.

But the routine was itself a sign of her support. I sense that Andrew mocks and jeers himself out of trouble: that brisk sarcastic self-chivvying gives him energy. His sister, joining in, boosts the charge.

Class Again

Once Andrew had passed his three A levels, he visited three Oxbridge colleges. June went with Andrew on all his visits to universities, and to all the colleges he tried at the university of his choice.

> *June*: They said we had to see this Dr Starmer. So we went up all this long passageway, and Andrew knocked at the door, and I said, this is Andrew Brewer—and he had students in there, and he said, can you wait a moment? So

the next moment all the students came out, and we go in and I didn't like this bloke when I first met him.

He was a snob—I only said hello to him—and we went in and it was beautiful, his study was wonderful, it was huge, with this big room adjacent to it.

The table was red wood: I always remember this huge big table and huge big chairs—

Andrew: Cut glass everywhere—

June: Everything else was very nice. It was a huge room— and he sat up there [June mimes position, suggests a distant figure] and we were sitting down here, and our Andy had his jeans and his shirt on—

Andrew: And my blue parka—

June: And his blue parka—

Andrew: And a roll-up.

June: Yes and a roll-up. And I just felt this thing about him. Then he started to talk, and he said, how many points have you got? I can't remember how many it was now—and you knew he didn't want Andy to go to his college straightaway. I could see his face: people give away a lot in their faces don't they—

Andrew: I got 13 points in my first year of A level, A, A, and C, and I would have thought it suggested I could handle just about anything, but he said he wanted two more As please next year, otherwise I couldn't go.

June: He got my back up—he really got my back up, and I really wanted to sock him, but I didn't. And I remember he was talking about books, and I had to get this little dig in about books, didn't I.

Andrew: I remember it well.

June: So I made this very sarcastic remark—I can smile and be sarcastic at the same time.

Andrew: Something about the *Confessions of a Window Cleaner*, as I recall.

June: I can't remember how the conversation came round, but I really wanted to thump him, because I thought, you arrogant pig, and I knew he wasn't any better than I was, I was as good as he was, in fact I was better than he was because I behaved better than he did.

He really got on my nerves, because he was looking down on Andy and I could see it. So we came out of there, Andy, didn't we?

Andrew: Um—we did.

June: The snobbery was obvious in the way he looked at Andy, he went in with his jeans, shirt, and roll-up . . .

This encounter offers a further glimpse of a theme of the last chapter. The worker meets the don in his cut-glass and mahogany stronghold. The worker and his supporters— Andrew's sister-in-law was with them too—are awed by good furniture and by the size of the rooms; but in the end repelled by snobbery. The don does not see beyond parka and roll-up. Both were tests, which he failed.

The premature conclusion of the school careers of the two returners in the last chapter can be explained by history, to some extent. But Andrew—and Sally whose story follows his—went to school at a time when many would imagine their opportunities as good as anyone's: in the 1960s and early 1970s.

Andrew went to a comprehensive. He left it with no qualifications at all. Sally picked up a handful of modest CSE passes at her secondary modern, which she attended in the late 1960s; but as qualifications, they were pretty well useless. So, with these next two returners, there is an enigma to solve. Why did their schools miss them?

I talked to Andrew first in his college room, not long before his finals.

Andrew's Schooling: Wars in the Library

I was born total. Congenital cataracts. The story goes that when I was 4½ I was being walked by the hand by my granny, and I said, Granny, what's that? And she said, it's the town hall you silly sod, and we kept on walking. And then what I'd said hit her. This was some weeks after an operation that was either supposed to work or to fail completely—and it worked. She was a dumpy old bustling granny, lovely character, used to wear aprons and do her cooking in big dishes: that kind of granny.

Well, she took me the length of the whole street and told everybody, he saw the town hall, he saw the town hall!

And this was nice. I had reading sight at school, not blackboard sight but close book sight, so it was a matter of sitting at the front of the class. Primary school was all right. I remember running around the playground a lot and shouting.

It's possible that I wasn't bothered until I had to do things that I couldn't see to do properly: that's only a thought.

I enjoyed school at first. I was in the A and B streams, and it was going along fairly well. I was good, I enjoyed it—but I was never an outstanding academic pupil: it was never a matter of: this boy will go far!

I've always had a thing about history. I don't know how that interest started: it was just there. History has always been fun. No, it wasn't from anyone in my family. My father was an aircraft riveter, my brother's a carpenter, and my sister works in a petshop. I'm not knocking them: that's what they do and that's fine. But there's no academic tendency in our family. Yes, there was a good history teacher at my last school, the comprehensive. I turned up for most history lessons: it was good, it was fun.

French was diabolical, I have the ear for languages of a housebrick. Bloody hopeless at languages, I haven't got a clue. I needed French to pass prelims here, and it was a matter of memorizing whole chunks of stuff.

No, up until secondary school everything was lovely.

I think it was something to do with woodwork: I could never get things straight, and the line always seemed to move when I was sawing along it. And I got pissed off with this. We had a teacher who used to like to say, and now Andrew will show us how it's not done. This was when I still had reasonable sight, reading sight, but not precision sight—and I'm also cack-handed; and if your vision's not quite right, hand–eye co-ordination doesn't develop properly anyway. He was a sarcastic sod—he'd say, you can all now talk for five minutes; so I'd start talking, and my neighbour would say, shut up, shut up. But he's just told us to talk, I'd say. But he didn't mean it. It was antagonistic teaching. It was not the way to teach. It was wrong.

So I began to skive off. There were a lot of other things too—my mother pissed off when I was 5. That's all in it somewhere. My father was at work; my brother was at work all day; sister was married; no one around between seven and five: dead easy, stay at home!

When I was at school, I spoke regularly, a lot of it rubbish, but I was often the person who said, hold on, chief, that doesn't make sense!

I remember once we had to change verbs into nouns, when I was in my fifth year. We had to turn sweep into a noun. So I said, Sooty hit Sweep over the head. I thought that did it brilliantly!

The teacher was not pleased. I thought—if you don't like it, tough.

And there was a dreadful book called *The Pearl*. Not really what you call full of excitement. The only thing I did really like was the history with Mrs Armitage. She was fun. It wasn't just history. It would be history sometimes, and then she'd chuck in something else, just offhand. She'd ask us what the capital of Iceland was, and then some more history, and then she'd say what kind of currency do they use in India. And then back to history. And then she'd shoot off again. You couldn't just lock in on one line. It keeps your head moving: you never know what's going to hit you next. Wonderful stuff.

But I was an awkward bugger. I wasn't often there, in my final years, and when I was there I was asking, why why why all the time. You get a nice reasoned answer. Then—why? again. And it was bound to get irritating. With classes twenty-four strong or more, they were probably getting heartily pissed off with me. And there were dozens of others in the class, and here's me on the rabbit, and two or three others on the rabbit as well, trying to be funny and often failing dismally—the kind of thing that 15-year-olds often do, if they think they're a bit smart but they ain't, or else they're smart but haven't got the ammunition: whatever way round it goes. We did not get on.

I don't really know what teachers said about me. But I was hauled up in front of the truancy board or whatever it is. They said—the thing 15-year-olds hate to hear—you're very intelligent, why are you wasting it? But when you're 15, who wants to be told that sort of cobblers? So either they were saying this as form, or else they meant it: that I was pigging around and blowing it. But I just wasn't interested in what they said. I didn't think about it: it was just the stuff they churned out to 15-year-olds, and I didn't want that, thank you. I just took an instant dislike to the whole lot sitting at the table—for no reason. They wanted me to go to school and I didn't want to go, so I didn't like them.

But I didn't have any idea of the future then, anyway. I just thought I'd leave school and get a job somewhere and that was it. Factory farming.

Why didn't anything reverse the trend? It's a factory. I don't mean that they were insensitive at all, but if I'd gone to them—mind you, who would at 15?—and said: something's going radically wrong here, I don't find your lessons all that hard—that's the kind of dreadful thing I would have said—can we sort something out here? Then, who knows? But why should they bother? Given that they've got all these other people in their classes, why bust their gut when I'm not even trying that hard, and I'm not there very often? I can see it from their point of view—it's like making an appointment to see someone, and you turn up and they're not there, and you think—well, sod you, up yours sunshine, I'm off.

Andrew's explanations are persuasive. He truanted because his terrorist woodwork teacher upset him—much as Eleanor was upset by teachers making fun of her accent. Once he began skiving off, the attraction of school, never strong, waned completely. He did enjoy history; but it sounds as if Mrs Armitage pleased him much as a good fruit machine might have pleased him if he had been a different sort of truant. Her classes were fun because they 'kept your head moving'; you never knew what was going to happen next. It was the sort of fun, as an academic pupil, I was given at school as a rest from real work.

She did not offer what he really needed, nor did any other teacher. *None of it was hard enough.* Andrew was a victim of low expectations. But he cannot really imagine going up to a teacher at 15 to tell her so, and ask for changes to be made in his diet. It was impossible to imagine not just because it would have been blasphemous coming from a truant—but because he did not know what he wanted. All he knew was that he was bored; he did not know why he was bored; and he certainly did not think school could offer him anything—except from fruit-machine history—as an antidote. I suspect that he is right when he imagines that his teachers found him irritating. 'Arrogant' is a key word of teacherly dismissal. His cocky questions and answers would have been 'arrogant'. No doubt he timed them to tease and goad: bored children must amuse themselves somehow.

Secondary schooling has failed clever working-class children like Andrew again and again and again. Andrew had decided that school was a transit camp, a necessary evil to be outfoxed if possible. Meanwhile his teachers were committed to the futile in their attempts to help him, so that their help always felt like hindrance. 'Come to school,' they said—but school was boring. 'Don't ask so many silly questions, and we'll like you better', they said. But though his questions sounded annoying, his curiosity was genuine. Not to ask questions was impossible. And pride probably dictated that he try to amuse his mates by spicing his curiosity with malice.

Even if a teacher had set about him with promises and exhortations and interesting work, he might not have succeeded, because Andrew had already written down a rule for his life which said, 'You will leave school as soon as possible and get a job.'

His teachers did not respond cleverly to the revelation of how Andrew spent his time when he was not at school. They missed their chance to see through the generalities—of Class and Arrogant Behaviour—in which he was camouflaged; missed their chance to detect his unique set of gifts and needs—to respond to him as Eleanor's headmistress to her, or as his 'abbess' to Peter.

We used to do woodwork on Wednesday mornings, and I

began to not go in. Then it became all of Wednesdays. Then Wednesday, Thursday, and Friday. This is when I was in the second year. And once I realized I could do it and no one bothered, it just went on. I actually stayed away for eight weeks solid. When my father found out he went berserk. They wrote to him and said, where's your son gone? He didn't know, poor sod. As far as he was concerned I was going to school every day.

But the hours I spent skiving off school I'd spent in the library—there were big thick books on the Second World War. I'd sit down and read through all this stuff, and if anyone asked, you'd say you were doing a school project. And I think I learnt an awful lot of history in the library, just enjoying life. Reading books and books and books. I had encyclopaedic knowledge of ships and tanks and planes. I wasn't interested in why was there a war or the justification of it. None of it had anything to do with the history in school. The detail I was going into was enormous—and their history was standard secondary school history.

I'd wait until about ten when there was no chance of anyone seeing me still on their way to school, and the library was only a few minutes away from my house. Through the back door, along a back alley, over a couple of roads, and that was it—great.

My father tried to find out why. The woodwork was only a part of it—there must have been other things. The people at the tribunal asked me why I didn't go. I didn't know why—I just didn't go!

No, they weren't interested in the fact that I'd been in the library. In fact the headmaster found me there once: after the tribunal he knew where I'd be. Whenever I wasn't in school he'd find me in the library. He'd tap me on the shoulder, and say, come back, Andrew. Not: what are you reading, and why are you interested in it?—just: come back.

But that was what I wanted. I wasn't one of these people who charged off to amusement arcades. I didn't like those. I wanted the library and books please. By then they'd rumbled me. Then it was go to school. I even went to live with my sister who'd been married only months. Yes it was a surveillance job, I had to go, she was there. But it didn't mean you couldn't go to registration and then walk out again. I got caught once or twice but I kept on doing it. Eventually they gave me this piece of paper which had to be signed by each teacher you went to.

I blew the three O levels I took. I don't know why. There was a question in the history paper about the Pacific war. I just went berserk on that one. There were pages on it: there was bugger all on anything else, but there were pages on that. I didn't have much time for the other questions.

By then when I skived I wouldn't go to the library—I'd get books out and read them at home.

The irony is matchless.

When Andrew was asked at the tribunal why he did not go to school, he could not then have known that school was not educating him; that his true schooling was taking place in the library.

But being in the library was wrong, just as smoking behind the bikeshed was wrong. However, his teachers did not have to worry about him much longer. The skiver with his cocky answers left at 16.

Soon I was unloading lorries in a furniture warehouse, a retail place. Then I was out on the van delivering. Problems had started by this stage. I found that I couldn't read the invoices. You know when you get three layers of stuff—the pink one we used was the third one down. I'd say, why can't people write properly any more? I wouldn't think it was because I couldn't see these things; it was—tell them to press harder please! And I couldn't read street signs. The bloke I was working with had to read the map and drive and find the house numbers, and this was a bit much, even though I made up for it by doing more of the carrying. I insisted on it.

And then it was selling furniture—quite nice, rather good.

And then I started falling over the furniture. Embarrassing business. And it was a matter of: yes madam, this is rather a nice suite, yes it's—blue—a very lovely suite. [Andrew mimed peering very closely at the furniture to make sure of the colour.]

Eventually the boss took me to one side and said, what's wrong? I don't bloody know, I said. You can't stay, he said, because it's getting dangerous. If you fall over a coffee table with a glass top one day, you might die, and to put it bluntly, we'd get blamed. You'll have to leave.

I was tested again, and I had glaucoma.

I screamed and shouted and ran around. I was bad to live with for a long time. I was 21. I was mad as hell. This was not fair. What had I done? And I had this job and I was making money, and it was fine. And suddenly—out. That was no fun. There was a lot of drinking done then. How my father put up with me I don't know, because I was the most awkward cantankerous bastard you could shake a stick at. Think of a man, now in his early twenties, acting like a 5-year-old. Everybody knew what I was doing—but they put up with me.

But from there on things got rather better. I went to the RNIB place in Torquay and they sussed me out pretty quickly. I don't think I had much choice as far as going there's concerned. It was greatly preferable to the alternative: the county had something called Tom Foley. I just think his way of doing things is wrong. He's the mobility officer and he's got the whole county to cover, and I didn't want to do one hour per week thank you: I'd be at it for months learning in that way. And my father's at work, my brother's at work—what do I DO?

I won't be able to leave the house safely on my bleeding tod, if it's one hour's training per week, for months! Stay indoors all day? Stick that. So I went down to Torquay. I was scared witless to start with—but I decided it was better than a poke in the eye. Besides which they were going to pay me! It beat staying at home.

They were good. They don't make many allowances for you. They've set the thing up so they don't have to. I went down there two or three times while I was working with the blind myself. It's beautiful; it's done beautifully. They've spent a great deal of time working that place out. Lines where carpet stopped and floor began for instance—they would often be so placed that if you followed them they'd lead you to a door; which would teach you *how* to use that kind of guide. So you can stand up and just check your feet—and charge! And there's nothing in the way on that line, until you reach the end where you're back on to wood. Then you can reach out for the door handle. Open it. Close it. No stick—no worries. And nobody's going to leave anything on the floor down there because that's a criminal offence. All the doors shut automatically. They're balanced that way: if you open a door, it will close, gently, not with a great bang. And this is good, because who wants to walk into the edge of a door? Down there it isn't possible. You can't wedge them either—wedging doors is also an evil thing, because people use doors to mark where they're going. If it's open, they're lost, and it will look blind! They don't like it!

You had to do all sorts of weird stuff. You had to do pottery. It was occupational therapy as well, I suppose; but it's beautifully done. Bill gives you a big ball of clay and two bits of wood. He can do all sorts of things with pottery: he's good. What you do is squash the clay down first, and get really mucky: everyone likes getting mucky. It's great fun. Then you put these two wooden bits either side of the clay. Then you get a roller. If it stays on the wood you cannot roll the clay too thin. You roll it out, and it's fun. Any fool can do this. You rabbit to the person next to you, and Bill is telling dirty stories all the time.

The templates would come next—say you're making a cottage, there'd be one for the end of it, or for a window, and you'd cut around it. Straightforward. And when you've done it all you feel really clever, and you assemble it. Bill didn't tell you you had to assemble it yourself. A bit of a worry that—but he did help a bit, he would cut a furrow in the base bit, and you would slot the upright bit into it using slip as a glue—spraying yourself and everyone else with this stuff. But nobody minded, and Bill would make sure it was straight. Of course the craftsmanship is appalling, but Bill *doesn't alter it*—he makes sure the walls are straight, but he doesn't alter what you've done.

Then you can have a musical box thing put into it, and when you've done that, it's fired, and comes out, and you paint it. You have made it. And you've probably never seen a bit of pottery before in your life.

When you go home, you just casually produce this really

nice looking cottage—you can put ivy on it and all sorts of stuff—and you give it to someone as a Christmas present. You say, oh yes, I made it. Yes, I put the musical bit in as well, it was there to do, so I thought, why not. Very casual. And of course your mother, father, husband, wife—is going to think it's the best thing since sliced bread because you've never made anything like that before. And you're not going to tell them that it's just roll, roll, cut, cut, stick, stick—like a Lego set. They think it's great; they react differently to you—not a lot but a bit—it starts the game going!

There was woodwork down there, and a metal workshop; and lots of things you can do if you sit down and think about them; and they've done all the thinking out for you.

They've got a capstan lathe there. I never thought I'd use a capstan lathe in all my bloody life! I thought they were horrendously complicated. It's beautifully thought out. There are no obvious allowances. Someone asked one of the volunteers who work in the canteen, I can't cut my food up, will you cut it for me please? Judith, who was in charge, came over and said, you can't cut your food up? No, he said. You'll learn, she said. She left him. The whole place went stony quiet, as if everyone was thinking is he going to have a go, or is he going to be a coward and leave? Is he going to run away? But he started to try and cut his food up. I expect he made a pig's arse of it first time. I expect it went everywhere. But nobody was going to do it for him.

Another thing about the way the place works is that it's flexible. You have braille lessons—if you want them. You don't have to do them. You have a limited amount of say— though they know what you should be doing. But it's not: you will, but: we think it would be a good idea. The staff are good—the staff go around and watch how you're walking, for instance. But they don't come up and say: bad! They'll come up to you and say: you're still leaning a bit to the left when you walk. And they'll talk to the mobility man and tell him you're still leaning to the left.

No, there aren't many staff—which is why they use the longer-staying students, which is good for you as well. You learn, he learns, everyone learns; and the teacher has more time for the really bad ones.

The first thing you do with engineering is play with Meccano. That kills your fingers. Lots of blind people find work in light assembly—and it's a game: let's see how good you are at light assembly. They give you battalions of bits to use—and you have to put something together, then do five assemblies in a limited time. Don, in charge, encourages you not to shout to find out where he is if you need him: you go and find him. You normally know where he is because he talks almost as much as I do.

You do more and more difficult ones, and the last one they give you—shit, this is bad news. You're turning these screws and washers in and it's knackering your fingers up. You're going to read braille in the afternoon, and your fingers are a bit sore. But it's the best way for your finger to be! It's been prodded a lot. It's exactly the best way to have your hand: a bit red, which means all the blood's there and the nerve endings are right. It was only later when I'd been working for a while that I cottoned on. Crafty little bastards!

They had me sussed down there damned fast. Christ! One of the things they had was working outside, mowing lawns, helping the gardener, and I didn't like that much. I went to the boss, and asked to do more braille and typing and less outside work. He said, if there were enough people working outside, fine; and there were enough so I stayed in the braille and typing room and worked there instead.

This was great. And I was a good student. I had braille sussed inside three and a half weeks. If often takes people three months. But I'd been working all day on this: I couldn't read now! Reading sight's gone here now! I was desperate to read.

That's where I discovered I had the knack of helping other people. I was part of a group of eight, aged 18 to 60. After a while Jenny the braille teacher would say, could you go and help so-and-so a bit? Eventually the students would come and see me at night for more help. I thought, this is fun. I can do this.

Jenny was lovely. She really knew her stuff. She knew exactly what people liked. She's the only two-handed braille reader I've ever known. She can read one half of a line left-handed, and one half right-handed. I don't know how the hell she does it. That gives her double the speed. Mind you she's been blind from birth and she's always read that way. But damn! she was good. I thought I was fairly good. By the time I left there I was doing fifty words per minute, but Jenny could double that easily. Class.

She used to send her dog around the room: Matty, a labrador, a lovely peaceful dog. She had her box under Jenny's table; and when Jenny was working at her table she'd say—have a look, Matty. Matty would amble around the tables and have a look at you. If you were working she'd carry on, and if you weren't she'd stop and have a sniff and have a little look at you to see what was going on. She was an amazing dog. We all loved her. You could hear her coming round because she had a little bell, going tinkle, tinkle, tinkle. Again, that was learning: you'd start listening for this bell and then you'd start listening for all sorts of things. So you'd hear the bell and if you'd been clever you'd palmed a biscuit at meal time so you could slip it to her. Matty was a beautiful dog.

What's the braille speed like to start with? It's horrible. I was teaching someone once, and reading—D—E—A—D.

Deeyad, he said. So I said: no, there's no such word. Try and concentrate on the whole—I know you have to concentrate on each letter, but try and hold it in your head. D—E—A—D—It's still bloody deeyad!

I'm busting myself to laugh, because I'd hit this stage. I'd hit the word agriculture: it's put in deliberately. It took me a long time to read it, because by the time you reach the E you've forgotten all the rest. It's gone!

But cracking braille was good. Jenny was the kind of person you go for to try and beat her. You haven't a hope of beating her. Her fingers go like typewriter keys. You're sweating like hell to manage 35 or 40 which is a bloody good braille speed—and she's over the ton!

His speed was prodigious. He left others in his group behind:

Why are they stuck? I thought, this is silly—I was also showing off a bit of course, there were a couple of young females in the group.

And I thought, hang about, I'm better at this than they are, whay hay! Let's ram this in a bit!

The sound which I have presented as 'whay hay' was a triumphant laugh; not at his cleverness, but at success. He had not known much success.

Let's push. Three and a half weeks was damn near a record down there. When I realized I was good at it, I just charged. Then I was going to Jenny for things to read, please. She would ask me whether I'd read such and such, and I'd say, yes, done that. She was a bit surprised—and she said, how about Winnie the Pooh?

That was a deliberate mean trick. One of the lines started: poetry sign, poetry sign, open quotes, open inner quotes, then at the end exclamation marks, close inner quotes, close outer quotes.

You read this line flowing and then you hit: AR, AR, H, Funny H, FFFFFFF, Funny J, J. And you know that can't be right. She gave it to me deliberately to say, that's all very well, but you're going to get some real bad stuff here—which I needed because I was showing off.

I swear I wasn't going to go and ask Jenny for help—I said I could do it, and here was this book, and I knew that it was no good saying the book's wrong, the book's never wrong. Bloody hell, I was three hours on this thing—sweating, cussing. Eventually I had to go to Jenny, and say, Jenny, what the hell is this line here? And once she explained it wasn't letters at all and I wasn't thinking properly yet—well, the point was duly made. She was just saying, you're good all right—but slow down a bit. Think more.

I have quoted Andrew's account of the RNIB college at length not just because it is fascinating in itself, but also because it offers a contrast with his account of his schooling.

His explanation of failure at school is typically unsentimental and rigorous. RNIB college—above all—taught Andrew never to make allowances. For him, the greatest possible blasphemy is to let himself off because he is blind. Such rigour makes glib excuses—whether to do with blindness or not—always unacceptable. Sitting in judgement on his school career, he sees no reason not to don his black cap. 'I was lazy and never there: why should they have bothered with me?'

His explanation includes a telling detail: why, he argues, should his teachers have made subtle bids for his co-operation when they had twenty-four others in their classes? I had asked him why he thought no teacher took the trouble to try to catch such a bright pupil, however elusive, however 'arrogant'. His answer makes sense. Teachers have to weigh up chances of success. It must have been difficult not to decide to leave Andrew, that occasional visitor, to his own devices. And schools are prey to cruel pieties. INDUSTRY AND OBEDIENCE OR ELSE has always been the most popular school motto. It is still popular, despite discovery of the Whole Child. Schools sell themselves as subtle fishers of children—'We will hook talent however stubbornly it lurks behind rocks and sulks on the bottom'. But the reality is that schools still lack power: too many pupils refuse to bite. So they are relegated to generalities which allow them to be discounted: 'He's one of those lazy arrogant boys: why should I bother?'

Once Andrew could be thus generalized, thus discounted, his teachers probably stopped bothering to fish for him at all.

He was easy to discount—to label—because of his class. It must be significant that his great success at RNIB college was in circumstances where appearance and accent were likely to be irrelevant. His most important teacher of all—the wonderful Jenny—could not even see him, so could not possibly be bemused by parka and roll-up into thinking him not worth her attentions. At college there was true equality of opportunity. At school his teachers could look at the way he was dressed and listen to the way he spoke and not be plagued by the thought that he was sinking out of his parents' proper water. Teachers often have a sharp sense of the tragedy of a middle-class child failing academically. In collusion with worried parents, they will work hard at such a child's salvation. Loss of income, status, respect, is a middle-class terror. In saving the falling child of 'good' parents, teachers may be moved by their own fears. But Andrew's dilemma was less poignant, less urgent. He was clearly a working-class child determined to leave school for a working-class life. If that choice had already been made by the circumstances in which he lived and the expectations of his family, then they did not need to quarrel with him, except to shake their heads on ceremonial occasions like the truancy tribunal and lament waste of intelligence.

Parka and roll-up and vocabulary are now Andrew's chosen goads and teases—at his Oxbridge college he refused to refer to the dining hall as anything but the canteen; and at the interview at the college where he was not made welcome he deliberately addressed the gentlemanly don as 'chief'. He has won himself power and confidence to tease people to reveal their prejudice and stupidity.

But even when he was 22, full of confidence after RNIB college, he met mysterious reluctance at a college of further education when he applied to do O levels, as we shall see. He concedes that their reluctance to take him on was partly the crass assumption that a blind person must be slower, stupider, and less promising than a seeing student; but he adds:

> Mind you, when I went to apply, I turned up in my usual exciting academic dress—jeans, old parka, and roll-up, and it was natural enough they were going to think, who's wandered in off the streets?

But RNIB college was not only a chance for Andrew to enjoy genuine equality of opportunity. His account suggests that he had for the first time in his life found somewhere apart from the public library where he was stimulated and intellectually provoked. His respect for the cleverness of the way the college worked grew and grew after he left—especially when he became a social worker with the blind, teaching them mobility and independence. But his account suggests that he was impressed at the time, even if he did not quite know why.

For a start, the college was flexible, where school—swayed by the idiot pieties—was inflexible. When he was discovered skiving in the library, school hauled him back to boredom at his desk. But when at college he asked to work less outdoors and more in the braille room, his request was allowed.

Most important of all, college—from the outset—set the highest possible expectations. Andrew's account of the import-ance of doors is significant in this connection. Doors had to close and stay closed so that students could guide themselves from door to door with confidence. Blind people need to learn the benefit of bravery. The college was organized in such a way as to let students realize that they could strike out—'charge' is Andrew's word, from his stock of military vocabulary, so that a multitude is always a battalion—with no worry about obstacles. The stick and that lesson once learnt, the blind can take confidence out into busy streets, crammed platforms, and charge. But what Andrew suggests the students wanted to avoid most is *looking blind*. An open door—the sudden disappearance of a staging post—would force them to hover, to shuffle, and to ask for help.

In other words, the expectation was total independence, a life unconstrained by disability. All were expected to become autonomous. The invigoration of his three months of intense learning was great. RNIB college was like a Utopian school, where no second is wasted, all influences converge, where pummelling of the fingers in the morning cultivates the right degree of sensitivity in the nerve-endings for the afternoon's braille; and where even the bell worn by a teacher's dog can be subliminally instructive.

In my first book I made the polemical point that psychiatrically disturbed adolescents misjudged by their schools may have misjudgement dissolved if they are lucky enough to find themselves in a good psychiatric unit where they can be looked at afresh. The point here is the same: Andrew went blind, and found himself in an institution dedicated to the opposite of the generalizing tendencies of schools—in which teachers are prevented by large numbers and the urgency of their timetables from seeing all their pupils as individuals. The college insisted that students should not be constrained by what they had in common, should not just be The Blind. The college sought to make disability irrelevant.

Blind college gave Andrew the first inkling of the scope of his intelligence, and that he was good at difficult things: reading braille, and teaching blind people. Difficulty is a theme in returners' accounts. They like difficulty—of which they were starved in school; they thrive on exalted expectations. Andrew came to crave challenges; to scorn the straightforward.

I'm patient. It's a great feeling when they get it right, and you know that they're getting it right because you've shown them. It's the best kind of teaching—it's practical; everyday. They get it right, because you've done it right. But you need an awful lot of patience, because it is a desperately slow thing to start with. You don't have to be blind to teach the blind, that's a silly fallacy, but it does help a lot.

As the first step in his 'return', RNIB college was a huge success.

Frying the System

After RNIB college, Andrew says:

I came away from there really geed up here now: go for this! I went to London to be interviewed for a computer course. I'd done an aptitude battery first. I did fairly well: 75 per cent and 70 per cent on the letters and numbers business. And the man who ran the course told me I could probably do it, but without O levels they couldn't find employment for me. So I said, okay, Charley, if you want O levels I'll get you O levels. Okay smart-arse, I shall fry you. You watch.

Oh yes, I respond to challenges like that: if someone says you've got to do something, I'm going to fry them. Yes.

So I went down to the local FE place. I'd just done all that nice work at college and I was fairly good at it—so, charge! Keep it moving. Did June come with me? I expect she did, she normally does—to make sure they aren't being smart with me. But they were very sort of: I don't know if we can let you do an O level . . . June by this time would have been at boiling point; but she wouldn't say anything so as not to make me feel embarrassed.

But one was all they would let me do. History. So I do my one, and I was a good boy, and asked a lot of questions, taped everything and went home and braille-typed it. I taped the whole session. The alternative was doing nothing all day, sat there like a lemon. I had to do something; so I thought I might as well attack it.

When he passed the exam with an A, his teacher called at his house to congratulate him. As at RNIB college with Jenny, he made friends with teachers, and was appreciated and acknowledged by them. And as at college, circumstances were much more benign than the large classes at school.

His class was fun. He was a lovely man. He put up with my tape-recorders and with me turning him on and off—and he knew I was turning him on and off and he wasn't bothered.

It dwindled down to about eight of us in the end. It wasn't as much fun as English A level with Stephanie, but it was fun. He was a good teaching person: teaching from the front. And it was a nice big centrally heated building, and there were even canteens!

The syllabus was modern English and European, as far as I remember. No, he didn't do wars, it was the other bits; and once I got into the other bits, they were fun too. Now I had something to put in between my wars, you see. Then I began to cotton on that the big thing is the social and economic changes that produce a war. I was in now: history of all kinds was fine.

I'd read something, and I'd think—what did he do that for? I don't know when it happened, but that's how my mind normally goes. I'll find something I don't know, and I'll trot off and have a look. Then you've got to find something else to find out how this happens. Then it starts rolling: I like to find out how things work, and why they work and what they are; historical and economic things. Once I'm in it, I'm really in it.

And O level history wasn't that hard.

By the time he had taken and passed four more O levels, he had been trying to find work for some time without success. Then he began to have more experience—as a volunteer—of teaching other blind people.

I happened to be in the newsagent's one day and they said—there's a bloke a couple of streets away, and he doesn't seem to be coping: all he seems to be eating is mince.

Well, I met him and we got talking. I told him I'd been down to Torquay and learnt all this good stuff. And he said: how d'you do spuds, chief—because I'm a bit nervous about those big pans of boiling water—it scares the shit out of me.

I told him it scared the shit out of me too—and it turned out that he really wasn't eating properly. I went round to his house and helped to sort things out. So I was back in business. I decided I didn't want to do the computer course anyway.

It was a good experience. It got me back into thinking again. Jenny had put the idea of teaching blind people into my mind—why not have a go? she said, you're doing it now—but the idea had to cook for those few years.

I then did a course training to work with blind people in Leeds. I did my four O levels in June and I was off to Leeds in September.

You had to live on your own: if you can't live on your own how the hell are you going to teach someone else to do so? It was mean. Torquay knew about us. But Leeds couldn't have cared less. Leeds is a hell of a big place, and if you get lost in the town centre it's bad news. I did get lost—took a wrong turning and got utterly bamboozled. I phoned my girl-friend, miles away down south. I said, I'm cold, it's raining and I'm bloody lost! She said, stay there, I'll get my car out and come and get you. So I said—how can you find me if I can't find me? I started laughing my head off. It didn't matter after that. Sometimes when it's cold and you feel terrible it's some silly thing that saves you—and you start laughing your brains out. That did it. I went out of the phone box, and started walking in squares until I found a street name I knew; and went home. I phoned up Sal and said, I'm home now.

The Torquay lot looked after you; but the Leeds lot—well, it was: if you can't make it you're out, sunshine. There were sighted people on the course; and the attitude was, if you can't see, that's rough.

They teach you how to be a technical officer for the blind and partially sighted. It was bloody hard work: it was mean. Cooking and bed-making and baby-care. You would pair up, and one of you would teach the other. Baby-care for God's sake! But it was fun sussing out *how* someone can do this. If I'm going to live with someone and babies come along, I don't want to sit there and say, sorry, I can't do this. I want to do my fair share.

You've got to teach people how to do nearly everything really—then they can go and live with someone on equal terms. Me for example: there are some things I can't do, but most things I can do. No half-way please. If you play, you play their game. I spent this afternoon playing pinball—and I didn't lose every time. I beat them a few times. Not often—but I did.

No, no, I wasn't over the frustration of it by the time of Leeds: that's always there. I'm going out with someone tonight—she's 25, and I'm told she's very good-looking. But I don't bloody know, do I!

But yes, it was less annoying than just after I'd lost the job, because now I was sorting out ways of dealing with it. But it's love–hate all the way up. When they first gave me this wonderful reading machine, I was tempted to love it one minute and smash it to bits the next. It's a great machine and I love it and it's my idea, and it's good. But I shouldn't need it!

Pinball—it's cost me a bloody fortune learning that. But I've done it. I can play most people, and have a reasonable chance of beating them. But if I could see the ball—the speed I've got now and the way I know how the machine bangs off this and bangs off that—I'd burn them all! Damnation.

After Leeds I went job-hunting, and I hit the standard problem. I can't drive. Either I didn't get the job because I can't drive, or because I don't give good interviews. I remember one place where they said, if we gave you the job what would you change? I immediately launched off into about eighty-five pet schemes of mine. And afterwards I thought—you daft bugger.

The first thing I was going to do was have a survey done: ask all the people who were going to be my responsibility, what do you want? But suppose that what they wanted wasn't what they'd been getting for the last ten years. Who would be responsible? Not me—but the senior people. Think of the trouble this could cause.

I kept on launching these pet schemes. I wanted to show that I'd thought about my job, that I was going to do it well, and that I had it sussed. They don't like you to have it well sussed. They don't! You're likely to cause problems.

I was talking in one place about a thing they have in Sweden. If you are male you have no idea what a female is like. All over—have you? There was one bloke who thought—this is just a story I heard—that women had breasts on their back. And in Sweden they have this scheme where they employ models and people are told—touch! Feel free! It isn't mucky—it's just finding out where everything is. It was all carefully done, and there was a third person in the room. The models were professional people who posed for artists or that sort of thing.

A great idea: it should be done. But the reaction I got! Shock horror! Bloody hell! Think of the fun the papers would have with that, they said—groping sessions by social services!

That was a job in Surrey. I was determined to convert the whole world to the right way of doing things.

Yes, of course it hurt that my enthusiasm wasn't acknowledged. I thought they were all wrong and I was right. But they all want to keep their cushy little world going, these people. I got angrier and angrier, so each interview I went to got worse and worse and worse. I was defeating my own object.

I got the job back home because I started doing some voluntary work: I offered to do the work I was qualified to do unpaid. All I wanted was my travelling expenses. And they let me do that. Then they decided to create a post, and I was in there with both feet, thank you.

I'd learned a bit by then: I did the normal things, kept them happy. I did it for five years, and that was enough for anyone.

What sort of thing did it involve? There was one bloke who wouldn't go out, socially. Nobody knew why. It turned out he was worried about going to the lavatory. He said he got too close and splashed his trousers. So I said— simple answer, find the bowl and sit. Now he goes out. That kind of thing. Vital. Things you've never been taught. Things like what you can safely eat in company. Spaghetti and peas are the familiar ones to be avoided.

I taught someone who was better than me. You should have seen her! She was so good—I taught her everything.

She was married, and she had a great husband, fantastic husband. He took me aside early on and said, how can I help? And I said, check her typing for her, encourage her, and always tell her the truth. If she's missing bits on the washing-up, don't you do it. Watch, and if she's missing bits, explain; then let me know and I'll make sure she's doing it right.

She lost her sight—went through a car windscreen, and someone had the bright idea to pull her back through, and that's what did it.

She was like me; she was going to beat these bastards, please. Yes, damn right, I could identify with her. And she liked being taught the way I liked to teach: push them, not too hard. No doubt I've done things wrong, and pushed a bit too hard sometimes, and sometimes not hard enough. I'm always safe: they'll cut their hands now and then; but they won't kill themselves or break legs. And when they do something right, you celebrate: yes! That's a winner! Then do it again to make sure it wasn't just luck.

Then you go to them and pretend you need advice and say: how do I show someone how to clean a cup properly?

So then they show *me*: teaching the teacher: that's a big thing. They love to explain the way they've worked out for themselves.

Yes, there was great pleasure in it sometimes. You go home some days feeling bloody marvellous. One of the things I used to teach was shopping, getting people to the shops. I'd take someone to the shops and we'd start sussing out products. How do you tell a Red Mountain jar from a Nescafe jar. One's square and one's got rounded bits; and packages like that tend to stay much the same. The labelling changes, but the jar stays much the same. And how do you ask somebody for help—and what questions would you ask, to get the most from them? They're willing to help but often they don't know how to. You also have to be firm sometimes.

I was bloody good at it, and most of the time I enjoyed it.

But I was not a good worker. Good workers know when to leave the job. They're good while they're doing it, then at the end of the day, finish. I wasn't good at that. I was doing extra hours at night. I wasn't narrow—or brave enough—to say to people, sorry, no, my books are full, you'll have to go on a waiting list which is four months long. Instead I was volunteering to do more all the time.

And this could not go on. I just stopped one day and said, I'm not going. It was getting too much.

I wasn't popular with my fellow workers—because sometimes they would say stupid things. There was one there who had a nasty racist streak. I said, look, chief, it doesn't matter what colour they are, what sex they are, what size they are, or how many limbs they've got. If they're yours they're yours and they should get the same time and attention as the rest.

The same thing happens here: if someone says something stupid, I say, that's stupid. I don't laugh with them because it's all a good laugh—if it's stupid. If you will leave your plates on the quad lawn, they're going to close the lawn. They're going to do that—I would in their place. But it isn't appreciated when I say things like that.

So—I stayed at home for a few months after I left the job. I drank a lot. My father was still alive and climbing the wall by now because of me. I thought, what shall I do next? Let's go and study a bit, just for the hell of it.

I'd kept reading always—stuff on my job, every periodical I could find. And westerns, lots and lots of westerns. Some history, though less—still the Second World War; my interest is massive and encyclopaedic.

So I thought—let's fry 'em, let's see what I can do. The way I worded it to one of the teachers at FE was, if I put my foot down, how fast can I go? She said, you can try one A level. But, I said, if I do one at a time I'm going to be here for donkeys' years! All right, she said, you can try two—so I decided to have a swing at history and economics. So I worked out my timetable for these two and Tuesday morning was empty. There was an English class that met then—and they said if I felt up to it and had nothing else on, I could do it. I had to fiddle a bit to be under the 20 hours—the need to be available for work and all that rubbish.

Stephanie the English teacher was happy—she said, three in one year is a lot for anyone, but you're welcome to try.

So I thought—I'll have a swing at these, why not?

Just about Easter time, I blew it, badly. I was doing a test essay in history. I'd just been working too hard. I was tired. Three in one year is a lot. I sat down and did my test essay in my hidey-hole room, and nothing would come out of my head. I felt terrible. What would happen if it was the same in the exam? And they'd done an awful lot for me at the college, which made it worse. They'd found me the little room. I'd make notes in class, taped notes, and when there was a coffee break, I'd run off into my room—it was in fact a bookstore, but they found a table and chair for me—so I'd rush in there, load the brailler, cup of coffee, fag, tape on; and then I'd do my notes as fast as possible, and get to my next class. Lunchtime would be the same thing. Back into my room. Sandwiches out, coffee out, fag, tape-recorder, afternoon lessons—the same thing. Without that little room, it would have been a disaster.

But I couldn't write. It was all in there, but nothing would come out. So I picked up my typewriter, typed my history teacher a little note saying, I can't do this, and left. I told my sister and she said, if that's what you want to do, fine. I think it's a waste after all that work—but it's your choice. She's very clever. If she'd tried to argue me into going back, I would have dug in deeper.

Stephanie came to see me about a week later when they were certain I wasn't going to come back. I wanted to go back, but pride was involved now—I'd blown this badly. I was not going to go back. But Stephanie came to my house and said, it's bloody dull when you're not there—don't do the exam if you don't want to, but just come back and entertain the class.

So I thought—I'll have you, you bastards, and I went back and carried on.

Pride is a big thing—my ego is fairly large: I don't mean big-headed, but robust. Once I dig my heels in they stay dug in. Yes, I did get on very well with her. There were only about eight or ten of us in her class which used to meet in some little hut somewhere. There was a sort of frontier spirit about it. There was a small canteen down there and we all used to sit with her and have coffee and chat. It was fun.

She always offered me a lift back into town after class. She had to go through town anyway to get home. She offered to give me a lift out there in the bad weather, but I said I couldn't do that. I'd like a lift back. You walk out, because you've got to walk out: that's honour satisfied. Once you've climbed the mountain, you can take a cable car down. I used to walk about three miles; and I never missed that class. It used to piss down, and about a foot of snow sometimes. It didn't matter because it was a fun class.

But I would not go about half a mile for the school.

I did things for her I thought she'd like. We were reading *Mill on the Floss*, and I did a character list with little drawings and things to illustrate everybody's relationship to everybody else, and she photocopied it to give out to the rest of the class. It was good. We write now and then now—she's in America now.

When I went back I had to prove that I'd had a ten-minute panic, nothing worse. And I could fry this—no danger. I got the highest marks again. A, A, and C. I blew the English a bit. But it was still the highest set of marks anyone got in that class. Normally enough to get you into university anyway.

I thought—this is fun, this is bloody good stuff, let's have some more of it. Then Brian—who taught politics—asked me what I was going to do next. I hadn't got a clue. Think about it, he said. He'd heard from Stephanie and my history teacher. Obviously they'd mentioned a few things. And let's face it, I was not easy to miss walking round that place: I was far older than most, and with a stick and everything. So people would say:

'Is he . . .?'

'Yes.'

'How's he doing?'

'He's bloody good actually.'

This sort of thing was going round the staffroom. So Brian asked me what I was going to do next. So I thought about it. He taught politics, so I decided on politics and law. Let's do two, let's be reasonable, three was a bit much.

So at the end of the first term, Brian came up and asked

me to sign this form. What's this then? I'm applying to something, he said, oh fine, apply away, feel free.

It turned out he'd got me an interview in this place.

It scared the shit out of me. It was dropped on me from an enormous height. When he first told me, I said, I'm not bloody going there, don't be daft! You're joking—go away! Why not? he said. They're a lot of funny buggers up there, I said, I ain't going there! Stuff them!

I also thought I wouldn't be good enough. But my sister—who is an ace person and has put up with just as much from me as my father did—said, Andrew, get up there. If they turn you down it's their loss. She's done a lot for me, and I owe her, so I came here.

She always helped me, never criticized me. Never a bad word, even when I left the A level classes and went home.

So we came up here. One college offered me 500 quid to go there: they've got a scholarship of £500 for a blind student there. And that was nice. I also went to another college—the one where I wore my old parka with a roll-up going and called him chief. He was a snotty bastard basically. He set me a target of two more As. He did not want me in his college. But he couldn't say so, could he—he couldn't say, get out working-class peasant who calls me chief and smokes roll-ups!

Dr Mann who interviewed me here wasn't sure. How would I read, he asked; how will you get around safely? I get around my home town safely, I said, I'll get around this place. If I can't—send me home!

How about books? he said.

I can get braille books, I can get books on tape, and I can do some reading as well. In fact I can read two books at once, I can have a braille book and a taped book going at the same time. Showing off.

I don't know, he said, I suppose you could try. Which meant I'd better be good. So I thought—right, you bastard.

I think he was timid and reluctant because I was the first one here. And if I blow it and it doesn't work out, that's their fault. That's his approach.

So that was it. And the first college was bad—they offered me 500 quid! And everything was organized for me! There were readers ready for me. A number of other students had been through and they'd found it most enjoyable and most useful. Our services are good, they said, we have things organized which will work well for you.

And I thought—no thank you, Charlie. They want me too much. But Dr Mann wasn't sure—and you don't preach to the converted.

They gave me the place, and I thought, thank you very much. I'll sort you bastards. And now Dr Mann rather likes me, I think.

So Andrew lost his sight and found his mind—and much more.

But his story leaves an unanswerable question: how many of his uneducated contemporaries might also have reached university if a disaster had rescued them?

His account has a narrative zest that may distract from its gravest implication: that we are still very far from equal educational opportunity if schools fail pupils as clever as Andrew. He tells us what is still being wasted: seams of unquarried talent; intellect after intellect undiscovered—because comprehensives are if anything weaker than in the 1970s when his education took place: teachers were much better off then; and there was no recruitment crisis. And it is teachers—good ones, bright ones, rewarded ones—that make schools work. New exams and so-called reforms are unimportant in comparison.

His schools taught him much less than his experience—which led him to return to education in more helpful circumstances than his comprehensive could muster. He stresses the differences: the most important being that classes at his college of education were small and intimate (eight in Stephanie's class, and a 'small canteen' where they used to sit and chat with her)—in contrast to the large numbers in which he was taught at school, and which he sees as determining his neglect. It is no coincidence that Stephanie came to acknowledge and like Andrew, teaching him in these conditions. There was no pressure to box students into convenient generalities. She appreciated Andrew to such an extent that when he threatened to leave her class, she made an accurately tactful—and triumphant—attempt to persuade him to come back. In so

doing she offered him the powerful, subtle, parental attention
that adolescent pupils need in school, but may—like Andrew—
never find. She knew him; so her attention was accurate. If she
had said the wrong thing, he would not have returned to her
class. But in school, no teacher knew him well enough to sense
what he needed.

Losing his sight gave Andrew a hunger for difficulty.
Responding to the high expectations he met at RNIB college
and at Leeds, he became autonomous, as they intended. Their
expectations were quite different from those he met at school.
Being blind and lost in the middle of a strange city is an
example of the sort of benign trauma he never met at school;
the sort of challenge pupils never meet when depleted teachers
in depleted schools come to expect too little of them. Teachers
have to be rewarded and authoritative to be able to set difficult
or reluctant pupils high standards, apparently impossible
expectations. With so many to teach and so little time to think
(to the importance of which I come back at the end of Chapter
6) it is inevitable that such pupils are relegated to comparative
neglect. Andrew's teachers in school could not set him the
targets he needed. They had energy to teach those who wanted
to be taught; they had enough to shut him up but not to win
him over. Andrew is right to point to the number of his fellow
pupils as a large reason for his failure.

Learning his profession with new intellectual zest, and with
great dedication, he himself offered clients the sort of powerful,
challenging tuition he never met in school. He pushed them as
far as he thought he could: 'they'll cut their hands now and
then, but they won't kill themselves'. Such an approach was his
own experience put to good use; was application of the hard
lessons learnt at RNIB college and Leeds.

Andrew's is a story of capacity being demanded and
extended, enriching and being enriched by experience. Losing
his sight made him want to learn about blindness. When he
worked with other blind people, he says that he made it his
business to read everything he could about his subject. Life,
work, and learning joined in one curriculum.

His job with the blind seems to have prepared him for
academic history. It is possible to detect a kind of thinking very
like a historian's in the way he operated with his clients. He

was good at seeing a small essential detail that led to a solution; good at breaking down a dilemma into its constituents. His solutions have the quality of historical insight, when a jumble of apparently disparate facts becomes coherent. He seemed to exult in the power of small facts to release large freedoms—in the fact that coffee jars stay the same shape, and that sitting on a lavatory is safe.

We did not talk in detail about his studies for his degree. It was clear that he had enjoyed himself. Modern European history is still his passion. Despite technical difficulties—which he never allows to inhibit him—he thrived. He has a very small residue of sight, that lets him use his reading machine, which projects words on to a screen magnified sixteen times. But his reading speed is much slower than a fluent reader's with normal sight. At a seminar or lecture, the only way for him to take notes was to use a tape-recorder. Then would come the exhausting process of transcribing the tape into notes. To read the notes, to use them, must always have taken far longer than for someone with normal sight. But he made a speciality of the apparently impossible.

He mentions an incident which may well be a glimpse of the particular problems mature students can experience with tutors younger than themselves. He was studying the Dardanelles campaign—about which his knowledge was already extensive. A seminar passed without his feeling the need to turn on his tape-recorder at all. At the end, his young tutor said that he had noticed that Andrew was taking no notes. An uneasy exchange followed, in which Andrew sensed the tutor's anxiety at an implication Andrew was unable to disguise: that nothing of any use to him had been said.

He had come to university from the war of his own life, decorated and sure of himself. Like an undergraduate who came back to finish his degree in 1945, his presence must often have been an uneasy one. He speaks his mind. He did not suffer silly young fools gladly. He was brave enough to take it almost as a duty to inform ignorant youngsters who would leave university for influential jobs. He mentions another incident. He was talking to a student about the tradition that members of a rowing eight take an oar home as a trophy. 'How d'you transport the damn thing?' he said. 'In the car, of course'—was the answer. 'What if you don't have a car?' asked Andrew. 'Oh, everyone has a car.'

Andrew jumped. He pointed out that half the population does not own a car, himself amongst them. 'They should know these things,' he said.

But unless he had gone blind, this man's fine mind would probably have never had its chance. Next time you buy some furniture, consider that the man or woman who serves you may have a mind as good as his.

6

Sally: The Uses of Adversity

It is returners' fulfilment that is extraordinary; their gifts are common.

I carried out many of the longest interviews for this book in the evening after a day's work. It was usual for me to ring at a door feeling disheartened by tiredness before I began; resolved to keep the session short so that I could go home. Three hours later, I would set off in a state not far short of exaltation—not from a lucky encounter with an unsung heroine, but because the excitement of return is infectious.

But I do not want to suggest that after my work for this book, all I do is stand back in romantic inspiration at the delayed florescence of returners' lives. I do not want the subjects of this book to celebrate the individual in glory. I want them, more than anything else, to show what it is like when the right to education is taken up; I want them to underline the importance of seeing education as a right; to stress the importance of preserving and widening the state's responsibility to educate.

These lives represent possibility that should not be the monopoly of a few. The people in this book succeeded because they discovered that they could be obstinate, persistent, brave. Their qualities, inevitably and deliberately celebrated, seem heroic. However, it was not such qualities themselves but their discovery that was unusual; a romantic argument about their rarity would not convince me. Stories of return are romantic, because of their compelling characteristics: sudden reversals, transfigurations; dark nights of the soul; bad luck turned suddenly to triumph. Life during successful return expands—which is perhaps why returners so often become impatient with anything but the best, and ardent for difficulty—which guarantees further expansion, once met and overcome. Returners

acquire an instinct for quality. Eleanor the absolutist—
impatient with second-rate textbooks; vigilant for dishonesty—
is an example. Andrew's refusal to accept easy options, to go to
a college where everything was laid on for him and there
would be no one to enlighten, is an example of the same
phenomenon. Returners are people at their best; people as they
can be.

Without exception, their fees were paid. They could claim
grants. Without financial backing, none of them would have
succeeded. Their success was enabled by the state. The
opportunities they managed to seize were funded. But the
existence of a right is not the same as its availability. My
argument is that opportunity only came within reach by means
of a psychological quest or treasure hunt in which the clues
were often indecipherable until adversity burst into flame. The
clues then became legible despite terror—which turned out in
the end to be misleading. This is particularly true of both
Andrew and Sally. Andrew probably thought his life was over
when he was sacked by his furniture company; but this disaster
turned out to be the beginning of his self-discovery.

The romantic fallacy is that the excellence of life—its
heroism, its rarely imaginable heights—should only be attainable by the few. My argument is different. I believe that the
opportunity for intellectual and imaginative development
through education should not need a psychological quest before
it can be taken up in adult life. It should be more accessible. If it
were, enormous numbers of people would find the fulfilment
enjoyed by the returners this book celebrates. Opportunity, for
a start, needs to infiltrate communities and minds rather than
stay locked in a building, the approach to which can be far too
daunting for far too many people. I have more to say about this
matter in Part II.

Kerry, who appears at the beginning of this book and in my
book *Invisible Children*, describes herself approaching the
college where she applied at first to do remedial maths and
English. By then she was in her early twenties, divorced, living
on her own with a small daughter.

Things had been getting just the same week after week after

week. Out of sheer boredom I'd go and visit different friends who'd also got babies, and occasionally we'd go to discos, though we couldn't really afford to go out. But it got so boring sometimes, you didn't know what you were going to talk about. You'd exhausted all avenues of discussion. I think I wasn't the only one feeling the way I felt. It was just the boredom of week by week existence, not going anywhere or doing anything very much. Even discos were boring: who wants to stand there dancing and having music blaring in your ears? If that was the highlight of the week for me— which it probably was—I felt I had to do something.

I saw an advert in the paper—it was that open book: we'll help you with your reading and maths. And I thought if they're prepared to help people like that, they might be prepared to help me.

How did I have the courage to go? I don't know—I think the boredom overruled everything: it was heavier than me. I walked there. I didn't have a car—and it was going from one end of the town to another. Somebody was looking after Claire. It was a nice day, and I set off.

I tell you, I was shaking all over, I was really nervous, because it meant I had to admit I was really stupid, before I did anything else . . .

Sally, like Andrew, illustrates the treasure hunt through which many must go before they find fulfilment. I met her for the first time shortly after she graduated. She is of medium height, with fair hair, short then, longer now. I was struck by her emphatic way of talking, even while we stood in her kitchen waiting for the kettle to boil. Then we took cups of tea into the sitting room, where her daughter Josie was reading the *Guardian*.

Some hours later, as I prepared to leave, she put on her TV— to find a programme about the children of prominent Nazis: a programme trying to suggest what it was like to carry their fathers' burden; and, sitting cross-legged on the sofa, she suddenly leant forward to face the television as if, when she had thought of a good hold, she would do a judo pounce and throw it to another part of the room. Her attention was total:

she wanted to know; it was as if she suspected she would be told something unhelpful, so would need to concentrate to see the truth the programme concealed.

'Why should they blame themselves? It's terrible', she said, with an urgency that made it difficult to leave. She wanted to *know*; and her attention was so fierce that I felt I must stay, and concentrate too, and know and understand.

Her return has made her sceptical, curious, intellectually alive; has transformed a pupil who left school with a couple of CSE 2s, a couple of 3s, and a 4 to a good honours graduate in psychology, about to do a master's. Public money well spent.

But her argument is that it was only adversity of an extreme kind that led her to the self-belief without which her metamorphosis would never have happened.

I went to a church school from 5 onwards. It was quite a happy time, but it always struck me that we didn't learn very much. I failed the 11 plus. I was very disappointed and felt then that I didn't make the grade, that I'd let people down.

I don't think anything was stressed to us about the exam. Because I had been quite happy at school, I couldn't see why I hadn't got through. My spelling was appalling for instance, but it was never emphasized that because it was appalling I had to pull myself together. It was just left.

The only person I can remember who went on to grammar school was a boy who'd come from a different school and moved into the area, and come to our little church school that only had 24 pupils. It was a tiny village. He was the only one who knew things like his tables, and he knew how to spell. He knew most things, and he was pestered endlessly for information from the rest of us because we didn't know—the easiest thing to do was ask David. He was marvellous, he had the patience of a saint.

I can remember putting on a brave face and pretending that I didn't care anyway, but deep down I thought, Oh God. I think it was the first time I'd ever failed at anything that seemed to be important to other people. My parents had always said to me, we want you to do well at school, but just do your best, don't worry if it isn't good enough.

There was no method of self-discovery. There was no

adventurous learning like kids have today. It was always: this is your 7 times table, learn it, you'll be tested on it, and if you don't know it, that's tough.

So there was no fun in it as such, and there was no class discussion, no debate, no development on an individual basis. Yes, I did just do what was asked of me, without even thinking there could be anything more.

Home? There were always books around, children's books, not encyclopaedias. But there was never any—self-discovery.

My father's a farmer, and I guess maybe I was wanting more to be outside with my brothers, the only reason I was ever indoors was to help mum, and I'd do anything to get out of that. My brothers got treated one way and I got treated differently, and the way I got treated I didn't like at all. I was supposed to help her.

I remember feeling aggrieved right from about that time. I must have been 10 or 11. We'd been fighting at the sink and I'd said to my mother, why are they always allowed out? I thought it was because I was the eldest, and I was trying to get across to her that it was so unfair. And then finally it clicked that it was because I was the girl. And I wouldn't accept that. I wouldn't accept that that was how it was going to be. But then I guess I realized that things were going to be unpleasant for me if I didn't.

I don't think they were that surprised when I failed the 11 plus, actually. If I'd passed I'd have gone on to the grammar school, and I think they would have been really pleased. My father had a grammar school education, he's 56 now, so way back when he was doing his schooling it was quite something to go to grammar school. I think it was just taken for granted that—you know—she'll go to the secondary modern school. It was a new school, St Margaret's. My brothers didn't pass either, and I don't think it was that great a disappointment. I think as long as they felt we were happy, that was the main thing. If we were good academically, then all the better, but if not they weren't going to go overboard about it.

The only horrific thing in the first year was maths: I was absolutely petrified of maths. I couldn't even change a fraction into a decimal. I started in the A stream and by the second year I was down in the B stream, and the teacher had a different method in the B stream of teaching maths, and I worked quite hard and found him very easy to understand because he was a good teacher. In fact I did so well, I went back up into the A stream in the third year. So I deteriorated again, because of the same bad teacher.

Sally gives us a very succinct statement of the difference between training—instruction—and education. Like Peter, she regrets the lack at school of what she calls 'self-discovery' (by which I think she means finding out for yourself), and 'development on an individual basis'. There was no 'fun'; no 'adventure'. Neither was there any discussion. The small child's experimental openness, its love of questions, was abandoned in favour of Gradgrind.

Later, Sally met a different sort of maths teaching:

Pat—at college—was a brilliant teacher. The actual method was familiar from school, but there was much more explanation, and I could ask questions, saying, why have you gone from this step to that step? And she'd say, if you think of it this way—and she'd take me through it, and I'd think, oh yes, I can see it now. But the staggering realization, for instance, that algebra is abstract! *A* and *B* don't have to mean anything; whereas when I was at school I was in a constant trauma, thinking, why do they call this y and x; and what does it stand for? Nobody had said to me, look, let's pretend that this is a game, you've got x and you've got y, and let's see what you can do to them, we're going to balance up two sides of an equation, and we're going to do it this way.

Nobody had said that! It suddenly hit me that it's a game and it's got a certain number of rules: her approach was to say, let's play it, let's make it fun. So—she was a good teacher; but I also knew the right questions to ask when I didn't understand something.

With the teacher at school, the class seemed to lick along; and the clever ones set the pace, and it was a case of being left behind.

She was encouraged to think in an open, playful way. She was asked to do her own thinking. Her teacher's invitation refuted Gradgrind because it assumed that no one student's thinking would be quite the same as another's. 'Let's play this game together', said her teacher. 'I will suggest, you contest. I will explain, you question.' She was offered the same reciprocity, the same respect for her individuality, that we have already noted in the early stages of Peter's and Eleanor's return.

Intellectual emancipation is implied: a jump over the fence in Peter's story about the juke-box. Left behind at school, she had no way of appealing for help. She did not know how to ask. At college, asking questions was not difficult, and could become intellectually playful in a 'game' she had never before experienced.

She left concrete thinking behind as she sensed an exhilarating plurality of possible interpretations in the work—in her late twenties—she was giving her mind to do.

At school she had been incapacitated. Not just by such a common difficulty as enforced stupefaction in maths—but by a shawl of assumptions into which had been stitched some comfy but disabling rules. Her rules were different from those that governed Andrew's and Peter's education. One rule suggested: 'As long as you're happy, that's all that matters; there's no need to worry about your homework.' The grander rule that made this moderation possible was that because she was a girl, school was not important. Hers was a version of Vanessa's ladylike training at her first convent.

I liked English, we had Miss Phipps, she was like my school mum. She was always really understanding to the girls, she was the headmistress, she was always very approachable. Domestic science, needlework, no problem there. Art, there was no problem. I enjoyed it. I excelled at PE and field sports. I probably got a reputation as being good at sports but not academic. How did it develop? Well, from the age of 10, I wanted to be a dancer, so from then I started classical ballet here in town; so by the time I was 12 I'd had two years at that and I was quite athletic; and we'd always been a fit family, kept active, good at games, fed well.

I won athlete of the year in the third and fourth years. But there were also things like Christmas concerts; and if they needed a dancer, I just seemed to have the knack of beetling around a bit quicker and being a bit more graceful. Yes, I think I was above average. I was. I loved it, I enjoyed it.

Yes it was hard to escape that identity, especially since I hadn't shone academically.

How well was I doing? Bs and Cs; As for needlework. I think for a girl you need to get As all the time to get noticed.

I guess, thinking back, it wasn't a very academic school, it wasn't academically demanding. We had homework set, but there was never any status for it. I can't remember anyone in my class going out of their way to get an A because they wanted the status. You did your work, and if you didn't do it very well, then it wasn't the end of the world. Yes, tepid expectations. I think we were just let to develop the way we wanted.

We didn't have O levels. Now I feel cheated about that; but we didn't think so at the time. I thought to be doing 7 CSEs was really good!

No one actually explained the value of education and what it can do for you. To reach for the top, to go to university! Not one female and only one other member of our family have ever reached university. And when I got my place to go to London, it suddenly struck me. I was thrilled that I got the place, but then I suddenly realized! My mother never had a chance. She was dumped in at the deep end. She had to get a job in a shop very young. She didn't excel academically.

Nobody had ever said to me, you can do it; or, if you worked hard, if you keep your head down, think of where it could get you.

Nor had anyone actually said to me that I was going to grow up, get married, and have babies; but I've got a sneaky feeling that was everybody's expectation.

Well, I'd got my dancing, my mother had given me that, and she'd given me eighteen months' secretarial training straight after school, because she said I'd got to have something to back me up, I couldn't rely on my dancing.

I can remember her saying, try to get a job that's got a pension. Work for the Post Office or something like that, or be a telephonist, their jobs are good. And for years I used to think, oh the silly old bag what the hell's she talking about.

But then it struck me: my mum didn't have any insight either, her mum hadn't told her. Less was available to my mum than was available to me. And she was busy bringing up three children, she didn't have time to think of it.

She did the best that she could in that regard. So I ended up forgiving her!

I think I enjoyed most of school. I was quite sad to leave when it came to it. I enjoyed school a lot more than doing a secretarial course at college. One thing happened that I remember with deep horror. I still think of it. I was with my parents. We'd gone down to a club at Henbury. The headmaster of the junior school was a member of the club, he knew my parents socially. But his son was there on that occasion, and he must have been going off to university; because he turned round and he asked me:

'Are you going on then?' And I said:

'Well, yes!'

'Where are you going?' he asked, and I said,

'Oh, Henbury College', and he said:

'Oh', like that, with such a sneery tone in his voice! And it suddenly dawned on me, hey, hang on, this is a whole different game, he's been playing to different rules. At that time anybody talking with even a mildly middle-class accent I couldn't stand anyway. I didn't say any more to him, and he didn't really want to speak to me, which I guess was a relief on both our parts.

It wasn't unusual for him to think that girls go on, because he was the son of a headmaster. The girls he knew he obviously expected to go on.

Whereas from where I stood it wasn't obvious that everybody goes on. I was lucky to go on even to do the secretarial course.

This moment brings together several of this book's themes: class; the way school can trap a pupil in a demeaning generality; the belittlement of women. It was a moment when Sally dimly sensed that she might have been cheated.

Her return has made her too judicious to blame anybody. But it is clear to what extent her school colluded with her family's modest expectations for her future. Particularly interesting is the headmistress, so approachable and nice, presiding over her girls' moderation and sanctioning it; and no doubt full of praise for Sally's graceful dancing. Nice though she was, she and her colleagues played the same part in Sally's life as Andrew's woodwork teacher in his. Their influence was misleading. His teacher told him he was a clumsy fool and put him off school; her teachers told her she would make someone a lovely secretary.

Her teachers and her mother would pat the shawl back into place if ever it threatened to slide from her shoulders.

I didn't have any aspiration to go on. I didn't know anyone at university, I didn't know anyone who'd ever done anything. You had to be really brainy it seemed to me. I didn't think that I was good. I'd had no proof.

When I look back, I can vividly remember my mother saying, time and time again—we must have been noisy kids—oh, for goodness' sake be quiet. At school we had to be quiet, there was no self-expression, we had to be an orderly class. And when I think back to it, even though I find it quite easy to talk to you now, even though it's being taped, at university, in a tutorial, the last three years, I'd think three times before making a contribution on anything that requires a knowledge of a topic that we happened to be discussing. So there's still that thing about being quiet, listening, doing as you're told; it's still there, if I'm in a social circle and I don't know people; I still stand back rather than go forward. But that has got easier in the last—I don't know—ten years.

I asked Sally the same question that I asked Andrew: why does she think that no teacher went against the grain of her school and saw what she was really made of?

I think that sort of teacher is quite rare. In English, if we were given a title for an essay, you could write what you wanted; and I used to do well in that, because it was creative. But I don't think I ever felt any freedom in other subjects; and it was always expected of me to be something other than I felt I was. There was no room for expression because you had to stick within the rules all the time. And especially maths—totally rule-bound. But when you got someone to turn maths around and say, you can make it work for you, you can take an equation and you can draw a graph with it of a certain shape; that is creative, isn't it.

The essays? In the first year, I got my book back and I got a star on the front, and I said, what's this for? I can remember being very surprised. I'll tell you in a minute, said Mrs Main. And I had to read out this essay; and it wasn't bad, it was something about walking home at night—I lived on a farm, and I wrote about being miles from anywhere, with telegraph poles looking like invaders from space. It was quite atmospheric, I guess, and she liked it. But the essay title I had the week after didn't let me take off, so it was mediocre.

Geography I always liked. I enjoyed producing very neat and tidy work, and he enjoyed marking it, and I guess I always got good results because of it. He was always very neat and methodical, pencil sharpened, placed in the top pocket, impeccable time-keeper. He always said, don't ever ever waste any time, you don't ever get back the minutes you waste, which is true.

I guess I was always on the middle ground; so they probably thought, oh well she's okay. I mean, you get noticed if you do really badly, don't you; and you get noticed if you do really well. The kids in between are okay, but no more—it's very safe, in the middle. If you excel at anything, you're putting yourself up to be shot down. If you participate in a discussion, there's always somebody who will say, no you're wrong. We were never taught the skill of arguing or debating with confidence. Being very bad at something on the other hand got you into a lot of trouble, so you steered clear of that. I guess it was best to be in the middle.

It was safe enough to excel on the sports field. My fad was hurdling—nobody else could do it, and I was brilliant at it, you see, so I stuck to it and exploited that niche. And you can't argue with that, can you, if you hit the tape first nobody can say you're wrong.

I loved the art teachers' lessons. Mrs McLean was fantastic because she always smelt so beautifully, and everybody used

to go behind her, especially the boys, who used to say, cor,
Mrs McLean's been up the corridor again!

She was so calm. You used to go into her lessons and she'd
say, let's do some still life today. Anybody that's calm still
grabs me: it's a serenity, I love it. She'd say, what sort of
fruit would you like? So we'd sit there for an hour and she'd
talk about things.

General science was okay. The only vivid thing that sticks
out with me is that we did an anatomy class on one occasion,
for which the teacher had got a calf from the abattoir, and
not one person would volunteer to help cut it open, so the
whole lesson was about to be disbanded because nobody
would step forward. In the end I said, oh come on, I will.
Are you sure Sally? he said. Yes I want to get on and *learn*
something! I said.

And the boys were all saying, oh it stinks! I guess it helped
being on the farm, because I'd seen lambs being born and
gory things like that which weren't really that gory at all.

After the lesson it was quite fascinating because they all
stood well away, because it was quite pongy; and then the
girls seemed to come back first; and finally the boys when
they got used to it.

Miss Phipps the headmistress came up to me that
afternoon and said, what *were* you doing this morning, Sally,
I've been hearing all about you, what *were* you doing,
wouldn't the boys do the dissection?

So they must have been saying something in the
staffroom—Sally, what a strange girl. But I didn't think it
was that strange, nobody would help, so somebody had to
step in.

On this occasion the shawl faltered, and fell from her
shoulders. She jumped from the 'middle ground', which is
where it is easiest for teachers to be blind to individuality.[1] The
most lethal generalities are bestowed upon the middling:
'they're all nice girls'; 'pleasant average workers . . .'. Her
moment at the dissection was not repeated—so it could be
discounted as aberrant. But it was then that her present self

[1] Sally here presents the case I argue in *Invisible Children* (Oxford
University Press, 1988).

became briefly visible—to the consternation of her head-mistress, who sanctioned the restoration of the amenable little dancer, and banished the spectre of a flesh-slicing virago.

The occasion was rich in irony. The boys were squeamish; she was unperturbed. She took charge; and yet her action was still amenable: by doing so she pleased everyone in the room. All stood back as the cutting proceeded; but the girls returned before the boys.

The exam went okay, I think I got grade 3 CSE with it. Needlework was okay. I did quite well. My Mum was a good seamstress, and it always seemed natural to be good at it: you weren't a proper female if you weren't good at needlework and domestic science, so it didn't prove anything. If I'd been good at maths, the one thing I couldn't get to grips with, that would have been different.

I missed a grade 1 English by one point, my English teacher told me, which I wasn't very pleased with, because I thought oh God, one point, missed out again. So I got a grade 2. Grade 2 needlework, grade 3 geography, general science grade 3, maths grade 4: a miracle, thank God I got a grade at all. I think I got a grade 4 for something else.

But it meant I could go on to college.

At college she did shorthand and typing and O levels in economics and British Constitution, and law. She was bored by everything but economics which she enjoyed. But she was bent on dancing.

I left early, I didn't finish my two years, because I'd decided that I wanted to be a professional dancer. I'd taken all my dancing examinations from 10 to 18. I was successful at that. I had the ability to go on and do it; and I knew girls in the dancing school who were a bit older than I was, and one of them got me a job, got me an audition, which I passed.

My first job was a summer season at Pontins holiday camp. For a pittance—but it seemed a lot, and I'd got the job and I was on the way. I enjoyed it—it was nice to feel that I was doing something that I'd decided on. I enjoyed the discipline of having to be good seven nights a week and twice on a Saturday. Nights were taken up, and it was our job and we were paid to be professional. But in the days—apart from rehearsals—we had our own time.

A summer season is twelve weeks; and then we moved just up the coast a little way for a season at a night club. It was hard work—all the way through the winter. And it's cold on the Norfolk coast.

I was in digs with three other girls. I shiver thinking about it now.

You do begin to resent the grotty side of things, because it's not very glamorous. It's okay when you're out there performing. You get paid, and you eat well for two days a week, and then it's corn flakes and toast for the rest of the week. It's breaking out in spots and not getting enough sunshine, and horrible things like that. I got quite homesick. I took a week off—not very long—and went home.

Sally's voice was quiet remembering all this. Josie her daughter came into the sitting room again.

Sally: But that went on for about two years. And then I got pregnant.

Josie: Blame me . . .

Sally: No, I'm not blaming you, it's me!

I had to give up the dancing, and I went home and made the best of it, tried to fit in with my family again.

It wasn't a very happy pregnancy. And then she was born, and that was okay, wasn't it, Josie?

Josie: Umm.

Sally: We knew it would be, didn't we?

Josie: I don't remember [laughs].

Sally: So I lived with my mum and dad again until she was about 2½. When she was 9 months old, I'd managed to meet someone. We saw each other for about two years, and got married. We were not very happy—we stayed together for about four and a half years; and then we decided that the best thing to do was get divorced. I was relieved—it was just trying to get out of something that was really bad.

It was 1977, I was in my early twenties. I moved out of the marital home. I found a flat in Stembury, found a part-time

job. I was a butcheress! I was driving a van doing the meat
round. They were great in the shop. There was Fran, and
Alan the manager, and Roger who wasn't very good in the
shop: he always let you do most of the work, even scraping
off the meat block so that your back would be killing you,
while he would be walking up and down the shop with his
hands behind his back. He was an awful man to work with,
always carried by other people.

Later on there was Larry—poor Larry who was so accident
prone and ended up as the manager.

So I drove the meat van. Then later on they had me in the
shop serving meat, so I knew something about it. I wanted
to go on and train, and Larry said, I don't think there'll be
any chance of you doing it. It's unheard of isn't it, a female
butcher? I hadn't heard of one, but I just wanted to get on
and do something properly.

Well—they said no.

Yes! It was a great disappointment, because I couldn't see
any reason why not. The only reason I could see was
physical strength—I could cope with unloading pigs' and
lambs' carcasses off the lorry, but I couldn't cope with a
whole quarter side of beef—though it took two men to get
them out of the lorry anyway.

Yes, it was the male sex closing ranks on me. They were
great mates; but that wasn't enough. But it was an
immensely happy time at the butcher's, because they were so
crazy. I was never made to feel that I was 'the female'. They
let me have a go at anything. So within the shop, and out on
the road, they just treated me as if I was the butcher's lad.
And there was no sexual harassment. So I was totally free to
be me, and they became good friends. I've never had that
anywhere else.

After the butcher, I went to the chemist. I started off
serving in the shop, and then I managed to become stock-
controller. So that was quite hard. But he was awful to work
for, an awful man. If you stepped out of line once that was it;
any mistakes that you made in the normal course of things,
you'd had it. We had two scenes in front of customers when
he threw papers at me.

He thought he was doing us a favour. I guess he thought

that as I was a single parent and needed the money I would never dare step out of line.

It would have been all right if he'd been a fair employer, if he'd been a bit more considerate: he was just totally rude. I didn't respect him for it. So I thought I'd look for something else. A friend of mine looked through the paper and found a secretarial job and said, that's the job for you—so I thought I'd apply for it.

I sent in my application, and I didn't hear anything. I had a half-day on a Wednesday, and I went for a lunchtime drink and had three halves of lager. I went home, and the phone rang, could I come for an interview? Oh God, and I couldn't say no, so I said, yes, I will, at three thirty.

I remember rushing upstairs, dragging the portable out of the cupboard, cleaning my teeth—God, my breath smells of alcohol—and in between cleaning my teeth I was familiarizing myself with the keyboard. I was really quite tipsy after three halves of lager, and I thought this interview is going to be horrific.

But it went so well, and I got the job. My boss-to-be interviewed me. We seemed to hit it off from the start. He was considerate, and he knew my personal circumstances. He explained what he wanted. He was new to the job, and he wanted somebody to be his right hand. He took me on, even though I'd bungled the typing. It was a disaster, I hadn't typed for five years.

And from then on it was two and a half years. I'd been fourteen months at the chemist's. On Friday the 13th, I walked in, did a day's work and gave in my notice to my horrible boss. The money was a lot better, you see. It's something I've taken up since, gender-related stereotypic occupations that women get into, and it's given me great fervour to change things for women. Through my degree I want to go on and develop that interest.

I worked for two years with my boss. He was brilliant, he really was. He was very tolerant of my mistakes, and there were a lot to start with. There was no harassment, even though he knew I was on my own. He was on his own down here: his wife and children were in Coventry, he couldn't sell his house. He was good, a nice man. On one occasion I went to him and said: look, it's not worth my working, I know a person who's drawing benefit and she's getting only £2 a week less than me. And I'm getting up, and seeing Josie to school, and coming up here and working, and going home, and picking Josie up: and it's such a rush, all for £2 more than her. It doesn't get me anywhere.

He tried to get me more money. He said, you're not giving up, you can't just give up and go on benefit, I'm not going to let you. But for the next year I didn't know what to do. I remember 30 being depressing, and he helped me through that: he said, don't be stupid, you've got loads of time. But being 30 and not knowing what I was going to do! I didn't want to be a secretary.

I'd felt for a long time that status is important. We worked very closely with personnel. It suddenly struck me that there were different classifications of staff in the way they were treated. A kitchen porter got treated like rubbish if he stepped out of line. If a senior manager stepped out of line he would usually get away with it. The rules were different. My boss was great, we worked together as a team, he tried to help me, but because I was a secretary, there was no status, no clout, no building on it.

There's no individuality, and no decent pay without status, and that was quite vital to me. I had to survive, and feel that I was at least going forward.

This is a clear statement about frustration, and typical of the predicaments to which many women returners have to respond. It is depressing that Sally's expectation at the butcher's and in her secretarial job was sexual harassment—or, at any rate, difficulties with men.

Like all the accounts on which this book draws, Sally's is reflection in retrospect. She talked to me not only after university, but also after she had started to think about women. Her analysis of herself as secretary is cogent because it is well thought-out, backed by analysis of larger concerns. Her narrative—like all in this book—is interpretation as well as description. When she presents herself at this time as thinking about her 'trap', it is hard not to be prejudiced by her fluency into imagining that her thinking *then* was combative and clear.

Frustration is part of her argument; pain and confusion are not
so polemically important. But pain there was; and confusion. It
was only action that began to thin it out and dissolve it. But the
act she first chose was not well judged.

> I did an exam, a typing exam, I hadn't done one for years. I
> thought: right, I'll do the advanced. I got it with a
> commended. I thought I'd failed the damn thing when I
> came out. I was convinced I'd failed it. And when I looked
> back at the errors that I knew I'd made, there were only
> three, and they were single letter errors, really minute things:
> I'd blown it all up; I thought that I'd failed. I was so shocked;
> and I thought, right, if I can get a commended, what else
> could I do?

So Sally stumbled into the first move in the sequence that led
her to university. Typing was the wrong corridor to take.
Typing qualifications could only lead to being a better sort of
secretary. Blindfolded, she had taken the wrong door. It is
significant that she thought she had fallen with her first step
when she had not at all. Of course she must have failed her
typing exam!

When she talked about this year in her life her voice was
often full of astonishment that she could have felt as she did,
could have acted as she had. She is astonished now to realize
that she had so little belief in herself. Belief, however, was—as
we shall see—beginning to infiltrate her self-doubt. The process
took a while.

> There was just the realization that something had to change.
> It seemed like a year of trying to think, right from the time
> my boss said I mustn't give up work and go on benefit. And
> I didn't know what to do. There seemed to be nothing I
> could do, nothing I could really aim for. I was left with just a
> feeling, that something had to change, and most of all *me*.
> But I didn't know what direction to take.
>
> Well, one day, the general manager told me about his
> daughter, who'd qualified as a physiotherapist, and emigrated
> to Canada. With the first month's salary she'd managed to
> deck her flat with all the electrical equipment she wanted,
> and she'd managed to bank $250! I thought—Christ! This kid

had gone through a four-year equivalent of a degree course for physio, got qualified, and there she was, 21 years old, earning all that money. Who was the bigger mug, me or her? She'd got it sussed. But how had she managed to do it? I started to ask myself all these questions.

So I thought of education. Right, I'm an ex-dancer. Physiotherapy's not a bad job at all. I'm going to go back and study it. That's how it all started. I thought of my past experience as a dancer: I know what muscles do when they hurt, what's wrong, and why: I'll pick up anatomy and physiology, I'll just do it, I'll go back . . . but it didn't work out that way!

Here she laughed uproariously. By then in the interview I'd woken to the urgency in Sally's voice, the excitement with which she remembered this time. I sensed a jump from the girl who left the butcher's to the woman who took an advanced typing exam, even if she thought she'd failed, and who then decided she'd train to be a physiotherapist. I suspected that something must have happened. By then I had met a large number of returners. For many, the first step is prompted by revelation, by a miraculous parachute bringing a mentor at the right time—like Vanessa's American friend; by a cataclysm that changes all rules, like Andrew's loss of sight. I asked if anything had helped her to think so strongly.

I tell you what it might be.

I had my house broken into. It turned out it was this youth who lived four doors up. He'd switched out the light on the landing which was always on at night for Josie. She'd woken up; and I'd gone into her room because she was crying. I thought the bulb had gone. Anyway, to cut a long story short, he came up the stairs and threatened to kill me with a knife, and then he said he was going to kill her.

I thought, this is life or death. I guess I thought I was going to die, and that he was going to kill Josie.

He raped me. But we ended up fighting, I beat the hell out of him, and he ran off. I had a friend two doors down, and we took refuge with her.

It took me a long time to come out of shock and to try and—you know—get myself together. Josie felt it more.

But, I think, from that time on, I seemed to realize that life is too short, it's too damned short. That sense *is* a driving thing with me. There is no reason on *Earth* why you should expect anyone to give you something, you've got to find a way, you've got to be able to push yourself on, or be grateful for what you've got and just accept it.

I think I expect things of myself; I know now I can do things. I beat the hell out of that guy. I thought he was going to kill me, and there was no *way* that he was. When I began to get over the worst of that I thought: if only I'd done that with my husband! We broke up because he used to beat the hell out of me. If I'd beaten the hell out of him, he would never have touched me again: we might still be married today. But I was never confident that I would be able to defend myself.

I've been interested by the research that shows some women recover from rape trauma more quickly than others, and I think I recovered quite quickly, partly because I was concerned about my daughter's welfare—she couldn't sleep in her own room at nights. But it was also because I took control of the situation at the right time, and I used that control against the thing that threatened me; whereas most women in that situation think they're going to die—there's a knife or some weapon involved—and they're left with a feeling of total helplessness. And then they ask themselves: if only I'd done such-and-such, maybe he wouldn't have got away with it; if only I'd done that maybe this wouldn't have happened. Guilt is always taken back in. The difference was that I took control. In the end, it was me who changed the situation, and that's what I think I learned: that I could change things.

We expect ourselves to get over trauma too quickly. I was determined to get rid of the pain like a grieving process. I had to make sure Josie was all right, because she couldn't sleep in her own bed for five months. She did get through it. But she still checks wardrobes and under beds even here. It doesn't matter where we move to.

I can laugh about beating him up now, but at the time it wasn't very funny, it was something I had to do. But apparently it was the first good hiding he'd ever had; he'd just been left to run riot, and everybody'd suffered around him. And there was no way I was going to internalize all the guilt. But it was quite awful. I had a black boyfriend at the time, and he said to me, you're going out with that nigger, I'm doing this for your old man. I said, what do you mean you're doing this for Sam? That's your old man, isn't it? he said.

I knew that my ex-husband was slightly doolally anyway. I wouldn't have put it past him to get this kid to come into the house and kill me, you see. The guy hadn't been drinking, and as far as I could tell he wasn't on drugs or anything. I thought I was for the cop, he was going to do what he said. There was all this talking, and it was like a million miles an hour. He was going to clean up the street, you know, bloody niggers in the street, and I was a dirty filthy cow because I was going out with a black man.

The way he talked was frightening, because he was coherent, in a twisted logical way. Talking, talking, talking is very natural with rape. You try everything to start with. Well, he did rape me. I told him, you take what you want and then go. I thought, right: I've got to strike a bargain, I've got to get away with my life and my daughter's life.

It never felt like a price because I was still alive, you see, and my daughter was still alive—and I knew they'd catch him. I've been within four feet of him since then, and he's made a move towards me. If he does it again, it doesn't matter where we are I will give him the same if not worse than the last time. People really push their luck sometimes!

He got a seven-year sentence, and did three years. And the time he actually approached me was at the station. Actually I see him quite frequently, and I always spot him before he spots me. It's weird. It's like I turn round and he's there. It's like a sixth sense.

It was just a case of getting over it. My friend down the road, who let me into her house that night—well, I burst her door down, the chain went off the door—she and her husband were really the corner-stone. She said, don't sit up there night after night—and I took her up on it a couple of times.

The day after, I had an interview at a hotel and I said I

couldn't go. It was inconvenient. And the guy bawled me
out on the phone, so I told him to sod off I didn't want his
bloody job anyway. Then I felt guilty—I felt guilty after I'd
said all that!

But it totally changes your perspective on normal things. I
just think I'm lucky. I think if some things don't happen to a
person, then they don't go on. When I first went back into
education, there were single parents and married women; but
the women that dropped back were married, and I often
wondered if I would have got this far if I'd been married. I'm
sure I wouldn't. It's a disadvantage to have a husband.

I've known women who have just knuckled under and
gone home and put away the books as soon as the old man
comes in, and got the dinner—you know—and cannot even
study last thing at night because they're expected to be in
bed! All I had was financial strangulation when I was trying
to get through. I didn't have the mental torture and
restriction of not being able to study when I wanted, read
when I wanted, do what I wanted. You can nail somebody
that way easier than over money.

Sally's case, then, is full of irony. Would she have got her
degree if she had not undergone this terrible experience? The
question is repugnant, for suggesting hidden beneficence in an
act of extreme brutality. Not only an isolated act: she talks
laconically of her attacker's brothers giving her further trouble;
and of her husband's earlier violence. She had been victim of
male savagery. Just as she found her best, found deep reserves
of strength, so these men offered her their worst: violence,
racism.

Her argument about the effect of her experience is persuasive. Most telling is the delay between horror and gradual
realization that she possessed free will, and that its scope might
be limitless. The interpretative equation took time to form. 'If I
could deal so successfully with an experience like that, I could
tackle almost anything.' Interpretation accumulated through
further adversity. The chemist—a dingy rather than dangerous
male—was intolerable. In the end she had to look for other
jobs. When she saw the advert for a secretary, a small part of

the equation formed. Her first thought was that she could not hope to reach the necessary standard, she had not typed for years. Her second thought—encouraged by her boyfriend—was revolutionary. 'Why shouldn't I aim at something that seems out of reach?' She had been schooled in moderation. If you do not aim high, you will never be disappointed. It is safe in the middle. But when she was attacked she had done something that the voices of her education told her was impossible: she had retaliated. She had turned rape into rout. Nothing could have been more immoderate than her behaviour. Like Andrew, she now became extreme in her demands upon herself; immoderate in self-belief.

And when the next large step was there to take, again, immoderately, she tried to take it. Why shouldn't she train as a physiotherapist? By then she was interpreting her difficulties in a completely new way. Financial hardship was no longer to be accepted as a fact of life, a constraint to be met with stoicism. Her moderate 'That's life, isn't it' was being replaced by a triumphant, a Californian, 'Life is what you make it'.

I knew now that I wanted the financial benefits of a good job; that was the main aim. Also it would be nice to get the status that goes with it; but one usually goes with the other. And I couldn't do that without going back in and getting qualified. Physio was the first idea. To cut a long story short, I would have had to do two A levels in one year in order to reach the required standard to train. The college wouldn't let me.

I knew this guy, a captain in the American air force. He was black, he'd studied, his family had been poor. He'd walked around, as he put it, with the backside hanging out of his trousers till the age of 24. And he was on something like 50,000 a year. And for God's sake he'd made it, he'd done a three-year course in one year. Why couldn't I do two As in one year? Anyway they wouldn't have it, so I thought I'm not going to give up, I'm just going to have to do something else. And then Kerry said she was going to university. University, bloody hell—it still hadn't struck me that it was possible.

And I thought, God I'd love to do that, but it seemed so

above everything, and so unattainable still. But if Kerry can do it . . . but she's younger than I am. What am I going to do when I finish?

Then I thought, sod it I'll go for it. I want to go, it's harder, but I want to do it, and I'll gain more at the end.

We can see the new sort of interpretation at work in the above passage—and preparation, like Andrew's work with the blind, for the thinking she would need for her studies. She kept on reaching the right conclusions, and reading the evidence correctly. Examples could be built into her argument. A friend who was on her way to university was available for reference. But how easily her conclusions could have been pessimistic and damaging.

The only thing I remember of the first day is that I bumped into a girl I used to go to school with, and we did O levels together.

I can't remember if I thought I was going to do well in them. I didn't give a damn what anybody thought, not really, I was prepared to give it a year and see what I could do.

I loved it. The man I was going out with was a doctor. He was a great influence. He was 45. He'd gone to Vietnam, he'd come out, he'd gone through the police force, he didn't like it, so he did medical school at 35! I said, you couldn't do that in this country, you couldn't do it! And he said, why couldn't you? I said, it's not structured in that way, they don't want to let people succeed in this country, and he said, who are they—where are you getting all this from? I thought the idea of doing what you wanted at any age was fantastic. He just said go for it.

Again, a mentor just at the right time. Again, new evidence to review. Again, she gets it right. Again, she refuses the temptation to say, 'Not here, not me', her American boyfriend sanctioning her conclusion: 'Why not?'

I did human biology, and we used to sit in bed side by side and I'd say, right, test me on the valves of the heart. He used to say, God, I haven't done this stuff for years, this is complicated; he loved it too.

Ray had been brought up by an aunt, he'd had seven brothers and umpteen sisters; and he said, use your brain, use your brain. The guy I'd been with at the time of the break-in was dirt-poor as a child: he was the first one to say, you've got a brain, use it. He knew I wasn't a girl or a woman first, I was a person and I'd got a brain.

You say I must be strong, and I say I've managed to feel that way by looking at things that boost me up rather than push me down. Women who don't recover as quickly as others from rape trauma internalize pain; and what women in that situation can be taught to do is to say: no, I don't want that shit; this is not my load any more, you take it. They can do anything mentally to think, no, this is not my problem. It's a way of thinking: don't defeat yourself; there are plenty of people out there to do it for you!

Something that fascinates me—we did a half-unit course on depression. And we did it from the pharmacological aspect, looking at drug action and depression. When people are depressed, it seems that they have a much better sense of reality than when they're not. That means that when people are depressed they are looking at their life at face value, how it really is. When people are not depressed, they're conning themselves, that's all; and it gets them through. And I deliberately use a strategy of looking at things in a positive way. As a result, I'm a much better person, I'm healthier, I'm mentally more capable of getting through, and if I don't get through I'll have another bash tomorrow.

You're in control of the camera in that way. But when depressed you see everything from only one camera angle.

She talks of her two partners—one at the time of the assault, the other when she began her return. American, they tuned her thoughts to a wavelength on which she could hear voices telling her how to fulfil herself, quoting case-histories, and proposing what she now sees as the dishonesty of the optimist.

These voices became audible after an experience of brutal adversity. They were telling her that she should empower herself, take her chance.

So I did human biology, sociology, and English literature, and I got Bs. I did them in a year.

Sociology took me a long time to grasp. I wanted to get into the detail, like at school. Everything had to be in minute detail; that was how I was primed at school, so I was still trying to apply the same rules. Then all of a sudden I thought, ah! you have to stand back a bit!

Human biology was great because it was in detail: blood composition, cells, bone structure, and so on. You had to focus very closely all the time, you see. English literature was nice: getting back to trying to interpret what you felt about books you were given to read. The poetry was good.

The English teacher was very good, very thorough. I very soon learnt how to précis material. There was never anything negative at all, just room for expansion. Mo taught me sociology. Her approach was to give constructive feedback. I can remember telling people it's not at all like school, why don't you come back, you'd be surprised. And friends of mine were saying, oh I was hopeless at school, and I was trying to get through to them that it's not like school. For ages it seemed I was saying that to people. And I tested out information on people: what a drag, what a bore I must have been! Apparently everybody goes through it, saying, I read a book about so-and-so.

Sally's early reactions to her studies echo Peter's and Eleanor's.

It is interesting that her schooling had failed to teach her to 'stand back'. This is another glimpse of training: for people who will be told they are not paid to think. She had been schooled to be literal; to think of knowledge as detail to be learnt, not to be organized and illuminated by her—or any—ideas. Her revelation of what was needed in sociology was a crucial moment in her intellectual development.

Like Peter, Kerry, Vanessa, she wanted to talk about her new excitement—and she wanted to encourage others to join her.

I did biology and psychology for A level. The two years felt so long I didn't think I was going to make it. I think I wanted to be further ahead than I was at the time; I couldn't wait. I worked like stink the first year. Worked harder the next year. I felt already full, I wanted to take the exams in

December of the second year: I didn't want to wait till July. And I'd been pushing my health: I'd been doing full-time studying, and I had to take a cleaning job—and in the January everything exploded, into absolute physical and mental close-down. I just conked out.

I was just working too hard. I felt as if I was slipping back: my perspective of things had changed, I didn't feel as if I was moving forward any more, and I couldn't get to where I wanted quick enough. I was defeating myself. I had these really intense shouting sessions—just for five minutes. I just exploded one night. Then I found I couldn't physically move around. What was happening? It was just like a sort of mini breakdown. I hadn't taken any notice of the signs telling me to slow up. I was waking up in the middle of the night, and thinking, right, photosynthesis!

But I loved it, you see, I could do it, I could even memorize page numbers, even see the pictures and diagrams and the page numbers. It was all a bit much, so something had to go. Everything went. For about four weeks, I just said, I don't want to go out, and I don't want to see anybody, I just want to be indoors and that's it. A couple of friends came round and said, look, get yourself to the doctor. But I was so scared of going outside—it was really too much. And gradually I was a little bit kinder to myself. I learnt that lesson a bit late too, you know.

I must go forward, I must drive myself, was what I was saying. Now I say, I must, but—

I had a month or so off, and gradually got myself back into it; but I still felt that I wasn't going to pass, and such a lot could go wrong. I guess I was just a bit depressed. The doctor was no help—he told me to pull myself together and get back to my studies.

I faced the reality of it, you see; whereas before I was saying, if I fail it doesn't matter. So I just eased back into it, with a lot of help from the tutors.

We can see that for Sally, as for Eleanor, Peter, and Andrew, early reactions from her teachers were important. Constructive criticism was what she found; and the support she needed in her crisis. Her downfall was overwork, and reminiscent of

Andrew's crisis. But it was also a therapeutic recession, relief from experience of an intensity that was becoming unbearable.

Such intensity often characterizes the early stage of return. She loved her work. She loved becoming somebody who thinks and speculates and learns. But her mind's new receptiveness could be alarming. The comforting defences of deafness had been dismantled. She was in a state of perpetual astonishment at what she could hear, and perpetual anxiety to interpret it all.

Eleanor was overwhelmed too, though she met no one crisis of such gravity as Sally's. But her experience went through similarly defenceless intensity. Andrew, speeding like a drunk driver through his three A levels in one year, crashed when he looked at an exam question and could not think of anything to say. He was laid up for a fortnight.

Sally's crisis lasted longer, and was graver.

She passed her A levels, but her grades did not do her justice: a C and a D.

By the time she began university, however, her vulnerability was past. She was steady, and able to cope:

Worst was the financial strangulation, but that was the only thing I had to manœuvre around, because the last thing I wanted was to get into debt, which I managed not to do in the end. I always thought after my degree I'd write a book called 'How to Live on Fresh Air'.

When I got home after the first day, I was shattered. I thought I'd never do it. To commuters the journey in and back from work becomes essential. I got the twenty to seven bus the first year and that got me into Victoria just after nine. I read a lot, but you can't really write on the bus. Going in in the mornings I could read, coming back in the evenings I was too tired.

Josie was 14 when I started. I was quite worried about leaving her early in the morning and not getting back till late at night. But I arranged for a friend to drop in after she got home from school to see if she was okay. She said, don't worry, mum, see how it goes. But for the first two terms the first year, I used to leave in the mornings and say, oh God keep her safe; and I'd look back on the corner while I checked in my mind that I'd done everything. She had special instructions not to let anyone into the house.

I honestly think she knew it was something I wanted to do. She could see the sense in it. She also knew that if there was an emergency my mum was only eight miles away. And I've always worked full time, so it was like an extra two hours at the end of the day when she was on her own. I was always concerned about her getting up to an empty house. But it didn't seem to worry her. And the times I was at home, if we got up together all we did was get in each other's way!

She really did come up trumps. She obviously is insecure about some things. But she is sensible. But if I had two children I don't think it would have been as easy.

Everything revolved around the work. There were no weekends. Everything was structured around getting the work done.

The work was awesome in quantity. But she coped—and without the support, the close 'acknowledging' relationships that she had needed at college when she began her return. Like Eleanor, she had won the power, to a great extent, to 'direct herself'. This is not to say that she had no need of encouragement and a sympathetic approach from her teachers—and some returners, damaged too severely by the failure of their schooling, or beset by fears of different provenance, are far from autonomous learners when they reach university. Sally suspects her own would have been unable to provide the necessary rescue if she had lost her way. But she had become robust, capable, very organized; ready for difficulties, and to thrive on their defeat.

It all felt good at first. The second year was hard, the volume of work was over the top.

Teachers? You think by the second year they should have remembered your name. I don't know why they didn't. Maybe I wasn't strong enough, wasn't forward enough. I would only speak when I was pretty sure that what I had to say was worth contributing. I think you can sound very naïve at that stage.

I can remember having this adverse attitude towards the computer. I'd never been shown the implications of using the computer to develop models of how people think or might think when they're given a certain problem to solve. That's what I mean by naïvety.

I was more than prepared to take things in and just be like a sponge and soak it up—all of it, even the rubbish. But by the end of the second year you can recognize what is worth taking on board; your own ideas and your own leanings are just about to develop.

I was a bit disappointed about the teachers. I'd found before at college that some teachers cannot cope with mature students. Some of the tutors at university had no problem, but others did. Lots of them feel you as a threat, I think. There was one tutor who'd say, no, that's not right, no matter what I said. But once I said, Judy I don't understand, you'll have to explain—it suddenly dawned on her that I was a mature student but I didn't know everything. I was really trying to get a bit nearer to her, without this barrier of threat coming up. But she didn't really want to respond to my overture. She got on really well with the younger girls.

Lecturing is on the side. It's: oh God, I've got to stop my research and go and lecture. I think if I'd really had problems I would have felt absolutely unable to cope. I wouldn't have known who to have gone to, even though we had our own personal tutors.

It would have been nice to have more support. Maybe I didn't ask for it: I've always found it difficult to ask for anything, even from my family. I don't think I made any firm contacts—partly because I was in transit: I was never there.

Coming up to the end of the second year just before the exams, I had a horrific morning: it took me about three and a half hours to get in. I went straight to the Head of Department, and said oh God, can I see you? And he said, yes come in. I said, if I have another morning like this I'm not going to come in—is it okay? I guess maybe I wanted to say to somebody, look I'm having a shitty time. And he said, do you want to come and see me some time? And there was something else I wanted to see him about, so I said yes, and I made an appointment. And then I thought oh God, I didn't give him my name. But when I actually went there the next morning he had got my file and he had found out all about me and there was no problem.

I knew this girl who would freak out if she got an A and two minutes later it would be forgotten. But she'd go mad if she got a D and she would dwell on it, for days and days. I used to say what's the point, you got an A last week.

How have I become someone who doesn't operate like that? I try to practise enjoying a good mark more. If I get a bad mark I ask the relevant questions about the area of work—is it important, do I want to use it? It's just being systematic.

Lots of people look inside straightaway and find something negative. But if you want to succeed, I don't think it's very good to do that to yourself. You try and bluff yourself to start with. I aimed for a 1st—I thought why aim lower. I can't see the logic of aiming for a 2:1 or a 2:2 and then getting a 3rd, because I probably wouldn't have worked as hard.

Sally gained a 2:1. 'Finals were a dream,' she said, 'I knew exactly what was going to come up.'
Leaving school with no qualifications worth the paper they were printed on; ex-dancer, ex-butcher's boy, ex-secretary—she was now ready to do an MA.
She accepts that she is able; but she believes anybody could achieve what she achieved. Her experience has taught her not so much to revel in her own gifts, but to stress the importance of determination. Returners are usually reluctant to accept as a premiss for the distribution of opportunity 'some can, some can't'.

Yes—you can do anything, anybody can do anything they want. But you have to be able to test your mental development, your ability to cope. People don't ever test that, you see. You need to have succeeded at something difficult from the outset. I don't think there are many situations where people actually test that, so they never get the feedback of success.

I hate to give up on anything, I hate to fail. Sometimes I

have to admit that I'm not very good at something. But it hasn't happened that often.

Generalization about others is an integral part of her interpretation of her own experience. Reflection on her own life leads her to see implications for other lives. Her greatest intellectual excitement during her degree years was the discovery of feminism. She became so excited that she had to will herself to postpone further thought till after she had graduated.

The third year was just good from start to finish. I researched why males don't enter traditionally female occupations. That led me into reading lots of different stuff. Resentment started to build up. Stuff on children's moral development, for instance, is drawn on findings based on boys' moral development, and girls are totally different. And then I went into philosophy, and the lecturer we had was totally mainstream, and the way he outlined things was totally male: he looks on consciousness as a single thing, peculiar to the individual. It is—but we're not consciousness in isolation, we're conscious of other people, within relationships.

I got so despondent with this overwhelming realization that the male is the norm. And it gave me a lot of insight why things in the past have always felt so uncomfortable. There were connections flooding in every day. For a good month I felt really depressed, because I was getting overkill, bombarded with these insights, and I couldn't see anything other than male and female. I'd got stuck into it, and it was really hard for me to exist in a normal way. The tele would be on and I'd say, that's a sexist thing to say, why did they say that? And Josie would get sick of it, I'd get sick of it, everybody would get sick of it. But I couldn't stop seeing it because it was there. It was uncomfortable clarity.

Women internalize—we get guilty. It's true we haven't got history, women's history isn't in the books, we aren't taught it at school. I didn't know that women flew aeroplanes in the Second World War without any radar, at night! Brave women, heroic women. We're only told about the suffragettes because they intruded on men.

I thought—I'll go back to it afterwards and do a book.

Like Vanessa, her thinking unites her own with other lives:

> We're not dependent on men; we're made to feel that we're
> financially dependent on men and we're emotional cripples,
> but when it comes down to it we're not. But you're never
> given a chance to find out, unless you're in a weird situation
> where you're kept autonomous like I've been for eleven
> years.

She broke a relationship in her final year:

> The more I questioned his way of thinking and his attitude
> towards women the more flaws I found in it, and the more
> he hated it and the more I hated it and in the end he told me I
> was wrong and I was making myself very miserable so why
> didn't I come back to normal—come on, shake yourself up,
> Sally. That was just confirmation, and I told him to sod off.
> He'd discovered that all he wanted was a housewife, he
> didn't want a wife. It was appalling; everything was
> confirmed in about two weeks. I was asking all the wrong
> questions, wasn't I?
>
> I like making people comfortable and cosy, and we'd had
> quite a good relationship. I liked being domesticated: I
> cooked at weekends because he wasn't there during the
> week. I enjoyed all that, went out of my way, making
> everything so easy for him, never questioning.
>
> In the end he just sort of dismissed everything I said—I
> was just a female.

The intellectual emancipation that began with the revelation
that maths might be a game pushed forward again. Her own
life and the world fused in one urgent curriculum. Nothing was
to be taken for granted any more.

7

Self and Others, Class and School: The Themes So Far

For many women, examination of their past lives with a torch of feminism is the first, crucial, intellectual excitement of their adult years. Thereafter the habit of thought is too good to drop. Sally says:

> I get these questions, and it's a puzzle, and I sort of think—
> well, wait a minute, if I think about this a little differently,
> from a different angle, not taking the obvious . . .

She had been so busy learning since the beginning of her return that I sense that she had not had time for much uncontrolled thought. She had been absorbed in the task of commanding her own campaign of fulfilment, conquering new difficulties, pushing forward, reading what she needed to read, finding the most helpful abstractions to illuminate what she had learnt. Then in her final year she took up a topic for a small research study that led her into her own life, the lives of women around her, her mother's life, her relationships with men, the behaviour of her current partner. She wanted to think and think and think; but she had to stop because she sensed threat to her canny progress towards her degree—with all its careful allocations of time, its obstinate practicality ('Do I need to worry about this bad mark—will I need the topic on which the essay was written?').

But after feminism, her intellect was never the same again. She had become the person I sketched at the beginning of this chapter: glaring at her television, menacing it with her refusal to be conned.

Sally's story, as I have already implied, suggests her as a persuasive exemplar of self-promotion. At critical junctures,

Americans arrived in her life—just as an American became Vanessa's mentor when she needed her. Both women 'took charge of their own lives', 'discovered their inner strength', began to 'use their resources to the full'. Eleanor did the same, and her path—without direct American aid— could be similarly described.

Such formulae come glibly to mind, and feel as familiar as advertising slogans: talk about lives and selves reaches so easily for them. The air is full of a static of words from best-selling American paperbacks—each one offering a different therapeutic programme—from pundits on phone-ins, from columns in magazines. Counsellors multiply. The language of psychic hygiene annexes the most unexpected territories. On the radio yesterday, a professional propagandist of male skin care said: 'Everyone wants to make a statement: these people have found an avenue for self-expression through toiletry products'.

I sense two attitudes to this new repertoire for our thoughts about ourselves. One predicts nightmare: extrapolates from the fulfilled jogger, so attentive to his skin, the privatized self and the end of community.

The other attitude is pragmatic, mine, short-term, and simpler. In order to be happier and more effective, many people need to discard some of the rules and beliefs which have governed their lives.

The nightmare is of enforced restlessness, insatiable desire for 'personal growth'; dictated discontent and planned obsolescence for any happiness as soon as achieved.

But returners cannot be made to belong to it. Their impulse is not towards change for its own sake. Their will to escape does not feel factitious, a mere response to a general invitation to be discontented with your lot.[2] Sally's development, for instance, could be described as 'integration'—a word whose significance I come back to in Chapter 12. She made a gigantic discovery about herself which shattered her composure. The idea of herself which she had put together was no longer

---

[2] 'How refreshing it is these days to meet a contentedly undefined, a peacefully unaffirmed self', D. J. Enright, *The Alluring Problem* (Oxford University Press, 1988), 23. This suggests a danger: an almost aristocratic nostalgia.

credible, no longer large enough—like a calm, small house suddenly trying to give shelter to an elephant. She had no choice but to change.

The discovery itself impelled thought; was a kick-start for her mind. The way she rethought herself foreshadows the accounts of Laura and Julie at the end of the book. Her discovery forced expansion, revolutionary reassessment—new premisses entirely. The energy of her return—with her greed for challenges, her immoderate targets—was the energy of a woman desperate to reintegrate her life now that such surprising new evidence had come to light; in a hurry to establish a completely new sort of composure.

And, like Andrew, her experience forced intellectual practice for the work her studies would demand.

I suspect that it is misleading to think of returners as models of the therapeutic spirit of the age. The keys they find in the undergrowth and use to escape are not of the same order as a moisturizing cream that promises a new avenue for self-expression. Their restlessness is released curiosity; a child's restlessness, the will to know more. They are seekers after truth; they are not addicts of experience, saturated with anomie. Self-discovery is part of a much broader scheme of revelation. When one course is over, they seek another, not from sudden depression, but in the promise of further satisfaction of their curiosity. Before, they put up with lives which they had no chance to examine critically; now they realize that what they took for granted can be taken apart instead; and understood, superseded, or altogether abandoned. They are eager to find new myths to slice open, new problems to solve; eager to rescue those still bemused as they once were.

Returners are taking up the promise made to children by their parents, and to all children by state education: we will help you find what you have. For all of them, the promise was broken; and for most, early in their lives. Return lets them find their gifts and strengths; it renews the promise. If ubiquitous psychobabble helps to lead people to take the risk of breaking some of their rules in order to return, then there is no harm in it.

Sally says that her experience made her realize that *anything was possible*. In order to learn the scope of her free will, and her own 'responsibility for her endowments'—in Eleanor's phrase—she had to interpret her experience to herself—and discover, first of all, that she had a mind to use. With her American friends encouraging her, she found the wavelength she needed, and applied what she heard to interpretation of her own life.

Sally realized, 'you've got to find a way, to be able to push yourself on . . . I think I expect things of myself, I know now I can do it.'

But her self was only one part of her curriculum. She has not become privatized. Her interests are generous, communal. In the statement I have quoted above, 'I' and 'you' merge into each other. As she approached finals, she became mentor to a girl who was fearful of failing—so convinced was she of her own inadequate preparation and inadequate ability.

> I said, you're going to do very well this year if you got Bs last year from doing no work at all, you're going to get a 1st—your sister did, didn't she? Oh, she'd say, she's cleverer than I am. And then she did it. She was absolutely stunned, she couldn't believe she'd got a 1st. Her self-esteem has gone up, so that's been good: it's suddenly dawned on her that she's got something special. And I thought—don't waste it, Mary, please!
> I could see the kid had something, it was obvious, and yet she had no confidence at all.

Sally wanted to use her discoveries for others; she wants to affect women's lives. Her experience has turned her just as much towards others as to ruthless promotion of herself.

Eleanor is training now to be a social worker; Kerry's first job after taking her degree was in a children's home—and she has now been seconded by her employer to train as a social worker. Vanessa talks of the interest other women show in what she is doing, and suggests how readily she herself offers encouragement to others.

Peter keenly wanted others to do what he had done. All six of the returners I have so far introduced agree on the importance, in the early stages, of being part of a group. Vital for them were discussion, the discovery of common ground with other returners, the excitement of breaking the silence in the company of others beginning to find their voices. Self-discovery was a social as much as a private process.

Andrew's case suggests that returners may also be at risk from too ardent self-sacrifice. His zealous work for the blind burnt him out after five years. And I have yet to meet a returner without an intellectual vitality that turns naturally outwards in order to sustain itself.

Rules, Adversity, the Failure of Schools

> 'It seems so awful to be standing there, hour after hour, doing the same thing, day after day.'
> 'That's factory work. The operatives like it that way.'
> 'I find that hard to believe.'
> 'They don't like being shunted about. You start moving men from one job to another, and they start complaining, or demanding to be put on a higher grade. Not to mention the time lost changing over.'
> 'So it comes back to money again.'
> 'Everything does, in my experience.'
> 'Never mind what the men want?'
> 'They prefer it this way, I'm telling you. They switch off, they daydream. If they were smart enough to get bored, they wouldn't be doing a job like this in the first place . . .'
>
> (David Lodge, *Nice Work* (Penguin, 1988), 123–4)

It's a job which brings you down, and I can't see the sense in that. Doing something that makes you unhappy. Well—it kills you in the end, you don't live a happy life. Which is sad . . . (Rob, 29, ex-factory worker, now second year student at polytechnic studying geology. All first-year exams passed)

Finally, a passage in a television programme about Iris Murdoch, made by A. N. Wilson, who is writing her biography. I was absorbed, because I have read her since my teens, and like his biographies. An old friend of the writer's told us about Iris Murdoch as a young woman. Late in the programme she was asked what sort of people she thinks read the novels. 'Well,' she said, in her commanding, *educated* voice (ducks on a river beside which she was sitting in her deckchair

suddenly cackled. 'Can you hear my voice above the ducks?'
she asked; but she need not have worried.), 'I think bright
people, certainly—I don't think someone in a supermarket
would enjoy Iris Murdoch.'

But on supermarket check-outs and in factories work people
like Andrew and Sally.

Through adversity, they discovered their strength. With
their strength they broke their rules and found that the garden
they had assumed locked against them was theirs to enjoy after
all. I cannot play relativist about their lives. Sally is a richer,
happier person, with her curiosity and her scepticism and her
zeal, than she would have been had she not returned. Andrew's
mind would have been caged, in the end, by the work his
'rules' qualified him to do.

The misconception implied by Iris Murdoch's friend is
widely held. Those who do so imagine that, because education
is provided by the state for everyone, the lives people lead
when they leave school must be the lives for which their
abilities suit them—as Vic Wilcox in David Lodge's novel
assumes.

But for Sally and Andrew it was not their ability, but what I
have called rules, that determined the lives they came to lead in
their late teens and twenties.

I am led to remember the two Joans. In my twenties, I
taught English in comprehensives in Scotland and London. The
two Joans, both Afro-Caribbean, were in my O level class in a
south London school in 1978. They were very poised, very
attuned to adult absurdity. They were both able—and it was
hard to say who was the cleverer. They wrote fluently,
understood fast. There was no reason why both should not go
to university. Joan the first might almost have made you think
she was a good little girl, her uniform was worn so correctly.
Her rule was: scale the ladder. All her work was on time: neat,
and terse and thoughtful. Her cleverness was not just academic.
Many of her friends were of Joan the second's persuasion. She
made herself acceptable to them, despite her punctuality and
her hard work and her neat uniform and her attentiveness. I
remember finding a cartoon of hers that had been circulated—
of an elephantine erection with a sly caption. It was a good
example of her diplomatic skill; of how she camouflaged her

assiduity. I would be surprised to find that she did not go to university.

The second Joan had made a rule for herself, to break which my praise and my irony and my melodramatic pleas were powerless. The rule said that school was a farce; its values absurd; its laws fit for children and not for the adult she wrongly felt herself to be. She wore her uniform with sardonic inaccuracy: skirt too long, displaced tie, wrong colour shoes. She hardly ever turned up. Suddenly she would be there, daring me to be annoyed with her. But I liked her too much not to try to be subtle—uselessly—in my persuasions. I liked the air she had of a defiant prisoner. I liked to see her walk down a long corridor with her head held high, hoping for a confrontation with a teacher about her truancy or her dress or a piece of work she should have done two months before.

I left before she took O level. I doubt if she turned up for many of the papers. I can easily imagine her a little later at a check-out, a sardonic witty neighbour for the girl at the next till. I hope she has returned by now.

Rules fence class from class, fence women from men. Subtle collusions confirm their authority. Sally's deadliest enemy in her teens was the ethos of her school: be nice, be moderate, be happy. Joan's teachers confirmed her rejection of them by rejecting her. Together, in sudden unanimous encouragement, we might have swept her off her feet. Instead, she was cheated. The cheating continues because schools are so weak.

The Strength Schools Need

Much too little was expected of Andrew and Sally. People imagine that schools discover children's abilities, and cultivate them. Not at all. They discover for each child the *version* of his or her abilities on show at the time. That version can be entirely misleading—as I suggested in my first book. It concerned pupils whose schooling was dim and insufficient, because they never learnt who they were. They were benignly neglected, allowed to accept the despondent theories they had proposed about themselves: 'I am not very interesting; I am not very bright.' Each presented this misleading persona-version to teachers—who accepted it. In later life some of them discovered that they were very able indeed; which is why I began to be interested in returners.

I argued that an 'acknowledging' teacher could have begun the transformation of such a pupil's self-estimate. To do so would have meant drastic raising of expectations. (The inspectorate is constantly criticizing schools for their low expectations of 'average' pupils; and these misleading ones usually pretended to be average.)

Sally might have met a teacher who glimpsed her true capacity. Such a teacher would have had a very difficult job. Sally's school was dedicated to moderate aspirations; they governed its curriculum: this is not a grammar school! This is a school where girls ply the needle and learn contentment. Rescue, in other words, would have been a tall order.

I do not doubt that in a good comprehensive it would have been easier; though the rescuing teacher would have had to take on the rules that Sally's mother pleasantly enforced: 'Be happy, that's all that matters, and don't forget you're a girl.' But Sally's relations with her mother suggest capacity for rebellion. One could write a play around the missed possibility at the dissection table.

Suppose Sally's saviour is a good-going feminist, eager to subvert the school's timid regime. Suppose that she suddenly senses in the rapidity of Sally's response, her claim to want to learn, a different biography from the Dancer, from Another Young Wife. Sally suggests herself a different girl altogether. Her teacher becomes her crusading mentor. She encourages more assertive dissection; provokes Sally to take the knife to the simpering premisses of her proposed future. Out go dancing, office work, modest ambitions.

Such a revision of Sally's history is not inconceivable.

Andrew was at a comprehensive. He too could have been rewritten. But his rescuer would also have had to work very hard against the grain. All such saints need time more than anything else. Suppose a different version of Andrew's truancy. Suppose a guileful headmaster. Make him a historian, impatient with the paperwork piling up on his desk, much more interested in his pupils, and especially his misfits and enigmas. Give him a dash of 1960s idealism. Suggest that his two heroes are Bruno Bettelheim and A. S. Neill. What above all those two prophets gave the most intractable of the children they saved was time. To read Neill's autobiography[3] is to guess that he grew impatient with Scottish state schools because working in one *did not let him know his pupils*. Such knowledge, he knew, could only come from closer proximity, and far more time, than were possible in ordinary circumstances. At Summerhill, he was prepared from the earliest days to give a child unlimited time. His promise was: 'I am at your disposal.' He would become the good parent the child had lost or never had.

Andrew's historian saviour discovers his pupil in the library, poring over an account of El Alamein. Instantly he sniffs the kind of enigma that has always enchanted him. His first reaction is to enjoy the irony of the truant who escapes in order to further a secret specialism. His second is to think of his older cousin, who drove a tank in the 8th army. His third is to ring up his office, say he is unavoidably detained, and will they cancel the two meetings he was supposed to have before lunch. He spends the morning with Andrew. By the end of the morning, the interest Andrew acquired in his twenties into the causes of wars has already dawned, lent by his new mentor. He has been promised a meeting with the tank-driver cousin; and the headmaster has already worked out the next stage of his own campaign. He is determined that his school will not miss this boy.

So he becomes Andrew's advocate. He organizes his re-entry into classes, persuades colleagues—in long and painstaking negotiations—to raise their expectations of the boy, and teaches him himself on the sly. The cousin takes to Andrew. El Alamein becomes a blossoming project. Subtly and persistently the headmaster begins to interest Andrew in more than wars.

Just as Sally might have become a dissident under the stress of her biology teacher's interventions, so could Andrew's intellectual revolution have happened before, rather than after, he lost his sight.

But my imaginary example of how this might have happened shows just how extraordinarily difficult a 'rescue' would be. What teacher—let alone a headmaster tyrannized by

---

[3] A. S. Neill, *Neill Neill Orange Peel* (Hart, 1972).

the novelty of financial management—could afford the time for such subtle attention, or to persuade her colleagues of the validity of her view of the child she is trying to 'rescue'. A lifeline from one teacher is unlikely to be enough, unless the child concerned is ripe for revolution as—perhaps—Sally was. But with Joan the second, and with Andrew and with all such children, the task would be to challenge and try to change rules deeply laid down in children's minds. One 'acknowledging' teacher is powerless to bring about such change unaided. The imaginary headmaster who rescues Andrew only manages to do so because—as headmaster—he can use his authority and create the time to persuade other teachers to change their expectations of the boy. And not only do expectations have to change: a whole approach must be revised. Those who do not know schools well may find it hard to believe how lethally tenacious can be a 15-year-old's retention of a completely misleading self-estimate. Nor is it easy for the layman or laywoman to realize just how difficult it is for the comprehensive teacher to bring off a subtle alteration of approach. There is an urgent pressure on every teacher to foreclose her judgements of pupils—to generalize, to label—in order to get on with her work. If you regularly assess and if necessary revise your expectations of every child you teach, your work will suffer if you are not given extra time for such careful analysis and thought. Do not—if you are a parent—be misled by the plausible new methods of assessment you will meet in schools. A 'profile' can confirm and continue a misleading judgement of a pupil just as well as a termly report. If a pupil is determined that she is not clever, she will perform accordingly—in the new assessment tasks of the National Curriculum and in GCSE, just as in work under the old regime.

Assessment of pupils, done properly, depends on regular, sympathetic, focused attention to all the complex details of an individual pupil's demeanour and performance—after willed abandonment of preconception. Teachers are *not* provided with time to do this. If a teacher does want to change not just her own but others' expectations of a pupil, she has no time in her day set aside for the exhaustive discussions she will need with her colleagues if she is to persuade them to follow her lead.

The powerlessness of schools is grievous. Any class over 12

or 15 at the most is too large for scrupulous attention to individual differences. Any timetable that asks a teacher to confront—say—six crowds in succession is absurd. Teachers have less and less time as the job incorporates more and more administrative and clerical tasks, which accumulate at present like unpayable bills; and it is time to think, above all, that teachers need in order to relate accurately to their pupils. Without time, they are forced to react, rather than reflect; to relegate to a convenient category rather than always reconsider; to expect the same of an enigmatic or recalcitrant pupil rather than devise a new approach to crack the enigma or end the recalcitrance. Teachers are more likely than ever to make close relationships with those pupils who seek them out: with the attractive, the articulate, the co-operative, rather than those who are uncertain of themselves, and all too ready to accept the rules that others have written for their lives.

Those in this book were submerged in convenient generalities like 'the nice sort of girl' at school. Teachers cannot gauge the true ability of all of their absurd numbers of pupils, and thus pitch their expectations accurately. To know pupils as individuals rather than caricatures, teachers have to be free from the constraints that make their lives so difficult: large numbers; the need to exercise control; the punishing regime of class after class after class with no time between each to reflect. In a busy comprehensive today, it is very difficult to be at one elusive child's disposal.

Schools are crude machines, and miss too many of their pupils. Return must be made easier for the armies of the missed. Just as many are being missed now, because conditions have not changed—so that pupils are still typed, labelled, generalized; and abandoned to underachievement.

Walk into any comprehensive and eavesdrop at gossiping groups of 15-year-olds. You will find that the Sally, the Nice Girl with Modest Ambition, is a model of enduring popularity. Schools have always been and are still full of such girls; whose moderate expectations can only be raised by being challenged head-on, and challenged again, and deliberately and continuously questioned. But a harassed and demoralized teacher is much more likely to say 'she's *the sort of girl* who wants to be a secretary, they give me no trouble, they're always quiet, they smile sweetly, and isn't it nice to have some in your class who write their work neatly and hand it in on time—even if it's pretty ordinary stuff?'

An equally popular model is the cocky streetwise boy, the Andrew before his blindness. ('Streetwise' implies patronizing justification of the wastage of working-class intelligence: this boy is very bright, but bless his cheeky self, his university will be the university of life rather than the sort you and I went to . . .) He too needs his rules to be subverted: unanimously, by all his teachers—by a relentlessly demanding school. All his teachers need to raise their expectations, to denounce his aspirations, to enchant him with loud encouragement, to offer him difficulty in a way that challenges his pride: benignly to traumatize him so that his idea of himself and his life can be transformed.

But they will not have time. He will be accepted and labelled as he is: bright as a button, a pain in the behind, and going nowhere. We should be ashamed of the powerlessness of our schools; at the continuing feckless wastage of talent and intelligence.

This book is about past and present waste, and lucky restitution for some.

Sally's New 'Rules' Change her Daughter's Chances

Sally's family, between them, tell this story in microcosm. Her mother wanted no more than her feminine happiness; so her school and her family ruled in lethal alliance for dancing, typing, and early marriage; for freezing at Butlins, for intellectual darkness, low pay, and a violent young husband.

But the main phase of her daughter's education—from the age of 10 to her sixth-form year—began when Sally was beginning to discard her old rules. As a result, Josie's aspirations—the rules by which she thinks of her life—are quite, quite different.

She is now a law student—at the conventional time.

When we talked, she was taking three A levels. She was 17. Her mother had gone back to education seven years earlier.

I can remember having to be on my own when I came back

from school, which wasn't very nice. I used to put the radio on, but when she was at college it wasn't very long. And when she was at university I was older so it was okay, because I'd grown up a bit more.

I didn't resent it or anything. It was okay once I had my own homework to do because it distracted me a bit. I'd just wait for her to come home. Probably make my tea or something.

When I was in the first year at secondary school I knew a girl whose mum was also at college and we were talking about what our parents were doing. My friends were quite interested in what we were saying: I felt quite proud in a way, because their parents hadn't done A levels or anything.

I can remember my mum and I used to discuss what I was going to do—I was going to do A levels and go on to university. And other kids didn't seem to have discussions like that.

Yes my mum did talk about what she was doing—all the time. It got a bit boring sometimes. She used to come home and tell me all these things about biology. I remember her telling me about the *Sun* being a Tory paper, when she was doing sociology O level, and I didn't know that at the time, and that was quite interesting. I used to test her.

I can remember her reading the *Siege of Krishnapur* by Farrell when she was doing O level. He's a good writer, which is why I like *Troubles*, I think, which I'm reading for A level. She used to read funny extracts. She got quite enthusiastic about it. That would have been when I was about 12, in the evening when she was doing her homework and I was doing mine—well, I wasn't into homework then. She'd be sitting at the table and I'd be sitting on the sofa. Now I sometimes read her bits from *Troubles*.

I think mum's really clever. She talks about physiological processes in the brain; and most people can't string a sentence together. I'm quite proud of her. Especially now. The friends I have at St Mary's, because it's a sixth-form college—their parents are solicitors or doctors; they're professionals. If my mum hadn't done a degree I wouldn't have felt as comfortable with them.

I'm proud of her because they did it when it was easy

because they went to university straight after school. But she's had to put up with grotty jobs and then make the decision to leave all that. It's quite a big decision to leave work, and start something you haven't been doing for years. I feel proud when I think about it, but when I don't think about it I just accept it.

It's great that she can help me—with essay technique, and interviews, and things like that.

She always says if she can do it I can definitely do it because I'm brighter than she is. I've got the ability so I might as well use it. She gets quite irate.

Sally came back into the room, and conversation turned to family history. Sally's grandfather on her mother's side worked all his life for the Electricity Board.

Josie: My great grandfather was quite clever as well, he was a communist, and he was into mathematics and algebra, he had lots of books on it. He learnt Russian, didn't he? He had several contacts in Russia, and he went there.

Sally: He had one burning hobby—he was a radio ham, and I never realized it until he died, and mum had to sell off his equipment. First of all she asked if we wanted it. And then she came across all his log books, because you had to log all your calls officially. He'd got people all over the world—in Russia, South Africa. He had more knowledge and more outside contacts than we ever knew! He was just this little man locked away in his room who we went to visit now and then, and wasn't very forthcoming. He was interesting when you got to talk to him, but nanny hated it didn't she? They always used to have these great conflicts.

'Bill's in his bloody room again—BILL!! Sally and Josie are here!!'

'Who?'

'God!' she'd say, she got so frustrated.

Josie: He used to know every single poem that Robbie Burns had written, as well. He knew them all, he'd recite them in a Scottish accent.

Sally: He was in both wars—don't you remember when he went into detail about how you tie up your puttees?

Josie: He probably learnt Robbie Burns to escape from grandmother. I wish I'd talked to him—with my socialist tendencies. It would have been interesting to talk to him.

Sally: But you wouldn't have had much chance if nanny had been there, because she was so selfish with the conversation. D'you remember that argument we caused—what were we talking about? I think it was the war. She got heated, and he got heated, and we were just getting to the good bits, and she said, we're not talking about that any more, you'll upset him. And I said, we're not, Nanny, it's interesting. But she wouldn't have it.

Josie: She'd just bully him until he shut up.

Sally: And he'd disappear to his room, and switch on his radio, and then there'd be the noise [Sally screeches: the valves shrieking].

But one wouldn't have worked without the other, they'd got to that point. And when nanny was ill, he looked after her. It killed him in the end. He went like that—one day he felt ill, the next day he was in hospital; and then he died. Then nanny went four months later. His last words were, 'Make sure Nell takes her tablets.'

And three days after grandad had died I was talking to nanny. She said.

'And Bill going the way he did—I don't need this. I'm ill!'

'Nanny, I'm sure he didn't die on purpose,' I said.

'No, I don't suppose he did,' she said, 'but all the same, all this upset!'

It is as if Sally's grandparents had a marriage that was a forerunner of all the relationships now strained by education—about which I write in Chapter 11. Nell, Sally said, didn't like William's radio and his room, because of the 'competition'. His active mind made her uneasy, as he escaped to Russia from the Electricity Board, learning Burns, algebra.

Autodidacts sit proudly out on a limb two or three generations ago in so many family trees. But for every one of them, nine good minds were starved of even the pinched evasive fulfilment William's intellect found through his radio. The fear is that just as many minds are still being wasted.

PART II

Brief Lives: An Access Course

8

The New Way Back

Profligate wastage is the theme of this next—rather different—Part; wastage stopped just in time. The difficulty about talking to returners is that their company is enthralling. They are enthralling. They tell you their stories of lethal schooling with tremendous energy, imbued as they are with present confidence, the prospect of triumph. As a result, you are in danger of becoming desensitized to the horror of what they are saying. Just so could burnt and maimed but jolly and optimistic warriors tell you about their battles with so many jokes and funny understatements that the horror of war escapes. But waste of talent and intellect is horrifying; and shaming to a society that boasts its affluence.

This Part contains much briefer accounts of nine mature students who attended an Access course. The familiar lucky concurrence of benign disasters, mentors, good memories suddenly retrieved, great qualities suddenly discovered, saved their minds and their talents from waste. We have no reason yet to be proud of Access. Access did not find them; they had the fortune to find Access. It offers restitution to a small fraction of the missed and cheated.

Access offers an accelerated route to higher education to those without qualifications or with very few. It is politically assisted at present by the decrease in the number of 18-year-olds. What will happen when this trend is reversed is an open question: one possibility is that institutions may suddenly chill their welcome to returners. But the view at present is that adults need to come back into education and training—between which an old war is being fought again. Political hospitality towards the mature student is not as thorough as it might be; it has not for instance extended to generous financial support: return very often means debt, hardship, endless money worries. Access may not be forever. It needs defending. Those who think education just delays training for work are very powerful: an important industrialist called at a recent seminar for work experience to begin as early as 7 years old, and derided the sort of education this book is about. And while Access is funded, political irony is rich. I suspect that most governments would not much like an electorate of returners, who can become impassioned social and political critics. Loyal to new thoughts and hopes, many deride old assumptions. Accommodation becomes anathema. They prefer their politics hot and pure, not cool and compromised. Their experience has taught them empathy for all whose circumstances have been imprisoning; has turned them left, rather than right. Return gives them a language the better to express what experience has already taught.

Roger—who appears in Chapter 11—used to service washing machines. Access and a polytechnic will release him into the job market with a degree in micro-electronics. Much as he may dislike the fact, he is proof to the government that it has spent money wisely. But he is now one of the undeceived. His own personal revolution has purged his politics; though like many of the returners I have met, he is a sceptic rather than a Utopian. Sally's feminism could never be separatist.

The scope of Access is uneven. Provision is rich in some places, scanty in others. Its aim is a ladder. A 'Return-to-Learn' course, for instance, offers students a chance to realize that their minds do work, despite fear that they have rusted solid in years of apparent disuse. In a part of the country properly provided, a student excited by such a course would then be able to go straight into another more advanced one. Some—such as those in this Part—would go on to a one-year course, studying several subjects at an advanced level. If they pass, they qualify for university or polytechnic. Others might decide on a slower approach; might leave a Return-to-Learn course and take some GCSEs, for instance.

Access is, as I write, in danger. Many successful students at the beginning of the 1980s found Access hospitable in its early phase *because of* its informality, its experimental enthusiasm, its lack of bureaucratic regulation. Pioneer returners met pioneer tutors. There was easing affinity between students' lack of confidence and the inspired improvisation of what they were offered. At its best, early on, tutors, students, and the rare organizers of that time joined in a conspiracy with an intoxicating programe: the dismantling by example of so many of the false ideas, the incapacitating assumptions, the lethal 'rules' which service the inadequacy of our education system. Students who believed themselves stupid—test-failures, early school-leavers, convinced dunces—discovered their minds, and proved to tutors and organizers hopes and suspicions they had held for so long.

The danger is that as Access becomes regulated, a familiar part of general provision, hospitality to those it should reach is lost. The greatest danger of all is that it will increasingly build into itself intricate systems of exclusion, so that it will become no more than an alternative set of hurdles to GCSE and A level. A grand reception-desk will replace the improvised welcome of the early days. And if Access becomes the only, the official way back, older paths and means may be blocked. That would be disastrous. Infinite variety and flexibility of access to higher education is vital.

The pessimistic case about Access, put at its most extreme, is that it has already lost its way. The early years should have been the first stage of development towards completely open access to higher education. The optimistic case is that what Access has revealed may in the end be much more important than what it becomes. Like the Open University, Access provides evidence for the argument for continued change. Whatever happens now, or in the immediate future, that evidence cannot disappear. Nor should a great achievement be forgotten: the restitution for so many of a right lost when the school door slammed at 15 or 16; recompense for the cheated.

To find the cheated Access does not just advertise courses and hope for the best. It is common practice to recruit and publicize in an active manner.

Catastrophe, desperation, or both sent the returners I have described back into education. Taking the first step was not as easy as going to a travel agent and buying a holiday. The thought of taking the first step was not one they snatched from the air. For Vanessa, who went on an Access course, the thought formed out of lucky revelation—when her student lodger took her to a couple of lectures—and her mentor's example and encouragement. For Sally, return became thinkable after the worst experience of her life. For Eleanor, the thought was born of despair and her daughter's example. The thought was her last hope.

Not only was their return a matter of luck more than anything else, but they could so easily have failed. They brought to their studies intellectual energy which they had been storing up for years. Their circumstances added urgency; their excitement vulnerability: they could not stop thinking, learning, feasting; and such excess is dangerous. If Andrew had not been treated with tact when his confidence collapsed, his return might have ended. If Sally had not had sympathetic teachers when she hit recession, she might have decided that secretarial work was her fate. When Eleanor told her maths teacher that she could not go on, and he told her that if she gave up 'they might as well all go home', his faith may well have been what saved her. Hard times, agonizing doubts, sudden collapses of confidence often afflict returners. And what they are doing has no inevitability. Return is outnumbered by other sorts of life, which in moments of crisis can seem seductively easy (or depressing: the fate to which they will return) to the embattled returner. And returners are all too often beleaguered by people who think what they are doing is odd. Sixth-formers, young undergraduates, are buoyed up by a sense of inevitability. Surrounded by their like, they are doing what is expected of them. In ironic reversal of returners' absolutism and dedication, young students—as Vanessa's daughter suggests—can be unpunctual, lazy, indifferent, blasé. But such nonchalance flows from a sense of inevitability. The mature student, even surrounded by other mature students at a polytechnic, can feel like a thief about to be caught until the gown falls on to her shoulders on graduation day. ('I have stolen this luxury—being allowed to go into a library and read for hours; being told to think! None of this is real; I will wake up tomorrow and find myself at my typewriter tapping out my boss's boring letter, delivering milk again. My husband laughs at me; my parents think I'm getting above my station; when I meet my ex-colleagues in the pub, they make me feel like an alien.')

So return should have been easier for Eleanor and Sally and

Vanessa and Peter and Andrew. The thought of return should have been easier to think. Ghostly queues of the cheated hover behind each returner. Some put a toe inside a college door, and then scurry home. Kerry, for instance, persuaded her sister-in-law to go to college with her and do some O levels. She got that far. But she had the misfortune to meet a maths teacher who was the reincarnation of all the dismal pedagogues of her unsuccessful schooling. They had a confrontation over a piece of work she found difficult; and she left—for good.

But if return were common, were as usual as buying a holiday, as familiar as teenagers going to school, she would have demanded a change of teacher, perhaps, or dropped that subject, or approached another college. And her teacher would have been more used to the needs of adults and would not have behaved as foolishly.

But Access may, with luck, be a sign of an irreversible shift of emphasis in education in this country. Apart from Vanessa and Peter, the returners described so far went on courses not specifically designed for their needs; not designed to lure the cheated adult. But Access, like the OU, is so designed, is a special route to higher education for adults who left school early. One great difference—enjoyed and quoted in accounts in this chapter—is that an Access student is in the company of others in the same position. But Eleanor, Sally, and Andrew were outnumbered by youngsters. The mix of ages and experience can be stimulating and fruitful—as community schools that welcome adults into their classes can testify; but for the returner assailed by doubts, the company of her like can be critically encouraging.

It is interesting that the Access students quoted in this chapter found 'acknowledgement' as much, or more, from each other as from their teachers. The psychological need for reassurance in the early stages of return, the stage before 'self-directedness', could be supplied by students for students, one often taking the role of teacher for another.

The shift implied by Access is towards the *realization* of the principle that education should be a lifelong right. But the fact that successful Access provision can depend on outreach work shows that the right is not easily accessible.

Yesterday, I had an appointment at a playgroup. I have just

set up a Return-to-Learn course in a village. At the moment, I am appealing to mothers of young children; so I go to playgroups, mother-and-toddler groups, and trap mothers at the beginning or end of sessions, to tell them about the course.

Access provision is new in the area, though learning for adults does exist: the classes that take place in a very successful adult education centre. But the rules of many of those I want to persuade to try my courses have probably dictated that classes at the 'Centre' are not for them.

I talked to five mothers about my course. It is a seven-week taster course. It is free. A crèche runs at the same time. I explain that it is designed for people who are thinking of going back to work, but feel they might like to have a go at some qualifications. For people who might need their confidence boosted a little; who sometimes dream that they might be able to study more effectively now than at school, but wonder if the years at home have turned their brain into a sponge. You will read, discuss, learn how to use a word-processor. You will write a little. At the end of the seven weeks, you will be able to decide what you would like to do next.

Most of the women had seen the poster advertising the course; but it had meant little to them. Its message landed on the outermost rim of their minds; and before they had had time to look, it had vanished.

Such is the difference between the existence of a right, and its availability. One of the women who had seen the poster had two children, one 2, one 4. Before she had her children, she had worked in a chemist's, doing rather the same job as Sally had done: selling at the counter, stock-taking. She talked fast, urgently; said that she had to go back to work sooner or later, but that she could not bear the prospect of being in a shop again; said that she had begun to think about teaching in primary school, but did not know if she had the ability for the qualifications she would need.

As she talked, I gradually described the course, inviting her to come. But I sensed that what I was saying did not yet fit into a prepared set of thoughts; that her mind was not yet hospitable to what I was offering. But when three or four weeks have passed, she may well know someone in the village who has attended the course. When the next one starts, perhaps she will give it a try, so long as I or the course-tutor talk to her again on several subsequent occasions; so long as we reach out to her, rather than expecting her to come unassisted to us.

To argue that she should be left to sign up if she wants, or not if she does not, is to argue that her doubts and the bad memories of school that may well lurk behind them are her fault; and that the rules which may well have fenced her from serious education are her responsibility to change, and hers only. Most of the providers of Access would reject this line of thought. It is more than possible that, despite Access, she will not return, or that she would have to depend on the usual treasure hunt of coincidence and adversity. Perhaps her life will not provide the necessary charge of despair, the salutary crisis. Perhaps she will go back to the chemist's and put up with it. Perhaps her frustration will never be quite strong enough, and she will be cheated of Sally's escape from the shelves.

The Access course that features in this Part started two years ago, and lasted a year. It was full time. Every student had to take maths GCSE; and studied sociology, English literature, politics, and psychology. The standard and demands of the work were about the same as A level. Pause at that statement: people written off by their schooling as intellectually deficient can escalate their achievements very rapidly indeed if their expectations are lifted.

The purpose of the course was to matriculate for entrance to a polytechnic in a southern town, which was, with a college of further education, jointly responsible for running the course.

Each student was awarded a book allowance. There was a crèche. Let it be repeated: for each one of these students, cohorts of others from similar circumstances—equally able, equally in need—may never take up the right to return unless someone persuades them to do so. And if the preliminary courses the seven in this chapter eventually took had been put within their reach years before, their return might not have had to wait so long.

Apart from a brief introduction, a brief point in retrospect, and from time to time an interpolated summary of what they said, the students are left to speak uninterrupted.

9

Nine Successful Returns

Margaret, 41

There are many different ways to have your talents wasted. As with Eleanor, the facts of Margaret's history nearly wasted hers.

She lives in a terraced house with her husband and her two teenaged children. She has her hair short, and wears clothes of quiet colours. There is something neat about her appearance that her presence belies. She likes words, talks fluently, and sometimes with great exuberance. She is intellectually sharp and forceful, very ready to laugh, politically passionate; expressive in voice and gesture and face.

The range of her interests is very wide. As a child in Ireland, it was history that fascinated her—and she had a very good teacher:

> She was a great nationalist which wasn't normal in nuns, you know.
>
> She wasn't the dead type of historian, and she made it interesting.
>
> One of the reasons for my interest was there were still some people around who were figures in '21 or '19, or '16, and I knew some of them to talk to. There was one old boy who was still an independent TD. He was so sickened by the civil war, he always stood as an independent. I used to love listening to him talk.

Margaret left school at 16. She took the equivalent of O level. Her best subjects were history and RE. She had to go to work. Secondary school, at that stage in the Republic of Ireland, had to be paid for. Three years were affordable, but not more.

I applied to do mental nursing. You could do so then with intermediate certificate, which is what I had.

I hated it. The sisters were demons. I've never met nurses like those old devils. They were severe on rules and regulations. Some of the patients had to be fed, and sometimes there weren't enough people to feed them. You'd be trying your best to make sure everyone got enough, but you'd be told off for running over the time. To hell with poor Maggie who's choking over her last bite.

I spent most of my time with geriatrics and semi-geriatrics. You had a lot of them in Ireland, institutionalized patients, there from when they were very young, from 16 or 17. There were some characters. Lizzie and Maggie Joyce used to reminisce about their childhood. Maggie used to say,

'My father kept a huxter's shop, and we used to sell crêpe de Chine, crêpe de Chine, crêpe de Chine.'

She said it like that, in a very quiet voice, and it used to amuse me. I'd only read about crêpe de Chine in a novel.

As students, there were only a certain number of patients' records you were allowed to know. I was dead curious about some of the old dears who'd been there since 16. On nights when you were only supervised by a round every now and then, I used to read the notes. I used to love to find out where they came from and why they were there. Some of them were pretty sane, just institutionalized. I think Lizzie and Maggie were just 'wild'. One of them had a baby, and the other was cast as 'wild', and the two of them were put away. The mother was dead. It's awful, isn't it?

I'd long for a quiet night, so I could read the notes.

An old lady died one day when I was on duty, so I had to go over to the mortuary with the matron. A granddaughter was there. She said to the matron, I didn't know my grandmother was alive. That poor woman had been in there for donkeys' years and the family never knew. It used to make you cringe.

Yes, you're right, it was history.

But I hated mental nursing. I answered an advertisement in the *Irish Times*, for someone with nursing experience—didn't need to be fully trained—to look after a polio victim in London. That's how I came to England.

Soon, Margaret married. She and her husband took in lodgers;
two miners, for instance, picketing down south in the 1973
miners' strike.

The older one looked a lot older than he was, he'd worked
pretty far down in his younger days and he had rheumatics in
his shoulders. Not long before he'd been working in a seam
where he couldn't move his body! In this day and age! I
became interested, and started reading a bit about miners and
trades unions, and a bit of history connected with them.

I got interested in political programmes, but I never
thought of classes at that time. I would have been too scared.
But when my children got older I met more people through
schools in the same boat as myself, thinking they should
have stayed at school longer. Education had changed after I
left school back in Ireland, and my two younger sisters had
been able to go on: one went to university in Dublin. I began
to think—could I have gone if I'd had the chance? But I still
didn't go to classes because I was scared. I went to enrol once
and changed my mind when I got there and enrolled for
badminton instead, at the primary school.

We used to chat at the break times. I used to think I was
ignorant. I remember saying the only politics for me is
when I like hearing people talk, and the two I like best are
Arthur Scargill and Tony Benn. The others were professionals—and middle of the road liberal sort of types. They
went in hoorays of laughing about Scargill, and him being a
red; I hadn't really defined anything about him. But that
made me interested and I began to read more of the papers.

I was branded from then on. It was a Catholic school. I
said once that I thought Christianity and socialism were just
the same. It was good fun. Yes, it was the first time I'd had a
lot of that sort of discussion. But what abashed me—and still
does—was the feeling I hadn't got the knowledge to go along
with the argument. This feeling that I knew I was right, but I
couldn't really argue because I didn't know enough. They
used to enjoy getting me going.

I definitely used to listen to political programmes more,
and I began to know more about who was who in politics
and what party they stood for.

The next step was maths, at evening class in the local comprehensive school. She wanted to be able to help her children. But she could not keep up. This put her off joining other academic classes. She would read the publicity for evening courses, and would often try to find a friend to go with her to one she fancied. But her friends would 'make excuses', and she could not face going on her own.

She saw publicity for a Return-to-Learn course, and at last an advertisement was enough to attract her:

> I had the courage to respond. It was worded in such a way that no matter how little education you felt you'd had, it was for you.
>
> I was called for interview. I was petrified: again it was this business of going on your own. I was accepted, and I enjoyed it. There were two residentials. I had a chronic headache before the first—from fear, I think—that I was going to be asked questions, or something. Sue, who was my tutor, was very optimistic and very helpful. I did a piece of writing about church and state in Nicaragua—and she said it was very good. It was Sue who advised me to go for the Access course, when the chance arose.
>
> On the course, I liked politics best, and I did best in politics overall. I passed, and now I'm at the poly, where the politics still interests me most. My confidence has definitely improved. I will speak out now. There's a third-year student in one of my modules who's the next best thing to a fascist. He said people who can afford private health care should not be paying anything towards the National Health. That was a red rag to a bull, so I challenged him. Its politics like that that make me a socialist.
>
> The kids think what I'm doing is great. Paul my husband works for the Post Office. He's supportive, but sometimes he doesn't quite understand how much time it takes. He's a great reader. History would be very much his thing, I should say. I wouldn't be surprised if he did something part time when he retires.
>
> I think if you were married to someone who didn't read, they would find it hard to understand all the time you spend with books. I knew of someone who couldn't stay on the

Return-to-Learn course. The husband was so frightened, so scared that she would become someone he wasn't, that he was genuinely ill. Sue said, what do you do? I said, I'd have let him be ill, to tell you the truth.

I've heard other people on about their husbands—that they try to get their work finished before their husbands come home, because they don't like to see them at their books.

Like many returners, Margaret combined lack of confidence and determination at first. Like Vanessa beginning her Access course, Margaret was 'petrified' on her first residential: that she would be asked questions and reveal her ignorance. And yet she was determined; craved challenges. When she could not quite face evening classes on her own, she was determined to do something difficult, so she decided to learn to swim, even though she was terrified of water. And now her confidence is steadily growing.

William, 41

Married with two children, he lives in a council house on a small estate. Coming through a dark passageway, you arrive in a spacious room, with bookshelves, and ledges for his hi-fi, and for his massive stock of records. The walls are painted in dark colours. It is a comfortable room, in some indefinable way making me think of the 1960s. He is tall, and relaxed, but his talk accelerates with enthusiasm when his subject is the early stage of his return. His excitement at the feast of his studies echoes Peter's; he has won the same enfranchisement.

He was a strike leader at his primary school:

> We had a lot of kids from an orphanage, and the teachers decided they couldn't eat their sandwiches in the hall with us. So one lunchtime we went out into the playground and wouldn't come back. I was one of the instigators.
>
> We wrote WE'RE ON STRIKE all over the school play-ground. They gave in.

He left secondary modern for a spell of wandering typical of the late 1960s. Brief marriage ('Then I met the *femme fatale*'). Long sequence of jobs—mechanic, group's road manager, factories, engineer for fruit machines. Finally, by the time he was married again:

I went on the milk for five years, and that's when I got involved with the union. The senior steward left and no one wanted to take it on, so I did. I enjoyed arguments, discussions—if you know you have a principle and you know you're right, it's a challenge to get justice done. I clinched a new commission deal—a good one.

Then they sold out to another firm who don't recognize unions, and by that time we'd had Julie. That's when I gave up. You reach a point where no matter how hard you try you're not getting anywhere financially. I was panicking, I had 300 rent arrears suddenly thrust on me, and they issued a summons to get us out unless we paid it. If I'd done 'Intro Law 1 and 2' at the poly as I have now, I would have known they couldn't make a retrospective claim like that; but I didn't know. So I gave up work, got 700 superannuation and 300 holiday money, and paid off the arrears.

Then Karen got a job.

I decided not take a job until I'd had a look around. And when I started looking I just didn't have the qualifications, though I wasn't thinking about them yet. 1984 was show-down time anyway, everybody was getting out of work. I was determined I wouldn't go to work until I could get a job which would give me a fair wage for a day's work.

Karen got a teaching job in the school here, and so she went to work and I looked after the kids. I got pretty bored. It was interesting to start with, the role-reversal: the youngest was only very tiny, and it was interesting to see more of the kids. But after a while you get so frustrated; you're not thinking; everything gets to be a routine.

And I got bored. I didn't get bored, did I? [shouted through to kitchen]

Karen: You didn't get bored? You were unbelievable.

William: I started to get frustrated I suppose. Then I saw this advert for the Return-to-Learn course in the paper.

When I was on the co-op I did one of the TUC steward tests and I got a 90 per cent mark on it. It was just general knowledge and common sense. That encouraged me, and I used to look at all the bumf I got sent from TUC college in Slough and I'd think, you ought to do something.

The course was social-science based. I thoroughly enjoyed it. My tutor was a really good bloke. I was nervous as hell to start with. I used to go rushing off like a schoolboy.

I got an interview for the Access course—and a parking ticket. But I got a place, and I was over the moon. Karen's support was very important to me. I think she got more fed up with my political leanings—

Karen: You had them, but you didn't do anything about them.

William: I used to argue with the television, sit and shout at Margaret Thatcher.

Karen: But you didn't do anything, you didn't get off your bottom and do anything.

I just thought it was a terrible waste: he was so bored with mundane jobs. It just seemed so stupid that he should blunder along and not even think about anything, when he obviously wanted to. Ever since I met you you said you'd wished you'd had more education.

William: Earlier, the reason I used to give for wanting more education was financial; but in the last four years it's been much more to understand the why and the how of everything, not just for what I can gain out of it. In the last two years since Access, my attitude to education has changed completely.

What was best to start with? On the Return-to-Learn course, I think the library mainly, and talking. The atmosphere was great, it was like a club, not like a school at all. The library? It was the fact there was so much information available, and it was totally unrestricted; it didn't matter what you were interested in, you could find something on it.

It was like—waking up. There's a lot of censorship, out in the ordinary street. And suddenly to be confronted with all this information, easily accessible, just for the looking, just for the taking, was tremendous. In ordinary life with the tabloids and everything, you lead a very sheltered existence.

The reason unions are considered militant is that they supply information.

It just became an Aladdin's cave. I never read before, but we had to read books, and I started to learn how to read. Karen has a load of books, and I started reading hers.

Karen: I remember arguing a lot, and if he didn't agree about something he'd rush off and find whether he was right or not. We had a tremendous argument about the French revolution, didn't we, and he wouldn't accept that he was wrong. We had a great row in the middle of his sister's shop.

I thought it was wonderful. The change was so vast. He finds now he gets very bored with mundane conversation; he can't cope with people who aren't interested in the world about them. But he wouldn't accept that he'd changed so much towards people.

William: When I was accepted for Access my fear was all to do with structure; having deadlines.

Karen: And you'd never written an essay, had you?

William: I thought I'd do really well on the sociology, but oh dear I couldn't do it, all this hippy-trippy name-dropping, every single point has to be quote unquote said by so-and-so, and I couldn't come to terms with that at all. I had to learn the discipline of academic sociology; that was the nub of it.

Karen: You were dreadful, you used to come home—

William: I used to get really ratty about it. In the end I had to compromise my own opinions, and learn the art of making the right quotes. The psychology was the best because we spent an awful long time learning to write reports, and that stood me in good stead for writing essays as well.

The politics tutor was very good, he kept chastising me for wandering off into history. We used to get into some really good debates. The worst shock I had was when the social-fund officer stopped our money. I explained that the Access course was under the 21 hours so that I could be technically available for work. They asked me if I was available for work, and I said that if they offered me a job street sweeping I couldn't take it because of the course. She said that I was making myself unavailable for work, so she stopped the claim. So it took me five letters and three months to get it reinstated. I had to take it to tribunal level, and they refused to pay the rent during that period. And that was just coming up to the exams.

So far at the poly I've had one real confidence shock. They're trying to encourage more mature students because of falling school rolls. The woman in charge of mature students interviewed us all, briefly, about how we'd got into higher education. At the end of mine, she turned round and said, you don't seem to have stuck at anything for very long, do you think you'll stay here?

I nearly strangled her. I said, well, thanks very much. I don't like to put people into showcases, but she's middle class, she's gone through higher education—it was expected of her to do it. She's got her qualification, gone away and had her family, come back in on an administrative level—and she thinks all these Access groups are very strange.

But the tutors are very good. My personal tutor is a real case, I really like him.

The c.v. is a middle-class habit. Many working-class lives do not fit the conventions of the c.v. at all. Expressed as a c.v. William's life looked formless. The presumption of virtue for the 'sticker', the professional who runs his or her life to make it look good on paper, is inapplicable to the career of someone at the mercy of economic mischance.

A pattern of work that seems to veer and stagger is very common, and likely to reveal—if anything at all—that someone without qualifications is poorly proofed against business failure or recession. And we see that such a person is also vulnerable to institutionalized prejudice against education—rather than training—in the shape of the 21-hour rule.

Margaret and William: saved from intellectual malnourishment by luck, adversity, badminton arguments, a mentor-wife.

Harriet, 37

Now we come to a new way to be cheated: racial prejudice. Harriet is 37. She is married, with two children, and lives in a semi-detached house in a quiet street. She has a gentle, quiet manner of talking, which somehow adds to the impression she gives of settled conviction and strength. She feels no need to proclaim her achievements; but her composure suggests them.

After we had talked she showed me pictures of her recent holiday in the Caribbean. There were several of her grand-father's house, where her life began. She seemed lost in thought as she looked. She recalled how she and the other grandchildren tested whether one of them was telling the truth. She showed me a photo of a big tank you had to walk across on a narrow board: if you fell in, you were a liar.

Her younger son was in the room, just back from school, contented, smiling. 'Yes,' he said, 'and you couldn't even swim then!'

I went to school in the West Indies until I was 14. It was a Catholic school. I think it wrecked my whole life. They were all nuns. Every so often the teacher would come behind you while you were reading. If you said one word wrong you'd get it round the legs; and therefore I developed a reading block.

I'd read away and all of a sudden I'd make a stop on the simplest word. Even now I've got a block if I have to read aloud. I've been training as a counsellor, and on one of the sessions we were role-playing, and I was given the part of a probation officer. I had to read out this social enquiry report, and I was sweating. But I did it.

There were dreadful beatings. Bright spots? I suppose there were, but I can't remember any. I hated school. But I could get out of it quite easily. I would offer to lend my services to the farm, and not go to school. As I got older I did much more: we had a shop and I could virtually run it. I wasn't good at reading, but I could do all the invoicing and everything.

I came to England at 14. I liked it at school here. It was incredibly different. People actually spoke. But it took me a long time to open up and talk to anybody. I think I was dreadfully frightened to start with.

School was an escape. I'd joined a family I didn't know because I'd been brought up by my grandparents. I found my brothers and sisters really difficult to understand at first. Looking back at it now, I suppose I was a pain.

I liked most of my teachers, they were all very helpful. I was best at needlework, which was something I'd had to do: my grandmother taught me; and cooking, and maths. I took CSE's and went to college to do a pre-nursing course. But my mother had financial problems, and so I went to work at an electrical assembly works. The most boring job ever! I did it for just over a year.

I did my English O level part time at college and failed. Then I applied to do nursing. I got in.

I went to work in a nursing home. Nuns again, but it was incredibly nice there. The person in charge was Sister Mary. After that I did my Nursing Diploma, and I did much better than I thought I would. I always thought little of myself.

I took to Sister Mary because she didn't behave like a nun. You could laugh and joke together. She's the one who made me feel I could do things. And she taught me so much: she introduced me to study cards, writing things down on little pieces of paper. She taught me how to organize my time. She was special. I told her about my reading—but she said, don't be silly, I've heard you reading beautifully to the patients! I didn't know she was listening. Even now I still go back and see her occasionally.

I did start to feel differently about myself. I felt I could do things, that I wasn't as hopeless as everybody thought I was. I felt incredibly hopeless, because all my brothers and sisters had got O levels and I hadn't got any; and education does make you feel inferior. My older sister had passed the 11 plus and gone to grammar school and excelled; she was the family favourite who's got a degree—and I used to think, God, I can never do anything. But she hadn't had to cope with the change from the West Indies.

After qualifying I just worked and worked and worked. We bought a house when we could, in a new community.

One day when my eldest son was 5 he came back from school with a report that said he was aggressive. I went down to the head and said, how dare you say my child's aggressive!

We had a slanging match; I dealt with it badly. But the

head said, if you think your child's not being treated well you can come down and sit in the class. So I did. And of course he was as good as gold when I was there! I think the head was just trying to get rid of me and he thought I'd never come down. But that started me off going to school to help in another class, reading—I was quite happy to read to kids—and helping in other ways. Then I joined the PTA, helping to organize things. And when he went on to middle school, I helped there. I was asked to become a governor— but I thought there was no way I could do that. The others would all be educated people! It would be all posh! But I joined the Afro-Caribbean Association; my interest was education, and with another woman, we formed an education group.

The Association became more and more interested in education. I learnt a lot about how and why black people traditionally don't do well in the education system. For instance I found that people were pushed towards sport, which I was very much encouraged to do. I thought we had to get together to change things. I think we felt that our children had got to do better, had got to take more part in society. Therefore not only would we want them to get much more out of the education system, but we were going to have to provide role-models. Our parents didn't; they came here to work and make money to go home; and it didn't happen. Our kids' home is here. We've got to make them see themselves as British, and believe that they can go into any occupation they want to. In the Association today, I think that's our main objective.

If I saw a black kid out on the streets when I knew he should be at school, and I knew his parents—I'd go to them and say, I know several people who would do the same for my kids.

The focus of what we were doing was trying to make sure that kids got their exams. And we thought—if we're asking them to do this, we've got to do it ourselves. I hadn't got an O level English pass!

When the Access course came up—we thought, yes, that's for us. Our confidence had grown, you see, because we had been successful. We set up an educational conference for instance. It was very hard work, very draining. We felt we had to have black people speaking—black teachers, black writers, academics. We wanted to show black people could do these things. It came off. It put us on the map.

Access was terrifying. I got there and I was told to write an essay. The first mark was abysmal. But when you get the mark you need you get a tremendous buzz. I had to learn the whole learning process, how to read books—other learning skills.

In sociology, I went from a mark like 45 to 80 something, when I did an essay about the educational disadvantages of black people. That got me going, that's what I'd been studying for the last couple of years.

I enjoyed the course very much. I found psychology difficult, but it ended up as my best subject. The teacher was an exceptional person. She reminded me of Sister Mary, because of her enthusiasm for her subject.

Now I'm going to do a degree.

When I went on the training sessions on the counselling course, I used to come home and say to my husband, what on earth have I let myself in for? It was the women I found hardest. There was one I said hello to; and she said hello in a very funny voice, and that she was awfully tired because she'd been watching her son playing cricket all day. And I thought—my God, I've been to work at half-past seven in the morning, finished at four o'clock, then I had to be at the training session at six. I went off her. I suppose I shouldn't have. Since then I have managed to talk to her.

But I feel that if I do things like taking a degree it will help my children.

My husband's on a course now. His enthusiasm is terrific. He used to get fed up with me going on about Access all the time but now he can understand it.

My uncle says, you've got a nice house and a nice husband, why d'you want any more? As if a nice house was everything. I may not get much more with my degree than I do on my D grade as a nurse. Once material possessions were very important to me. Clothes—and my car had to be just so. Now my car looks like a tip, and it doesn't seem to matter any more.

The importance of expectation is deeply inherent in Harriet's account. Governing the educational work of the Association has been the proposition that the best way to insure children against the iniquity of racism is to make them think highly of themselves. To model the sort of expectations she wishes her children to have, Harriet has decided to expect far more of herself.

Lesley, 35

Lesley is also a trained nurse, and shares Harriet's determination that her children will not be confounded by prejudice. She came to this country from Jamaica when she was 11 years old.

She too gives an impression of strength that has no need to express itself forcibly. She is very calm, and sure about what she is doing. We sat in a peaceful room, comfortably furnished, with French windows looking out into a garden. I sensed that for her the Afro-Caribbean Association had offered intellectual liberation. She still feels the pain of her early experience in this country. But new understanding has given her a mirror in which she can see not just herself, but her kind—as if in a huge group photograph. She has learnt intellectual confidence as a result.

I was like an alien in the classroom at first. There were two of us West Indians, but the other girl was at the other side of the class. I was lonely. It was an entirely different curriculum. I didn't know England, or where London was. And I was thrown in at the deep end. Read that book and get on with it!

It was beyond me. If I put up my hand, I'd be dismissed. In the end I got so shy I didn't want to make myself look silly, so I just sat there.

They didn't want us to get on. All they thought we were good at was art and athletics. When it was time for games we used to come first, and so on—but so what, I didn't want that. I went to school to learn. That's what they said about all of us: artists and athletes. Why didn't they spur us along, with the others?

In my secondary school, the PE teacher was awful. 'The blacks are all the same'—was his sort of opinion. I used to feel, is it worth it, is it worth going on? If they've branded you, you might as well carry on and behave as they want you to behave.

I remember one time in home economics, we were making a Christmas cake. I said, the cake you get from shops is really hard—if I bring in a recipe from my mum, we could do it. She said, oh I don't know if they'd like *that sort of thing*.

I said, what d'you mean, *that sort of thing*? I do answer back—I'm very inward, but if you get me mad I will tell you. So I said, I'll bring in a bit of cake my mum's made and you can taste it. In the end it was only 'us' that got to make it.

There's no way I'm going to let my children go through what I did. I went through hell. I'm a governor of Morton school, where my eldest boy is. I'm an active governor and I go into school regularly. I can go in at any time when they're working. When I drop him off, I talk to the teachers. If you help out at school, they take more interest in your children.

Getting involved will help my children to achieve more than I did. I want them to. They've got to be three or four times better than a white child. No, they wouldn't have the same opportunity if I didn't bother. My God, they wouldn't—I know it. If teachers think you're not supporting your child, they won't want to know.

Being involved with the Afro-Caribbean Association was part of all that.

Access started, which is a way of achieving qualifications. And with the change in the way nursing's set up, my SEN qualification is getting pretty worthless.

Did I enjoy the Access course? I didn't have time to enjoy it. I just had to get on with it, there was so much work. Two girls who were on the course said to me the other day they didn't know how I did it with four children and working—I did two nights, Friday and Saturday. I'm still doing two nights now I'm at the poly.

The support systems were fair, but the students themselves were very good. When I was down in the dumps I could phone Margaret or Liz and say I'm feeling so down, and they'd say, don't let it get to you; or I'd show them an essay I was worried about, and they'd say, it's fine.

You haven't got time to enjoy the poly either, it's a lot of work because I've got a family, and I know I've got to pace myself because I don't want to fall behind. I'm very eager, because I just want to get it done.

No, I don't understand how I do it either! I study at night. My husband gets the children ready for bed and he reads to them, and I get to work. You've got to be good at planning your time because it's so precious. Some of the young students I do my seminars with are very different: I turn up and I've done my bit, and they don't turn up. But then they're young. They say at the poly that the mature students work too hard. My tutor said the other day, don't worry, for goodness' sake, what does it matter if you get a C? I say, I don't want a C, I want to do better than that. A pass is nothing to me, I want more.

I think the Access course pushed me on, and had that effect.

Lesley's demeanour at school made it even easier for her teachers to label and discount her. She says that she became 'so shy' that she 'just sat there'. It cannot be said often enough how difficult it is for teachers to make subtle attempts to encourage the unresponsive, especially when anxiety or disenchantment makes such pupils determined to avoid attention. So Lesley was trapped twice: by prejudice, and by the silence her unhappiness forced on her.

Lit up by determination, she will never be trapped again, never be cheated by demeaning expectations. She sets herself Sally's immoderate target: nothing is allowed to be impossible.

Sandra, 29

Most of the decoration in the sitting room of her third-floor flat has an African theme: pictures with an African setting; carved figures in black wood. She has three children. Her son woke when we were talking, and she brought him into the room. Like many of the mothers I interviewed, she could divide her attention expertly between a toddler and my questions. Her patience and her agile switches of attention were impressive. The greatest difficulty for a mature student with children is the need to juggle responsibilities, and to switch roles quickly.

Sandra is welcoming, talks easily, smiles often, so that you sense that her recent achievements have given her great contentment.

At school, she gravely underachieved.

I came to this country when I was 5. Even at infants' school I can remember not getting on very well. I can remember being too far ahead. A note was sent back saying I shouldn't be doing joined-up handwriting.

I think they had an image of how well you should do as a black person, and you shouldn't do better than that.

I went to a comprehensive. I don't think they encouraged you. I liked biology, but I used to sit at the back of the class and not do anything. Only three in the class got O level and I was one. I never revised for it. My teacher stopped me in the street she was so surprised. I wrote and I wrote and I wrote. I can't remember doing that for any other exams. In the English exam, I started all right, but half-way through I gave up caring, and I blew it on purpose.

No! Nobody talked to me about what I might do. Careers was a waste of time. I never knew I could go on to further education.

I stayed on at school after O level to do things like a secretarial course. But I hated it. I went for lots of interviews.

At the first interview, when I went through the door, the man in the room was writing, and he looked up at me and stared at me for a long time, and then he sort of shook himself. He said, can I help you please? and I said I've come for the interview, and he stared at me again. Then he recovered himself, put his pen down, and said, come and sit down. I sat down and the interview began. During the interview he asked where I came from. I said my parents come from the Caribbean. He asked me, what's it like over there? and I said, I don't know, I can't remember. He didn't talk about my qualifications but about the Caribbean.

I heard nothing. I left school without a job. I kept on

going for interviews for typing. People, especially white people, have an image of what black women should do. When some people find out what I'm doing now, you can see the shock on their faces. People often assume that my husband's job is at the works—but it's not, he's a research technician.

The first non-typing job I went for was at a dry-cleaners, and I got it. I stayed there for six years.

Race has been very important to me—I think I started thinking about higher education when I worked for the dry-cleaning firm. I went in as a press-operator. Then, you never saw black people at the front of the shop. After that I took small jobs, crèche work—I even set up a crèche a couple of times. But it seemed that wherever I worked, I could only expect to get so high. Most times it was prejudice, but their excuse was qualifications. I thought—if I get some, at least they won't be able to use that excuse.

The other major influence was being a woman. That and being black were two influences almost pounding on me, telling me, YOU SHOULD DO this or this or this. I decided that my personality didn't let me stay at home, I'm just not that sort of woman. I used to get into dreadful moods because I wasn't doing anything with my head. Once when my husband was working for the bus company I used to get a free bus pass and I used to put my child on the bus and just go somewhere with him—anywhere.

One very important person who did influence me was Joan. I used to take my eldest boy to this Saturday school when he was 2. She worked there. I went to work there as a volunteer. One day she saw me talking to this group of children about a ladybird we'd found, and she said, you seem to have a natural gift for working with children. She said I was so bright I seemed to have tremendous energy about me, and I should push myself. She's retired to Trinidad now, but then she was behind me all the time. She said I had so much, I should put it to use. She went on to my husband about it— and she may have helped him to change his attitude. When she heard I'd got to the poly she was really pleased about it, as if she'd put all her money on me. She was a very inspiring person. I didn't have to tell her anything about myself: she would tell me. She would say, why don't you do this, do that—you're quite capable? I respect her so much I almost bow down to her. She's the person whose judgement I respect most. I miss her when I'm down, I miss being able to talk to her.

And it's only recently that I've really aimed high.

Sandra's start was evening classes, four years after she left school. Dressmaking first. She did so well she bypassed A level to do her City and Guilds. It was very hard work—sewing to strict deadlines.

There was a drive in me. I enjoyed learning, I enjoyed the homework.

I was doing the teacher-training for FE when I heard about Access. They chose me for interview. There was a maths test, and I passed that with 80 per cent, and they accepted me. It was only then I discovered that you could end up going to the polytechnic, which was something I had been thinking about. But I still had this idea that only clever people went there and that I wasn't clever.

People I was going around with socially weren't doing what I was doing. And my husband used to say that people at work asked him why he let me go to college because it was a waste of time.

We did have arguments about housework and dinner. I would have deadlines, and he would still expect me to cook. Now near exam time he tells me that he'll cook such and such a night. And he tells me off for wasting time. He realizes the importance of it.

When I have time off, he wants me to fall back into the old role again, and I don't want to fall back into it. But he keeps telling people about me being at the poly, because he's proud. It's embarrassing for me because everybody takes it differently. Some people say I'm showing off, and they criticize me for not looking after the children; some reactions are really quite nasty.

By the time of Access I knew I was pregnant with my third child. I felt as if I had a terrible amount of work to do. I studied at night and I kept on falling asleep on my books. My husband did everything while I did my homework.

When Christmas came, I asked for work, so I could get ahead, so that when I had my third child, I was well up with it.

Education I found most interesting. I could identify with so much. I never found it difficult. I made up my mind to become a teacher. We covered a lot about race in education, even considering the attitudes of the college teachers. I hurt my leg badly, and was invited to use the lift in college. A teacher once saw me get out of the lift and almost shouted at me—can't you read the notice, it says teachers and disabled students only? I let her have it; I said, I suppose you think that anyone looking like me couldn't possibly be a teacher.

We could choose books in English, and we chose books by women writers and by black people. I felt part of the course. They were talking about me. The white people on the course were finding out a lot about black people, they were learning how to accept me.

I've really enjoyed polytechnic, but sometimes my thoughts are dominated by child care. We've gone much more deeply into sociology—how people think; it makes you think about yourself, and how you fit into society. I just find it totally interesting.

I'm doing okay. I took eleven modules and passed them all. I really wanted to get some As, and I really pushed myself. I felt everyone around me was getting As. But I just got B-pluses. My husband was really pleased with my marks!

I just feel I'm meant for something, and it pushes me on.

I feel that the people I was with on Access are changing. I can feel myself changing all the time, and for me it's totally positive. It's hard work; but the feeling I get out of it makes it all worthwhile. I feel inspired about it.

Race prejudice creates the cruellest generality of all. Lesley's anger is with schooling that never touched her as an individual. But in adult life, Harriet, Lesley, and Sandra have all begun to discover themselves. That is what Sandra means when she says she can feel herself changing all the time. Like Sally, education helps to revise assumptions and expectations so that they protect her development, and prompt more.

For all three, life and learning affect each other. Their first education cheated them, so Sandra and Harriet find the study of education compelling. The subject illuminates their experience; but their own lives help them interpret what they study.

Sue, 31

I met Sue at home. She has brought up her 8-year-old daughter Chrissie on her own. She talked about the pain and difficulty of being a single parent and a student: the conflicting demands, the incomprehension of others. She sometimes feels nearly overwhelmed.

As soon as we began talking about her schooling, she mentioned her worries about her daughter's school. The class was out of control, Sue said, and Chrissie was made a scapegoat by the teacher—in Sue's words, treated as the 'class beast'.

> She was accused of stealing sandwiches, and because of her reputation, of course they put the blame on her, and she didn't do it, and she was talking about the unfairness of it and how she didn't do it three months later.

Sue went to complain. Like Harriet when she first approached her daughter's school, she accuses herself of having been too aggressive. But she says, 'What was so horrifying was the prospect of it all happening again'. Luckily, Chrissie does now have a teacher with whom she gets on well.

Her mother was also a victim of the ruthlessness in school with which some pupils are relegated as unworthy and unteachable.

> The very first thing that came out in the Return-to-Study course was the way I held my pen, which was different from anyone else. And I remembered that when I was about 9, a teacher used to slap me over the hand with a ruler because of it.
>
> I could see the same sort of things happening to Chrissie at 6, and that was really horrifying. But because I'd been through it, I could recognize the signs.

On the whole my primary schooling was really nice. I used to read a lot as a child but didn't at all as an adult until now. It was the school all my brothers and sisters went to. Then I went to grammar school which I hated. All my friends ended up going to the secondary modern, and I felt terribly isolated. I think there was snobbery about being working class. But my feelings had a lot to do with being isolated; and the school was a long way from home.

I was there for two years. Then they asked me to leave. When I went to the secondary school I'd wanted to go to in the first place, I remember going into biology, and they were cutting up a plant. I thought, for Christ's sake, what are they doing, we did this two years ago. I felt devastated. I honestly don't think I learnt anything from that day on.

I can't really say why they asked me to leave. I can't in all honesty say I was that disruptive—maybe I was, but I've seen worse. They very much kept everyone in line. I'm not clear about it really. I did tell them I didn't like being there— I was bolshy enough to do that. But that's a challenge, really, in a way. They should have been able to deal with it. They told my mother I was a born leader. Yes, I suppose they should have wanted to keep me!

One thing that didn't help was that the history teacher had left. She was lovely, everybody liked her. The other subject I liked was art—and the art teacher probably didn't have all that much push in an academic school.

My mother said she wanted me to be happy. I've got no criticism of her, she's a wonderful mum in so many ways, but she so easily says—as long as you're doing your best, that's all right. She does it now, when I tell her about something I'm doing and that I'm worried about doing it right. I get really angry with her.

For me, it's almost like accepting defeat—to say as long as you've done your best, it's all right. She had a completely different existence from mine, and that's why her values were different. She met my father and married him when she was 18, and they had six children. He was the provider and she was the mother. My father—who I think is in fact very, very bright—came from Ireland and had no education after the age of 14.

I don't blame them. They didn't know the system. I didn't realize at the time that I could have gone on to CFE. I had a careers adviser who never ever suggested that to me. He said, do you want to be a nurse, or do you want to go and work in a factory? And I didn't want to do either of those, so for a little while I didn't bother getting a job.

The secondary school was more of a social experience, quite honestly, than an academic one. I don't remember it being anything in particular. I do remember maths, not getting on at all. It related to stuff I did in sociology last year. Boys doing better at maths. It's so true. The boys were always up there. That teacher must have realized that I wasn't doing what I should have been doing, wasn't going at the right pace or whatever. He sat at his desk at the front and you took your work to him when you'd finished it, so invariably I just sat at my desk! He should have picked that up.

Things weren't demanded of you much really. I didn't stay long enough to get an O level or anything.

Blame? I don't know. Maybe I had to wait for the right time for me. The grammar school had much better facilities and I learnt far more, but somehow it was so channelled. The secondary school had nothing, they just had no facilities.

I started going back to education when I was going to a mother-and-toddler group. We did photography, which by its nature allowed people while they were developing their films to talk to each other. We were all women who didn't know each other. That was extremely good. At the mother-and-toddler group you just talk about whether your kid has got spots: that's the level of conversation, it really is. But in the class you're not talking about the children, you're talking about the photographs you're developing, and discussing why certain things worked or didn't.

And in the Access group last year we learnt how to share each other's work and so gain each other's knowledge. It really quickened the pace of it.

Now Sue is full time at a polytechnic. The stress she puts on her photography class suggests again how important it is for returners to be able to talk—especially in the early phase. She found herself working, learning, discussing techniques. When the course ended, she wanted more. The serious absorption of learning had very quickly become indispensable. She felt herself changing. Meeting and talking to others in the same position helped her to find the courage to go on. To have stopped would have been to take her self-portrait out of the developing tray before its time.

Shirley, 35

She is bringing up her two boys on her own. She talks emphatically and neatly, suggesting a mind fond of order and clarity, possessed by a woman who knows who she is and where she is going. She is very alert; her smile of understanding is a quick one.

She had moved house days before we met, and we sat in a bright room lit by a window overlooking her garden. I wondered what the room would be like, once she had found time to arrange and decorate it. I could imagine exact and clever ways of overcoming lack of money. I sensed that whatever she planned would work: she would bring it off.

I only remember bad things from primary school. Within two weeks, at 5 years old, I'd been refused the sugar mouse everyone got for being able to tie their shoe laces, because I couldn't. There was this lovely jar of them. I remember being dragged right across the room by my pony tail and thrown out for talking.

My mother was keen for me to pass the 11 plus, because she knew that I had what it takes. She can hardly write or read, but she's very bright. She plays bridge, she's one of the top players in the county, but she couldn't write a cheque without making five or six mistakes. She can't spell. She never reads books, she doesn't even read the paper. No, her education didn't touch her at all.

I was put in the bottom stream of my grammar school—I passed the 11 plus. I came from a working-class family on a working-class estate. There seemed to be all the working-class kids in this lowest stream. It was very expensive to go to the school: the hats, the ties, the blazers, tennis rackets, hockey sticks. Money was very tight. My father was on the assembly line, and he was often on strike.

There was definitely a class structure to the streaming. Those with professional parents were in the top two streams, and the working-class kids were dumped.

I had problems fitting in. I felt a misfit. There were only two of us who passed from my primary school; I had no friends to go with. I think the 11 plus was a nonsense. Tests are a nonsense, full stop. I was coached to pass it.

I rebelled. I was awful. I was snarly to the teachers, I called them rude names, I made teachers cry—very easily. I used to upset their routines. We used to use the gym when it was out of bounds. One day we tipped tar all over the place. Me and three others. But I was always the instigator.

I remember my biology teacher telling me there was no way on earth I'd pass because I hadn't kept up with the work, and I'd disrupted her lessons all the time. I got an A in it. I was determined. It was my favourite subject.

Nobody ever pulled me out and said, come on, we'll help you get over this, or, why are you like this? I just remember being labelled a rebel, and I kept to my label, and worked for it, and confirmed it. Wherever I went I confirmed it. People expected it. Oh, she's in our class today, we'll have some fun.

How my mother didn't kill me I don't know. I threatened to leave home. I used to have tantrums at home if I couldn't go out. I'm repaying the debt I owe her. She had to struggle, taking me to school when I'd had an accident, in between working before I went to school and working when I came home. All the things she did for me! I broke my leg; I was off school for three months. The first time ever I skived off school, I went to my boyfriend's, and a friend of his gave me a lift home. We were knocked off the motorbike.

There was my mother waiting at the gate. This experience has something to do with my going back into education— because what I did to my mother then was terrible.

I just wish someone had sussed me out. It seemed that wherever I went I had the better of them. Perhaps I wouldn't allow them to. The one that could have done—the biology teacher—didn't want to know. I never thought I gave her a hard time, because I loved it. She should have seen me in the other lessons. Hers was the only class where I sat in the front, always put my hand up to answer questions; but I was never, ever asked to answer. Probably if they'd looked at my record, they'd have seen that biology was the area where they could have caught me. They could have given me responsibilities; asked me to clean the animals up, or tidy the lab. You can find something in any child—there's always one area that any child's interested in.

I left. I went straight into secretarial college, and then to a factory. I stayed there for eleven years, until my eldest son was born. I loved it. I had a lot of responsibility.

I got married when I was 21, to someone just like my father: someone who drank a lot, an introvert, very quiet, working at the factory with a dead-end job. My mother kept telling me it wouldn't work, she knew the relationship wasn't right. I think I knew it wasn't right, but when you go around with a group of friends, and every other person is married, you jump on the bandwagon, don't you.

Then I had my first child when I was 26.

I stayed at home for a year, and that decided it. I thought, 'I'm not cut out to stay at home and hoover and hoover and clean and clean and hoover.' I didn't want to leave my husband, but I needed something else, so the first thing I did was Chinese cookery. Then I did a computer class, after doing calligraphy. The third year, I thought, let's do some certificates. By this time I knew my marriage was dead.

Of course the idea of me bettering myself didn't go down well in the home. His technique was ignoring, rather than arguing. Once or twice he'd say, what are you going to do with all these certificates, what's the point? I said, I don't know yet, but I've earned the money to pay for the courses, so all it costs you is the two hours you stay at home when I go out.

I think it was fear of me being better than him.

I did maths O level. I got a B, so I thought, if I can do that I'll do two the following year. I did sociology, and a data-processing course.

Then I tackled English language at night school. I knew

someone who worked on reception at the poly: I picked up a
prospectus and saw you had to have English. I got an A, the
only one in the class. It was wonderful. I couldn't believe it.
That was the last one I did before the Access course.

By this time I was going in a completely different
direction. Paul became the outsider. I didn't need his
support, I could do it on my own. Arguments were flying,
and everything was my fault.

I decided that I had either to go to the poly, or go under.
By this time Paul was denying me money, out of spite. A
friend phoned me and said, go for Access. I decided I would,
and they accepted me. You can imagine the panic, I was told
on Friday afternoon I had the place to start on Monday.

It was organized around children, nine to half two, and
four days, so those on social security didn't beat the 21-hour
rule. You were given a grant and a child care allowance and a
book allowance of £100, and I spent it all on books, the only
books I'd ever had.

It seemed that I was with another lot of rebels just like at
school! I was just like I was before, this obnoxious person in
the classroom. I must have seemed a tyrant to teachers who
hadn't taught mature students and were only used to
conforming 18-year-olds. I'd say, right, you're looking at it
from a middle-class point of view, you've never been
working class, you can't actually see what it's like to be
working class. An 18-year-old wouldn't have said that.

The first piece of work was in sociology, and I was very
blasé. I thought—I've done that, it'll be easy. Needless to say
I nearly failed that piece of work, so I thought, this isn't as
easy as it looks, you've really got to buckle down. So I
worked really hard.

When I go into a classroom people think, oh, she's very
aggressive and extrovert and doesn't care; but I'm sure that's
a cover up for what's inside, and most people don't see that.

Most of the time I had outside problems constantly on my
mind. Solicitors writing me letters—and sometimes I went to
lessons almost for relief. Psychology was my subject,
because I'm interested in people. I got on with the teacher
like a house on fire. Perhaps because I have a logical
mathematical mind—most of the others didn't—it worked

well for me. You didn't have to have this airy fairy stuff and create something from nothing. As soon as I did the first report, most people didn't have a mark but I did, even though it was appalling.

It was interesting, and it was new, and anything new I like.

The support? People were helpful all the time. Most of the time I wouldn't let them help me. I'm still the same here. If I can't get the answer on my own, I'd rather not do it. I don't know why. I have to do it on my own.

At the end of the Access course I came down with pneumonia. It was pure stress. I was desperately ill for a week. They didn't discover what it was. I thought I was dying. I went down to six stone. This was exam time. I forced myself in to two of them, but they wouldn't let me. The two I did were fine. I was worried, because if you didn't get 60 per cent on the course, you couldn't go through.

By that time my husband wasn't speaking to me. If I came in he went out, and if he came in I went out. But one day I must have looked like I was dying, because he did offer to get me a hot-water bottle.

Shirley wishes a teacher at school had tried to rescue her. Like so many returners, she has an unerring appreciation of the importance of the 'acknowledging' tutor. She is witness also to the great variety of the motives adults can have for return. Hers is penitential; and her penance must be solitary. To accept too much help would dilute what she wants to offer her mother, to make up for the past. She wants to arrive on her mother's doorstep with a degree rather than a broken leg.

Shirley—like Peter and Eleanor—exemplifies a further theme in returners' experience: marital breakdown under the pressure of one partner's change—usually the woman's. The best bet for Shirley's husband would have been to follow suit and do some changing himself, like the two men in Chapter 11. In every university, polytechnic, and college of higher education, this story is familiar.

The man's attack on his partner is best understood, of course, sociologically rather than psychologically. Roger and Dave in Chapter 11 illustrate this point very vividly.

Alan, 36

Single, now a student of development studies at university, I met Alan in his mother's house, where he was staying for Christmas. Talking to him, as to William, felt familiar as only conversation with a contemporary or near-contemporary can. I could easily imagine him in the early 1970s, his curly fair hair grown out into an Afro.

Hesitation and diffidence sometimes surface through his intellectual zest, the pleasure he takes in interpreting his experience. Then, it is as if he is overwhelmed by the feeling that he will not be taken seriously, that he's bound to be rumbled. Most of the time it was hard to imagine that his higher education had been delayed for so long.

My brother had done very well at school, but I didn't. I didn't much want to take on the competition. I went to a private school. They didn't push me, I did all right in class, but when it came to exams I just didn't get them. I did O level and passed two, and then spent the next two years getting three more. I was just stuck at that level. I also pursued some A level courses. I did all right in class, but I couldn't write essays. I found a letter to my mother from school saying, he can't write an essay, and we don't understand why not. I think what I was doing was not being sequential, not arguing it through, tending to get interested in details and missing the main question.

It was important to write my own essay rather than the one required; I think that's what I was trying to do a lot. The essay is a tyrannical form. I was trying to take a quirky view, thinking—I know what you want, but I'm going to give you something which I think is much more brilliant. So I got Ds and Es, which makes you think—they simply don't understand. I wasn't going to accept that the essay was at fault. I took it as them being slightly fuddy-duddy.

It affected the way I saw myself, and the first set of failures helped to reinforce the lack of a sense of adequacy intellectually. I categorized myself: I don't pass exams. And I fulfilled that prophecy in the end.

I wanted to be distinct: my brother had been academic, so I became sporty; and disruptive in school, in a reasonably pleasant way. But I wasn't easy. Two teachers could cope with it, and they became important, and I went on to do their A level subjects. But the others didn't want me near them.

And of course that was at the time—in '68, '69, '70—when we were likely to think that education wasn't all about passing exams. I was reading John Holt and A. S. Neill, reinforcing my idea that slogging to get a lot of Os and As without questioning them was in some way to let myself down.

I don't know what I would like my two teachers to have done. I thought of them as a couple of friends; the tenor of the school was not to push; it was very liberal. Two people did tell me that if I worked I would get on, and I resented that extraordinarily, because it seemed to be saying, toe the line, play the game, and you'll be all right.

I'm not at all sure that I would have been open to benign bullying from people I did like, such as the two good teachers, who taught history and English. I think I was pretty hard to bully because I was very touchy.

The things they gave me did last. I was a voracious reader for twenty years after leaving school. A lot of what I was doing was stuff I'd picked up at that point. My interests mirrored some of what we did together and read. I read a lot of novels, and social history. And a fair amount of poetry.

When I was leaving I said to the history teacher—where d'you start now? And he said, read everything you lay your hands on. And I did, and still do. I always thought it worth reading a book even if it was a bit difficult.

His life after school has been busy and varied, and he talks about it not quite dispassionately. Were his twenties and early thirties a waste of time, or unusually interesting? He cannot yet decide.

First, assistant editing for the BBC; which he left in the end because he disliked the institutional life. Off to France. Factories in Paris came first. Then his interest in agriculture dawned when he went to work on farms: 'tobacco, walnuts, asparagus'. Just as he thinks he has found his future, his relationship ends, and he finds himself back home, self-employed as a painter and decorator.

It was the lowest point on the curve in my adult life. I didn't want to be in London painting. I knew there was better to be had, and rather regretted chances I'd blown. It's at that point you meet your ex-BBC friends, and they've got a house and a car and isn't their life easy, and I'm renting a flat and it's all a bit tacky.

I spent three months on the dole without really looking for a job thinking what to do next. Then a friend said, why don't you do a degree?—because she was doing the one I'm doing now. She thought it would interest me, and she gave me some bumf, and I read it, and I was very, very doubtful about the whole idea. But the three months had prepared me a bit.

But when I phoned my university, they said, come and see us. The person who interviewed me said, you absolutely ought to do this, it's an excellent idea, because of your experience and your background, your reading. But you've got to sort out what went wrong at school. I suggest an Access course. I said, what are they? and he explained. He was incredibly positive.

I think he sensed that it was my experience twenty years before that was making me doubt, and that by being positive he might at least kick that out of the door. And my travel, and experience of the media and agriculture were relevant. About 30 per cent of us on the course are mature students.

The first bit of work I did, I was terrified that I was going to get back with 'rubbish' written on it. We had to write something about childhood. I tried to write about coming back from holiday when everything seems familiar and yet strange. I found it extremely difficult. I think the biggest hurdle I had to jump was to write it and give it in. It went brilliantly: 18 out of 20! I couldn't believe it.

After only two weeks I felt I knew everyone, and became a talker again, and started shouting and saying what I thought. We were a small and cohesive group. And right the way through the Access course essays were never a problem. My written English was fine—and I know through my reading what is grammatically correct. I also had confidence, I suppose, and I worked a lot harder because I was fearful. And I think my ideas were in order, which they certainly weren't at school. Now when I write, I spend some time thinking and making notes and saying that goes there, this here.

In a school like mine you don't organize anything—so you can be totally at sixes and sevens, without any experience of having to be organized that might help you write essays.

But by the time of Access I'd learnt by reading other people, and thinking, this is good, this is bad. Some people had read a lot less and had more trouble.

They had lots of people who had trouble with structure. It was taken as something you could either do or not. The tutors have to learn how to help people with their writing, because some people didn't do as well as they should have done, and the tutors didn't know how to help them. If you've got someone who's apparently intelligent, but whose essays are not what's required, it doesn't mean to say they're not any good. It can all be in the head, but there can be terrible difficulty in getting it on paper.

I got on well with the English tutor; and the politics teacher was very sympathetic, a great diplomat, and a good supporter of people. He really wanted it to work. The psychology teacher was a good teacher used to getting results, and we weren't ready to be put through the machine like that quite yet, and that gave her a shock. She wasn't used to the fact that we would answer back. We'd say: no, that's rubbish, you can't say that.

There was the great argument with Liz about evolution. I can't recall what the tutor said, but it was, don't be silly, we're taking this as fact. This created two camps right from the beginning, because no one could tell Liz what she could or couldn't believe in that sort of way.

After that she continually found that she'd say, this is how it is; and people would say—why? She got better at dealing with it, but always found it difficult.

The sociology teacher made mistakes right at the beginning. For instance she gave William a very low mark on his first essay, and he'd worked incredibly hard. I think he'd got the wrong end of the stick as to what was required. She should have said, all your thoughts and ideas are valid; they're just not what's needed for this essay. Instead of which she wouldn't even answer his questions. She talked to him for a couple of minutes, and said, that's not what we want. It destroyed him for a long time, and always made me a bit wary of her. She gave me a low mark too for the first one, and again, she didn't really tell me why.

She won quite a lot of people over, because she became more accessible.

In English, people said—not surprisingly if they'd read books to pass the time—well, what is this? A book's a book. How can we spend four weeks asking questions about it? I'd done that at school, though I'd fought against it there; but I could accept it.

The English literature had the most discussion; but there was a lot for sociology. The psychology was far more cut and dried like an A level course. But it would have been much more sensible to start each topic with a question-mark and get the discussion going.

Yes, the course was very intensive. My first term at university has been very much more relaxed, though people who have gone to poly have found that it's fairly intense too.

I got good marks, but I never quite believed it—until the summer term I kept thinking it was all going to turn to dust. That it wasn't quite real, they weren't really testing it. I'd spent so many years thinking I wasn't any good—and I couldn't believe my luck. I went to university thinking—they gave me good marks; what will these people do? Still feeling I might be rumbled.

As a group we did cohere—through battle, in a way. A lot of the people on the course were fighters. That's how they'd got to where they were in life. We got over being polite, because of the subjects we were dealing with—talking about politics, gender relations. Two in particular were very verbal, very aggressive, and helped to do that. We got over inhibitions, we became much more like a family.

The support came out of individual friendships—I became very friendly with Sue, and we helped each other; and Lesley asked me on one occasion if I could come up and help her with some work. Sue and I would often have a drink at lunchtime, and we would help each other.

Alan's account is rich in implications about the way adults learn. The psychology teacher, for instance, did not respect Liz's experience, or acknowledge the validity of her thoughts. In a sense, adulthood itself was denied by this teacher's didactic certainty.

Returners—Peter comes to mind—usually lack intellectual technique at first. Essays, reading, and note-taking can all be taught, as Alan suggests. It is absurd to expect such skills just to appear, like growth on a plant.

Alan suggests that William's sociology teacher did not take the frailty of his confidence into account when she gave him back his first essay. Hers was a very different approach from the one taken by Peter's first tutor. She criticized Peter rigorously; but he sensed her faith in him, her respect—and her encouragement; so her criticism was never destructive.

The point Alan makes about the importance of confidence is echoed in the next account.

Anne-Marie, 38

She is Norwegian. She has one child, a son, whom she brings up on her own. We sat in a room full of plants, with a bird in a cage, and loaded bookshelves, and surprising objects in corners. Again, I thought of the 1960s, feeling completely welcomed, not just by her warmth and hospitality. Her fair hair is long now, and I guess it has been so since then. Her English is so good that you forget she is Norwegian. She has a terse, almost clipped way of describing events and feelings, and laughs often and abruptly when she sees absurdity. Things are going well for her; but the way she laughs sometimes suggests she does not quite believe it.

My father had great hopes for me and I didn't comply with them. I wasn't interested in the school he wanted me to go to—his school. And I failed the exam. He said I was stupid, and so on, and that didn't help. From when I was 12, things were pretty awful. My sister was the opposite, she had to be top, and I just didn't care. We used to fight a lot. She would do anything to please; and I would always ask, why? She did very well at school. Teachers didn't really like all my questions.

I went to a comprehensive. We had masses of tests, and my father used to help me with my work. He is not exactly patient, so that made me hate school the more. There was a fire at the school, and I remember being really pleased about it.

In my early teens I became one of a group of friends, and I spent most of my time in their houses, or out with them. Boys, motorbikes. I never asked them home, because my father would interrogate them. But I did do well in subjects I really liked, like physics. If I got on well with a teacher, I would get on better. The history teacher for instance. He liked people, was interested in them.

Relations with my father got worse and worse. My brother had heart trouble; he was very ill, and so my mother was totally involved with him. And I think I must have been awful.

I left school at just 18. By then things were unbearable, and my mother arranged for me to come to England.

Life then flung her about. Her child was born in 1977. Then she was deserted by his father. All manner of different jobs followed. Then, at a very low point, she attended a WEA Return-to-Learn course. She was very anxious at first, but the course was a success, and she decided to go on to Access:

Before Access started, various things happened. My son's father died, and that was very traumatic. Even though we weren't living together, we still had an intense relationship; and after he died, I felt different, I wasn't looking over my shoulder all the time. It stopped me hiding. The year before he died he'd written to ask to see the child, and I thought that would be terrible, because he was the sort of person who would see him when it suited him, and then walk out again. You cannot do that to a child.

After all that, I really felt I had to do something, and Access was what I chose to do. I got a place. I was amazed. It helped that Liz was also going. She had been on the WEA course with me, and we got on well together. On the first day of the course I was as sick as a dog—partly to do with nerves. So I missed the first day.

It was good. The group worked well because people liked each other, though there was a lot of aggression as well. But the personality clashes were useful, they led to debates.

We used to help each other a lot, ringing each other up. Most of the help I needed was with the literature. I didn't get on with the teacher after he asked us to recommend books and I suggested Doris Lessing and Margaret Drabble, and he said, ah, middle class, and rejected them.

To some extent we would share each other's work, reading each other's essays. That was very useful. Liz helped me—she came round here—after I walked out of a psychology session. I was really near to hitting the teacher, I walked out, when she told me that a piece of work I'd slaved over merited nothing. She was so tactless. After that I couldn't be bothered with the subject, so I did ecology with Roger instead. That was great.

Sociology was what I enjoyed most. I enjoyed putting the essays together, and I enjoyed doing the projects. It was the one thing that I did well in. I liked the teacher, I really liked her. Though I didn't like politics that much, I really liked the tutor, I thought he was very nice. Teachers are there to teach you, and as an adult you tend to be not very confident anyway, and you need if not boosting then definitely not undermining. Negative comments can really put you down. And labelling people like one tutor did at the start by saying that foreigners tended not to do well because of the language problem—was not helpful. Right at the start, when you are wondering whether to do the right thing, and you might just give it up!

The sociology teacher was very encouraging and likeable.

Anne-Marie vividly suggests the transitional phase in returners' development—before confidence extends to their learning; before 'self-direction'. She was as needy on her Access course as she had been as an adolescent when—she says—she did well in history because the teacher 'liked people and was interested in them'.

But her frail confidence was assaulted by her psychology

teacher; and by her English teacher's haughty reception of the books she recommended. His response was dishonest. He offered the reciprocity adult learners need. 'Make some recommendations yourself', he said, 'I don't want to TELL you what to read—we'll decide together.' Believing him, she made her suggestions—only to have them disdainfully rejected as beneath consideration. This was a demeaning put-down, and blasphemy against the sacred rule for teachers of adults, particularly in the first phase of their return: to remember that the person you are teaching has good reason to lack confidence—*which is what she most needs*. For her to gain it, you must respect what she says, what she feels, what she hopes, what she fears. Do not reject the words she says, the suggestions she makes, or what her experience has led her to think. Accept what she offers; and only after acceptance say how your thoughts differ, and offer information or suggest where it might be found; information she may then use to support, develop, or change her own thoughts.

And in spite of a returner's increasing self-reliance, she will go on benefiting from her teachers' respect. Self-direction is not an irreversible state, like puberty. Stephanie's experience, quoted at the beginning of Chapter 11, suggests that autonomy can be very quickly dismantled under the pressure of a teacher's unremitting disdain. If Eleanor had been taught only by the Monk—who so bitterly scorned her unconventional essay—she might have abandoned her studies, with her confidence in pieces, and her growing self-esteem cut down. Many students who arrive at university or polytechnic after an Access course meet demeaning, deeply stupid attitudes and approaches. Alan, for instance, near the end of his first university year, asked for the first time for an extension of an essay. His tutor agreed; but he had also to ask his director of studies, as each essay would contribute to his degree, and deadlines are strict. But this particular essay interested him greatly. He read very widely before sitting down to write. It is often more difficult to organize thoughts about something that you find fascinating. He soon found himself blocked; overwhelmed by too many thoughts, too many possible ramifications. Try as he might, he could not come up with an essay that satisfied his high standards.

His director of studies reacted to his request with impeccable stupidity. 'Why should I give you an extension if you can't be bothered to meet a deadline?' was the gist of what he said. He added with scorn that when he was at Oxford he had written all his essays in three hours flat.

He assumed that Alan was either lazy or stupid or disorganized. He treated him as if he was an errant 18-year-old going to too many parties. He did not consider him as an individual at all. Alan's growing intellectual self-reliance, his growing belief in himself, were profoundly challenged. The academic's memory of effortless Oxford essays made Alan angry, which helped him to argue his case. He explained what he felt, and was granted his extension. But what the encounter taught him was how lethally destructive it is to be treated not as an adult but as a naughty adolescent, making you feel as you felt when your education was failing.

10

Some Further Implications

An adult learner's early lack of confidence is usually the result of inadequate schooling. Memories of poor schooling haunt these nine accounts. But biographical accident can also wreck chances. The advantages Alan enjoyed were powerless against the fact that his brother had been an academic success before him. Anne-Marie's sister haunted her too.

At a distance from his adolescence, Alan could see that he needed to work in a very different way. Planning took the place of relentless idiosyncrasy. His adolescent need to be his own man was so strident that he could not answer *their* questions; he had to answer his own.

Organization is an adult habit, on the whole, which many adolescents acquire in time for academic success. But for an adolescent plagued by the need to differ, as were Anne-Marie and Alan, disorganization can be pathologically important. It seemed that all Alan was offered was his brother. Answer the question, and be your brother. Pass A levels, be your brother. The only way he could refuse was to disorganize each invitation not to be himself; to break each one down into its laughable components. He had to scatter and dodge. 'Do your O levels, learn how to write properly, listen to what we say, then do A levels, pay attention, do plenty of homework . . .' Such proposals were offered as parts of one coherent programme: how to grow up properly and be a serious person. But the programme meant one thing only to Alan: because his brother had carried it out with such success, if he did so himself he risked becoming *a poor version of someone else*. To someone intelligent and talented, that was an oppressive prospect. An adolescent who needs to differ is a little like a dissident under the old regime. His or her intelligence mans a radar of irony to disclose false connections so that all sorts of plausible parts of the Great Programme are scattered. The teachers Alan liked must have realized that the only way to educate him was to acknowledge his need to differ. They let him talk; they let him scatter. If he dodged their questions and answered his own— well, too bad. His scattering was intelligent; it must be doing him good; he was reading plenty.

Rather than help to push him into rejection of everything to do with books and learning—everything that had the faintest taint of the Programme—they made sure that reading became an essential pleasure. They played the same part in his life as Peter's Aunt Liz, and Dumas.

But Alan needed all his teachers, not just two, to unlock his brother-fix. Schools are full of children cornered psychologically. We should ask of their teachers the parental concern and subtlety they need in order to escape. Alan's account bears witness to the great variety of dispositions pupils bring to learning in school. His teachers should have been able to offer an approach that took his disposition into account. Two treated him with parental sensitivity; but others undermined their work, strengthened his self-defeat. They said, 'Work, boy, and you'll get on!' He heard a command to be his brother. He resisted the generalizing tendency in what schools offer.

Shirley hankers in retrospect for parental rescue at school. Her plea is for one teacher to have understood her—to have 'sussed her out'. She knows that her disposition could have been cleverly subverted. She wishes that a teacher had refused to be persuaded by her antics that she was stupid and unteachable. She regrets that no teacher saw through her behaviour to notice her lack of confidence, her working-class unease in a 'nice' school. Accurate response to her disposition would have called her bluff. United, her teachers should have worked on the assumption that she was an extremely clever girl. They should have trapped her in what psychiatrists would call paradox: the more she 'snarled' the more they should have praised every sign, however small, of her gifts. Her behaviour was experimental: she gave her teachers a hard time in order to discover in their reactions what sort of person she could or should be. But she was threatening to teachers unused to her

sort of antics. They reacted with defensive—perhaps vindic-
tive—hostility. Shirley concluded that she must be a bad girl,
and acted accordingly.

Her case takes further the argument I developed at the end of
the last section about schools. Teachers do not have time,
occasion, or necessary conditions to act as strong parents with
all their pupils. To react accurately and with strength to an
adolescent's experiments teachers need to reflect, and to co-
operate. Strength comes from a sense of unity with colleagues.
Such unity is possible only if teachers have time to talk to each
other regularly and at length about individual pupils, in order
to devise a unanimous approach. To have blocked Shirley's
attempts to prove herself stupid, teachers would have needed to
act with great strength. A full class, just as much as lack of time
for reflection with colleagues, makes it difficult for a teacher to
act with any forethought at all. Large numbers enforce short-
sightedness. To pin a disruptive pupil in a planned paradox—
which that pupil then meets in class after class, until the desired
message is understood—a teacher needs to feel very powerful.
Such power is very difficult if twenty-four other pupils are
asking attention to their particular needs. But subtlety,
restraint, paradox need authority. The baited snapping Shirley
won from her teachers was weak, more than anything else. Her
biology teacher was saying, in effect, 'You have been horrible
to me, so I will be horrible to you.' The conditions in which
teachers have to work make such weakness very hard to avoid.

In order to outfox a pupil like Shirley, power and unanimity
were indispensable. Without them, united only in weakness,
her teachers successfully devised her failure. She was cheated by
the utter inadequacy of the conditions in which her teachers
were expected to act *in loco parentis* to cultivate her gifts.

Horticultural metaphors are inescapable. The randomness of
schooling—unchanged since Shirley's day—is as if one were to
buy a garbled miscellany of flowers and shrubs, and plant them
taking no account of their different requirements. Some thrive;
some wilt. Alerted by drooping leaves, one harassed gardener-
teacher will try a little pruning; drop on some fertilizer without
time to discuss with others whether it is the right one to use.
Even if the leaves perk up, a depleted colleague will spray a stiff
solution of the wrong approach altogether, and the leaves will

droop again. There is no time for subtlety; less time for unanimity. Teachers are constantly on the run; small wonder, then, they deal in guesses, long-shots, quick assumptions, prejudices, lazy generalities. Most of his teachers told Alan he was a lazy so-and-so. Shirley, no doubt, was just a 'disruptive little bitch', or a 'foul-mouthed troublemaker'.

We have to see most of the Access students as trapped by schools' weakness, by their teachers' ruinous failure to discover their individuality, and give them the accurate attention without which they could not flourish. What they achieved in one short, intense year of adulthood should be repeated: a level of attainment that qualified them to enter university or polytechnic. It was very hard work, as Alan has just testified: harder work than his first taste of university. Huge strides were taken. William began as someone who had never written an essay, and ended disputatious, articulate, endlessly interested, and a competent writer. They all had to take such strides. How many thousands of children leaving school with a modest GCSE or two are equally capable of such supersession: of everything they take themselves to be, everything their teachers accept them to be?

Themes laid down in Part I surface again in these accounts.

Margaret and William both talk eloquently about ignorance. Margaret's inability to base her political beliefs on knowledge embarrassed her. William talks of ignorance as enforced 'censorship'. He sees the uneducated as excluded in ignorance and by ignorance from the 'Aladdin's cave' of knowledge that he has begun to explore. This image echoes Peter's account very closely indeed: his description of the first stage of his Open University course was, 'It's like Aladdin's cave; complete enlightenment'.

Mentors appear again. It seems clear that for Harriet, Sister Mary was critically important. She talks of her gratitude to her mentor with the same fervour as Sandra talks of Joan, now far away in Trinidad, who told her that she had a gift for teaching. The mentor is authoritative, a 'parent' whose attention is accurate and optimistic. The mentor rescues his protégé from generality. The mentor says, 'I know you and want the best for you.' Her authority is to proclaim, 'My grounds for believing in you are better than your grounds for self-contempt.' The mentor dissolves misjudgements, makes expectations soar; belatedly, she gives what Harriet's and Sandra's teachers should have been able to provide at their schools.[1]

Lesley's, Sandra's, Shirley's expectations have become as uncompromising as those of Sally and Andrew became. In order to fulfil them, they will work as hard as necessary. Difficulty does not defeat, but invigorates them. It is almost as if they force adversity to serve their needs: the scarcity of Lesley's time for study makes her more organized, clearer, more determined.

Overcoming difficulty and constraint has given them courage and conviction echoed in the accounts in Part I.

The difficulties Alan and Anne-Marie had to tackle were to do with their families. Margaret had to overcome history—which moved on just too late, to release her younger sister to go to university in Dublin at the usual time.

William—to use Andrew's phrase—was 'factory-farmed' by his schooling. Shirley and Sue were working-class misfits in schools for nice girls. Harriet, Lesley, and Sandra tell a distinct story: of having to surmount the iniquitous generalities of racism.

After their experience, they are very alert to the dangers in schools. What they say returns us to the importance and the powerlessness of teachers. They know that if you let things take their course, your child may not get her fair chance. Lesley says that if she did not get directly involved with their schooling, her children 'would not have the same opportunity' as others: 'my God, they wouldn't'. She understands—completely—that teachers do not have time to think; so she helps them to do so. 'Look well at my child', she says; 'don't you dare hurry past him and assume that when he's in difficulties it's because he's just a good little athlete. Don't you dare trap him in one of your lazy, provisional guesses, your demeaning generalities: he's not "that sort of child"; he's unique.' I have met many returners who show the same

---

[1] In a planned mentor scheme based at Islington Sixth Form Centre, reported in the *Education Guardian* of 24 July 1990, a 17-year-old protégé says of her mentor: 'I was really shocked by what was expected of me, but with some help I found I could do it.'

determination that their experience should not be repeated in their children's education.

Lesley is witness to the continuing powerlessness of schools. A friend of mine has just been told that her child is not 'ready' to read. Sharp and Green have disclosed the meaning of such a statement.[2] All the child's teacher means is that she cannot attend to all thirty-one of her charges with equal thoroughness, so it is convenient to account some unready. She is admitting to her irresistible need to trap pupils in generalities.

Teachers—with the weak, provisional inaccuracy their constraints enforce—accepted Lesley's and Sandra's underachievement. Ah well, what can you expect? Even their racism was implicit, hurried, unthinking—and more difficult to weed out as a result.

Teachers chucked Sue out of her grammar school. Her mother was told she would be more 'comfortable' in a secondary modern. Judging conclusively, they organized no concerted campaign to keep her; to make sure that a girl who they said was a born leader should have a fine education to fulfil that gift. No, no. A common girl: let her be with her own people.

Sue also understands how easily a child slides into the snare of misjudgement, and is terrified that her daughter will repeat her history.

Finally, Eleanor, Sally, and Vanessa have born witness to the ways in which women's education can be determined by prejudice. Sue's mother echoes Sally's, telling her not to aim too high, telling her just to be happy. Shirley's husband feared his wife's 'betterment', which he stubbornly resisted; sulking in his discomfort and his sense of defeat. Her education terrified him.

In Sandra's account a much more accommodating man resisted her change at first, trying his hardest to make her fulfil the old requirements while the books piled up on her desk. But now—at least—he is proud of her.

This clever woman found the 'old requirements' very claustrophobic. She felt her brain going numb at home, and took random bus rides to escape her frustration.

[2] R. Sharp and A. Green, *Education and Social Control* (RKP, 1975).

Education does break marriages. In Part III, I look in closer focus, at first, at two marriages under threat from books and curiosity and ideas. Liz was on the same Access course. She too came to fear ignorance almost more than anything else.

PART III

Themes and Conclusion

11

Regenerations

Each returner can benignly infect other lives. But resistance to the idea of education, and to change of any sort, often makes husbands fight infection vigorously, as Shirley's story suggests. The wisest course is complete defencelessness.

In the fight, some of the significance of return can be more vividly seen than in any other way. Margaret has already mentioned women who put the books away before their husbands get back from work; Shirley's return led to divorce; Sandra was fought but won. Roger and Liz take this story further.

Roger and Liz

This is Liz, mother of six, talking of a revelation before her return began:

> I remember looking up and it's like snakes, and they're enclosing somebody, who can't get out—and it's ugly, I'd never seen anything so ugly. I remember walking out and thinking it was the worst thing that I'd ever seen. It was called IGNORANCE—that was the name of this picture on the ceiling. I thought it was what was happening to me. I was shutting doors instead of opening them: it frightened me. I suppose I just saw it as the ugliest thing in man—and you couldn't get out of it . . .

And from my notebook:

> We've been talking about the poll tax. As always, talk has accelerated and intensified, until the room is full of it, and children come in, pause, listen—enjoying it—and either join

in or depart again. Roger has a terrific command of logical invective: an oratorical way of surrounding some piece of idiocy with an army of good arguments, and then sending out squads of them, angry and logical, to attack. The poll tax, and an entire political philosophy, stood no chance. The vitality of his mind; and yet he was bypassed by his schooling; ludicrously denigrated, belittled, unfulfilled.

Liz advances her own arguments. A pincer movement on Thatcherism. When Roger asks to borrow her car she says no, she's selfish, she's learnt the lessons of the eighties, self-interest dictates that he have nothing to do with her car.

It's clear that the fervour of the early stage of her 'return' has waned, now she is busy with accreditation, now she feels the machine has got her. But then she talks about anthropology and how it fascinates her, and you know that her mind is still doing its stuff: this good mind eager to understand. Returners are keen to understand.

We talk, Sally the middle girl comes in, in a pouting sulk. Liz lets her stew for five minutes, and then charms her out of her sulk in about thirty seconds. Rachel sits beside me while the tape turns making small rissole-shapes out of a dead bit of pastry she found in the fridge. She sings, chatters, natters to the mike, sugars the rissoles—and is altogether friendly, as she was in the garden.

This long note followed my last visit. I first met them over a year ago. My note then says:

I can't quite explain what it is about their home that so appeals to me. Their liveliness is from adversity. The sense of a continuing fight is strong, and the terrific energy this fight calls out from them.

And all the time children came and went. Rachel sat on the floor and played with the mike. The interview was not to be something kept away from their children—partly because of the geography of the house: kitchen and sitting room in their smallish house are one open room. But this sense of free coming and going was an expression of much more than lay-out.

I want my depiction of their intellectual life, and the stories of their education, to include their house, their children. This book should suggest settings for intellectual life at odds with those that may come most easily to mind.

In Chapter 4, Vanessa's elder daughter speaks of an evening when she and some friends sat talking in the kitchen after the pub. The scene is familiar. The director of a television play might easily choose such a setting for students talking in a vacation; and the designer would dutifully provide shelves of jars, knives pinned to the wall in arrangements that please the eye, a platoon of wine bottles, an expensive coffee-maker, enough chairs around the table for three or four more students to join them, a door opening on a wide passageway where pictures glimmer.

The mother joining in is less familiar, but becoming more so. A mother in the setting described above might still be pouring coffee, or even making a wry face to camera to suggest incomprehension, tolerant amusement, or a studied good-mum sigh because she just wants to *get on*, but thinks it is rather nice to see students doing what you expect them to do. But we are just about prepared for 50-year-old Vanessa to ignore the coffee pot and argue instead. She should do so standing, in order to look provisional, a little guilty, ready to depart for her proper work. We are not quite ready for her to sit with her daughters and their friends for an unplanned hour.

But we are much less ready for the kitchen in a small crowded council house (the whole downstairs is about the same size as Vanessa's sitting room) to contain anthropology, or a critique from a washing-machine engineer, striding and eloquent, of the way computer science is taught at a polytechnic.

I suspect we are even less ready for him than for his anthropology-enchanted wife and mother of six. Shouldn't he be brooding in his van, his mind inflamed with thoughts of tearing up books?

After the second meeting with Liz and Roger:

> They're not completely harmonious when they talk by any means. Because they're at roughly the same stage of intellectual exhilaration there isn't enough space for them

both to talk. There's always a sense, when they both deliver, that there won't be enough time for it all to come out. One of them will have to wait. Their fluency is hectic.

I can remember from early on my sense that their intellectual energy flows from their need to understand their experience. Understanding can only begin for returners after they have abandoned a diffident fatalism about themselves. Sally's account is the best example. Rape taught her that she need no longer accept, fatalistically, comfortably, that she was a good little dancer-secretary. The deals that express such disappointment are not just psychological, but sociological. To repeal them is not an act of individual supersession alone; it is also a defiance of the rules that they enforce. Such defiance is hard to bring off on your own. Peter, of all the returners so far, seems to me to have had the hardest job. He was the loneliest, the one who found it hardest to feel one of many. But for a woman who wants to end her disappointment, defy the voices of her upbringing, allies are there to be found. She will go out and find support (another key word, almost a cant-word in our dealings with each other). She will try to fulfil in her own life the promise of familiar images of solidarity: circles of women holding hands; women hugging; women proudly smiling at each other; women talking in a group, their faces full of revelation.

The bid to end disappointment feels sinful at first; is never easy; nor am I saying that because help is to hand for them, it is easy for women; Eleanor's account alone suggests the opposite.

But for a woman who wants to end her disappointment, any change—circumstantial, intellectual, emotional—fits and belongs to a wider alteration. The 'personal is the political'. The changes brought about by Liz have been immense; but I believe that Roger's revolution may have been both more difficult and lonelier. Whence has come the help for a man—a working father of six—subverting most of the assumptions by which his life was governed until his wife attended an eight-week course run by the WEA?

Their first education tells the familiar story of barbaric inadequacy:

Roger's Schooling

We had a seminar at the evening Access course I was doing, and a lot of us had horrific experiences at school which made us think: I'm not one of the clever people, therefore my place in society is to do something menial like push a broom. An awful lot of us had had experiences like that.

I went to a secondary modern school, Batsford Mount. When I first went there you were only ever considered for CSEs. The maths teacher was an absolute swine. Because of that I have a real blockage about maths. He was terrible. He used to pick on the weakest boys in the class. He also just happened to be a PE instructor—a double swine. He was almost fascist in his outlook, the way he regimented the class. And he had boys who were pets. And they were boys who were excellent at PE which I obviously wasn't. And then you had to meet this guy in the maths class. So all this is compounded until you feel you're no good at maths, you're no good at PE, generally you're a pretty worthless person. And that's the worst effect of that type of teaching, that you feel worthless as an individual. That affects your attitude towards what they're trying to teach you.

You felt in maths that if he was doing something on the board and you didn't understand it, you daren't ask, because he would encourage the other lads to have a good giggle; and secondly you felt you were the thicko in the room anyway; and thirdly if you asked you didn't get a sensible answer. He would throw out a general question and he would pick on you, you see; and you daren't say anything. You might actually know! But you daren't say it, because you weren't confident because by that time your confidence had been so bashed that you daren't ask, you see, for fear of getting it wrong anyway. If he asked you, you'd say something stupid in sheer panic. Then—hopeless boy, useless lad!

And then he'd ask someone else who'd be the pet boy, you know, who scores a hundred at cricket every time he goes out or something.

I was always the fat boy in the school, so I was always the one who had the mickey taken out of me. If you were in the

showers you were always the one the boys poked fun at, and
you weren't that good at games. But you see the whole point
was that it wasn't that you weren't that good; it was that you
felt conditioned to believe that you weren't that good.

Roger's use of the second person in this account is telling: he
looks with grief at his schoolboy self and talks of him as
another person, as 'you'. But the pronoun is also plural.
Roger's account suggests an army of the drearily undereducated; suborned troopers at the mercy of their trainers' sarcasm.

I went for a job interview at the Electricity Board. I'd done
quite well in the entry test, physics and that sort of thing.
Anyway they'd written and said to two of the teachers did
they think that I was good material for an engineering
apprenticeship rather than a craft apprenticeship. I always
remember these two teachers stood there with me and they
laughed, they thought it was a real joke. They laughed!

It's worse than being in the army—and it was absolutely
dreadful. That kind of system only helps to classify people
and put them into groups, whether it's class or the type of
jobs you do. It drove it home that there was no way you
could break out—it was a big joke to try.

And for somebody like me who comes from that working
background: the first day at poly I thought, what the hell am
I doing here? I felt embarrassed, I felt clumsy, I felt stupid, I
felt I was sticking out like a sore thumb.

And if you say to anybody in my family, oh I'm going to
college, they say, what do you want to do that for? And
that's bad, because then you can come to despise education, a
lot of people round here despise it, not because they
wouldn't have loved to have done it, but because they have
to justify themselves in some way.

It was like a long-drawn out murder trial where you were
the accused, and at the end of it you were judged whether to
be let off or not. It had that judicial feel, it set people into
groups, and you were adjudicated at the end as to which
group you were in. And having been put into that group,
people for their own self-respect had to glorify that group.

Education was something that took place between 5 and 15, and that was it. After 15, you'd finished. It was never ever impressed upon us that education continues.

I wonder what it would have been like if someone had ever sat down with me when I was 12 or 13, and said, come on, okay, you're quite artistic, you're good at this, you're good at that—so let's see whether we can draw these capabilities out of you, acknowledging that you're weak in some areas, but good in others. But you never had that opportunity: you weren't looked at as an individual, in the sense that someone sat down and told you what abilities you had.

Roger recapitulates earlier themes. His education took no account of him as an individual. He was categorized by failure in the 11 plus; categorized in school as not very able; and when a vocational test suggested he had been wrongly categorized, his trainers took his success as a laughable aberration.

He most poignantly shows us the regret of the generalized: that no one 'sat down' to discover what gifts he possessed; to decide how to cultivate them.

Liz was a misfit in her secondary school:

Liz's Schooling

I went to a secondary modern. It never even entered anyone's head that they could stay on. Most of the girls used to work in Woolworth's, or somewhere like that.

We used to have corporal punishment, but I wasn't afraid of that. I was afraid of the embarrassment of being made to stand up.

I remember teachers who disliked me and you knew there was nothing you could do. I remember somebody shouting at me, oh you look so innocent, and accusing me of doing something which I definitely hadn't done. It was the way I looked. She would always pick on me. I never knew why she disliked me. I would often get sent up for the cane. If you tried to explain you knew you'd already been found guilty. To me the only way to cope was to play truant an awful lot. I just wouldn't go.

I had to become worse than the others in a way. I suppose by the age of 14 I was worse: I never wanted to look good or stand out—because you'd be a swot then, wouldn't you. I had a posh accent, I arrived in the school late from a boarding school. I didn't want to stand out. I was taller than the others as well.

I'd always sit at the back. Now I always question everything—if there's any injustice, I'd be the one to stand up and say. But not when I was at school.

I did make trouble for the maths teacher, that was when I was 16, near the end, I lit up cigars in the class.

Roger: Nothing's changed has it?

Liz: But it had taken quite a while to get to that. Before that, when I first went, I was quiet and I'd always sit at the back. But I knew I was different, I felt different, probably because of my accent; because I wasn't from the town, and my parents didn't live together, my mother was single, and there weren't a lot of single-parent families then.

But the schools are so big—how are they going to notice one child? My stepfather died when I was about 13. But you couldn't talk about it; and the thing is you're afraid of being emotional as well. My daughter Rosa has social studies and they have talks about life. They're actually allowed to air their own views. It's encouraged, much more in small groups. We never had anything like that. I don't remember anybody getting us together in small groups and that being an important part of education.

I mean to me education isn't just your head, it's your whole being, isn't it, it's learning to cope with your whole self. Then it was just kind of off pat; everything was learnt off pat as well.

I always say with my children—you have to be aware of their emotional state as well. If they're upset they can't learn. Rosa just loves school, and I think that's a lot to do with the fact that we got very interested in it a couple of years ago and started getting more involved with her, and visiting the school more, becoming more interested in what she was doing; and I suppose because I stopped being afraid of going. For years I would avoid entering schools. I still have a fear of teachers.[1]

I very rarely attended classes in the end, I just—

Roger: You were asked to leave, dear.

Liz: I think they were very relieved when I did. But they wouldn't have noticed if you were there or weren't. I played truant for six weeks once, and it was only on the last week they actually noticed.

If somebody says to you, you can do it, you CAN do it; I always say to the kids now, if you want it, you can do it, you actually have free choice. I never believed you had free choice before, but that it was kind of mapped out. I actually know that it's up to you, now. But I'm 37 years old!

Liz's schooling was as limiting as her husband's. She too recapitulates earlier points. She dealt with the difficulties of school by truanting. Her teachers' lack of concern for her absence she explains in the same way as Andrew: 'How are they going to notice one child?' But she was not known by her teachers. She too regrets that none of them bothered about her as an individual, and that she did not express what she thought.

She was on the same Access course as Harriet and Lesley. Like them, she has learnt the advantage for children of making your parental presence felt. She feels that if she and Roger had learnt that lesson earlier, the education of her two older children would have been the better for it.

Now 37 and 43, Liz and Roger married when she was 17 and he was 23. They have six children. Roger worked as an engineer looking after washing machines and fridges. Liz stayed at home looking after her children, and doing part-time jobs: barmaid, waitress, chambermaid. It was Liz who made

[1] Rosa also has her mother as a wonderful role-model. She has just done extremely well in her GCSEs. She likes what her parents are doing. She is forthright, in her mother's style: 'I'd be quite angry if my mum gave up college now. I would never just leave because I hated school. Although I'm proud of what my mum is doing, I don't want to do it at that age. I want to stay on and perhaps go to poly or university. Even if I didn't know what I wanted to do afterwards, I'd have an education, so I could make a choice. But I always used to think I'd leave school at 16.'

the first move. She was 35. Like Shirley Valentine in Willy
Russell's play, she went to Greece.

> I just decided to go, one Friday—I set off on the Monday. It
> was absolutely wonderful, it was like the beginning of
> everything. I knew that when I came back things were going
> to be different. I think it was the space. I can remember
> sitting on the beach and thinking, there's nobody—it's so
> big—it's like having your eyes opened.
> It's as if the world is bigger than you make it, more than I
> was experiencing. I went on my own, without the family,
> and I was really frightened, but it was amazing.

Roger says of their marriage that at the beginning:

> I saw it as my bounden duty to take care of her and look
> after her. I think I decided when Liz wanted to do something
> different that I had to sort of—let her go off and do it. That
> meant letting go of everything I traditionally held to. But at
> the same time I felt quite excited about what she was doing.

Liz agrees:

> I was only 17 when we got married, and because of my
> background I was quite unstable, and Roger was stable, and
> in a way he was like a father-figure to me, and it was more
> difficult for him to let go because we hadn't married as
> equals. I grew up in our marriage, but it was very difficult
> for Roger to see that I had grown up or that I was changing.

After Greece there was to be no going back:

> After Greece it was as if I saw things in colour not just in
> black and white. When I got married, I used to read, I loved
> books, I used to escape into books, but gradually my
> concentration seemed to have gone, and I'd stopped reading.
> But what was worse was that I'd stopped *looking*—d'you
> know—that's what had happened to me. I had reached a
> point where if something didn't change I'd be stagnant, I'd
> have retracted to a world which was just the kids, and I
> knew that there'd got to be something more.
> I was very frustrated. Being at home and having kids,
> everything has to work round them, you're nobody, in the

end you've lost your identity. I used to wake up depressed at the thought that this was another day. Somewhere along the line, you think—who am I? What am I doing?

Like her husband, she talks of herself, in powerful images of blindness and stagnation, as one of many; of many mothers, many women, their lives chopped small at home.

Before she went, she had plucked up courage to contact the WEA about a Return-to-Learn course. It took a year, she says, before she dared to phone. The course started when she came back from Greece.

I had become frightened of change: that's why it took me so long to phone. I didn't have the confidence to be interviewed. You're safe at home, aren't you?

But the WEA course was great, because there were people from different walks of life, and none of them had any confidence. Most of them were women in their thirties, and they were coming out! The important thing was the encouragement we all gave each other, and nobody put you on the spot. It was all positive: I couldn't believe it, it was really good. Even in maths they made sure you knew you WERE capable. That was the big thing about it: that you've got a lot to say, that you're good at this and good at that. All through school nobody had said that you're good—at anything. I couldn't believe maths could be so interesting. There were about ten of us; it was absolutely brilliant. I hated maths at school—and I thought, if I can do that I can do anything. The course lasted eight weeks, and I thought, I must do something else now. I did an assertion course next, and then I went on a six months' free Second Chance to Learn course. They had child care, and Rachel was quite little—so I didn't have to worry about her. It was a full day each week. We covered politics, literature, history.

We had debates, and various things began to have meaning for me: women's issues, politics. I used to think even the word 'politics' was horrendous before that; then I came to think it was about everything. It was because they made it applicable to you.

'You' again, not 'I'. The personal is the political:

You realized that a lot of decisions that had been made and which really affected you, you'd had no say in. You were unaware of everything happening higher up. It all suddenly made sense why you had been feeling so frustrated. Examples?—oh, women's issues of any sort, economic issues, even the stock exchange. I started to realize that some people had much more control over their lives than I had. I felt we didn't have control over a lot of things; and we'd always been poor as well.

I'd always felt guilt because you had to be at home for your children to be their mother, and if you took a job you were neglecting them in some way; but now I was clear that it was other people making the decision for me that it was my place to be in the home. And people had been telling me for long enough where I should be and what I should be. I just wanted to be myself. Suddenly I felt freed, and that nobody was ever going to tell me again what I should be.

It was vital that I met people who were struggling and needed the same sort of confidence. They gave it to me, and I'd give it back to them. The friendships you make are lifelong.

Suddenly you could learn all these things that I had been cut off from. I just became interested in everything I thought I never would be. I just loved all of it. We had a residential weekend, and no one went to bed. Everyone had left their kids and their things behind: no kids, no husband, nothing.

But it was not only Liz who felt disappointed, frustrated. Roger too was 'restless'. His wife says that from time to time they would discuss whether to go to evening classes instead of the pub. And Roger, she says,

during the marriage had got much more into reading and looking at things, whereas I was losing interest and not being able to concentrate. He started reading an awful lot about things—archaeology and photography. He became really interested whereas at first he never used to read a lot.

Roger: I read the Bible a lot, and books about the Bible, and you get quite hungry, the more you read the more hungry you become, you develop an appetite to learn. And I suppose we had reached a point in our lives when we were restless with life generally. I did make a couple of enquiries about courses, but I didn't get replies.

Because of work, Roger would have felt that a day course such as Liz began to attend was out of the question. Such a step was too big; impossible to contemplate. But Liz began a revolution in their life together. Revolutions unlock old assumptions; make insuperable obstacles dwindle.

At first:

Liz: We used to fight the whole time: I tell you, it was horrific. I just was not going to let go of it.

Roger: And I was quite resistant to what she was going to do for a while—even though I'd looked in the paper during the last two or three years from time to time when the polys were advertising, but I used to think: well, I'm not qualified to do something like that. So when Liz started heading in that direction, and going to WEA, I did feel quite excited by what she was doing.

Liz: But if it was for me it was for him as well, really.

Roger: In a way I felt frustrated that she was breaking free from the mundane, and I was left carrying the can, being the traditional provider, while everybody else seemed to be getting liberated from the mundane life: still having to slave away, bringing in a crust, doing it all traditionally. And I was 42, and going through a weird stage anyway, and thinking, oh God, I'm going to die soon.[2]

And I thought I had two options: I could either stay as I was and put up with everything and be an automaton, or I could do something else, run off and have a wild affair—

---

[2] There is a middle-class version of Roger's dilemma: a professional man in his early 40s may already be able to see the end of his promotion prospects. At the same juncture, his almost unqualified wife may be able to see the end of her work as a mother. She may decide on a new life entirely; for him to make a similar decision is likely to be far more difficult. In a sense, she has the advantage of having nothing; but to change his life, he has too much to give up: all sorts of 'rules', a high salary. His wife returns. Oppressed by her excitement, he may be too weak to resist the imperative to undermine her. Unless he changes, they will part.

Liz: But he couldn't find anyone: I kept introducing him to people—

Roger: Then my father died; and I always felt I wanted to do something like this for him, in a way. But everything was weighing against me. Being working-class people, traditionally you never went to university or got a degree, and you've got no qualifications, but I began to discover that you had lots of qualifications, not necessarily academic ones, but valuable in their own sense. You see, I'd been thinking about education for a while, but I think I never really had the courage to see it being a reality; but by the time Liz had applied to do Access, I thought: maybe this is not so out of reach, maybe this is something I can do. I took courage from her. In that sense she led us: she really gave me the inspiration or the courage to take the final leap.

Liz: It caused an awful lot of fights, and I even regretted—

Roger: But I was supposed to be the provider, and I was thinking of throwing all this up and living off a grant. Gradually it seemed quite feasible that I could get a place at the poly—I discovered about the part-time Access course from a handbook, and I enrolled for it. I enjoyed it all, but ecology was brilliant.

Liz: But we did do a lot of fighting. We used to argue more, after my course day.

Roger: You had to be more careful what you said. She spoke up for herself more.

Liz: Yes! I used to be so different. If Jehovah's Witnesses came to the door I used to buy *Watchtower*—I never said no to anyone. Can you believe it? I'm really aggressive now.

Roger: You used to make salads of weeds up the garden. Liz has changed a lot. She's very fiery now about political issues, especially when they encompass women.

Liz: On Access you had to do projects, and I did all mine on women: women in politics, women in literature, women in everything. So I was unbearable to live with.

Roger: Actually, I found it quite interesting. I hadn't consciously thought about women's issues. She was studying sociology which I found interesting. We used to talk about it a lot and argue.

Liz: If you've got kids you really are second-rate as a woman; you're offered 1.80 an hour, and you're the one who cleans the loos, works behind the bars, has to wear a short skirt. I worked in one which had a big notice behind the bar saying 'Wear short skirts.'

One night I was working there with Sarah, my eldest daughter. She was waitressing—and these blokes were really awful, they would not go, they waited outside for her, and we told the manager—and he said, it's good for business.

Roger: What was it like when we began to talk?

Liz: As a male he thought he was being attacked.

Roger: Primarily or primevally, as a man I felt, hello! What's this? You don't become paranoid, but I think you have moments when you feel quite frightened.

Liz: He's a threatened species.

Roger: I was nervous, thinking, where is all this going to end up, where's it going to leave our relationship? But Liz had made it quite clear that she was determined to do this anyway, so there didn't seem any point in arguing or fighting. And I did feel that she was entitled to do what she was doing anyway.

Liz: It was his freedom too.

Roger: Yes, it set me free too, you see.

Liz: The thing was, I'd made my mind up, and I would have put my marriage at risk.

Roger: I could have said, I'm not going to re-tax your car, so you'll have to take the bus. But she'd have walked.

And in spite of my natural reactions, inside I felt that it was good for her to do it.

Liz: The thing is—

Roger: I think she should find her own place as a person, because men and women lose identity within marriage, they become husbands, wives, fathers, mothers. She needed to know who she was.

Liz: You see reality when you step out. When you're in these four walls there are a lot of myths about what actually happens, and the myths you've produced that make you feel safe start being challenged. Myths about women for instance. Roger probably thought that all the women I was going to college with were raving lesbians, which is far from the truth. Feminism is just women.

Roger: When she came back and started talking about women's issues, and 'I'm determined to lead my own life, do my own thing, go my own way—'

Liz: It wasn't quite that bad—

Roger: No—I'm putting it in a nutshell. And you think— what a lot of trendy lefty weirdos, smoking dope, bleeding communists. This is how it suits the masculine world to portray feminists, because it becomes a façade behind which we can hide. They're all loonies: how convenient, compact, and tidy. But if you really have to face up to it and say, what are these women really saying, and who really are they? then you have to face up to the fact that they're saying something that really matters.

I mean—we did have some horrific

Liz: Rows.

Roger: Rows. I can remember times when Liz was leaving.

Liz: My behaviour was extreme in those days. I think it's more moderate now. I'd be angry with Roger and my son, and it wasn't really their fault, because I'd allowed those pressures to build up, until they'd reached a point where I couldn't cope any more. I broke out, so I was angry. Roger had to suffer the consequences. I felt I had to fight them to find myself, I had to fight them because they were the people who represented all the pressure.

Roger: I represented everything to Liz that she was discovering. I hadn't consciously considered women being paid less for doing the same work as men, and so on.

Because Liz was thinking about them, I did too.

Liz: You have to talk things out, anyway. Every big thing that we've been through we've learnt from. We're not afraid any more. We were afraid before: afraid of role changes, of not being what we thought we were—which was totally untrue anyway. But life is about change anyway, and education's forever, and should always be forever.

Roger: Whereas when I was a kid, there was education, there was going to the doctor: it was in that sort of category. It wasn't life, it wasn't you: it was something outside of you.

Roger has let us glimpse in these discussions the full range of his response to his wife's return.

- I was resistant./I was excited.
- I was frustrated still to be the provider./I'm 42 and what about death?
- Education is not for the likes of me./Maybe I could get some more education after all?
- It was like being attacked./Actually I found it interesting.
- I could have stopped her./She was unstoppable.
- They're all loony trendy feminists./What women are asking for is important.

Before these thoughts began to fight each other, he describes their state as 'restlessness'. The answer was motion, which Liz began. She moved to Greece, to a course; Roger, emotionally and intellectually.

Liz studied. She came home. They argued. Roger was astonished and enraged—but he was interested too. My guess is that the key to the vitality of his response was intellectual, so that 'interested' is the most important word he uses.

She called his bluff: he had been dreaming about more education for a while. Fed, his intellect began to thrive—and its activity to feel regenerative. Their arguments must have been intellectually satisfying. Liz brought ideas from her studies which forced Roger to think. He talks as if his strategic withdrawals, even his all-out Dunkirks, were as stimulating as victories. Liz lit up prejudices he probably did not even know he possessed until he watched them being strafed by salvoes of feminist sociology. And as he ran to defend them, with gallantry under fire, he could not help being intrigued to note how irrational was their rickety construction, as they fell apart.

In a sense, it did not matter what his intellect was forced to tell him; what mattered was its activity.

Intellect became vital. They became enfranchised.

Liz could call on a movement to confirm what she was doing, and give coherence to what she said, thought, and hoped. But Roger had to accept her leadership, with no ally in so doing. There was no movement to join at first—until he was in a class with others cheated by their schooling. He throws light on the many husbands who do fight to keep their wives as they are. They fear a sort of cuckolding, as their wives come to know their own minds. To follow your wife is dangerous and isolating. The cuckold is alone and foolish. But following his wife's lead has been Roger's triumph. When he read this chapter his response was almost a hymn to the regenerative power of education.

Liz's response was pity for the sulking man, cheated by prejudice about women. She is clear that Roger, lonely though he felt at first, has immeasurably gained by letting himself be swept up by her reclamation of the right to learn.

I see her as a pioneer. She is very direct. She will always state her belief. She will take you on. A teacher on the Access course told her class that evolution was a closed case; was proven. Liz said, 'Nonsense, it's no such thing.' A battle then began. Liz was defending a position she would die rather than yield: 'The right I have reclaimed at long last is the right to think about all that's taken for granted—because I have escaped from a world others have made for me, and I am going to remake that world afresh by *understanding it for myself*. Damn all old men with beards. Don't you dare tell me "because I tell you so".'

Every person you meet has got something, and should be learning constantly. But all education—anthropology or literature—should be part of life, not apart from it. Education is lost if it doesn't go to the people who desperately need it, the ones still living with the myths. Some of my friends are still living with them, and are afraid of that kind of jump.

Anthropology broadens the intellectual work she took on when she began her return and asked the first questions about her own life. It is a subject for a pioneer.

Social anthropology is asking why—why do people do that, why is that society constructed in that way? It challenges everything in you, because every group is different, and you can never generalize. It's great. In one way the world becomes more attainable; but in another, it becomes vaster, because there is so much *difference*, the amount is fantastic. The questions will never stop. Anthropology extends and can never finish, because it challenges. I've never stopped enjoying that.

Roger's choice of another subject to combine with electronics follows suit. To begin with he chose physics and electronics because they would lead to good jobs. Sociology allows him to go on asking the questions that came to interest him in the early days of his wife's return. The questions are important; he is not so concerned any more to take a subject that can be respected as a means to a good job.

Helen and Dave's experience echoes this story.

Ultimatum

I met Helen some years ago, when I was researching for my first book. Her return had just begun. Now she is teaching in a comprehensive.

Like Liz, she is authoritative, determined. You can always depend on her to say what she thinks. She talks volubly and emphatically.

Her family moved from London to the country; she went to a secondary modern.

I was amazed. It's surrounded by grass, really beautiful, and there was this bench and I sat on it, and a teacher came up to me and told me to move, I said, I ain't moving! Just do as you're told, she said, you're that new girl from London, aren't you?

She was typecast as troublemaker:

I used to wear a bright green jumper and a green miniskirt, and blue socks with yellow stripes round the tops and shoes with clicking heels: it used to drive them mad. Red shoes.

They used to echo in assembly. If they hadn't been as worried about what I was wearing they might have been more interested in what I was doing.

My sister went to grammar school and got O levels, and I was always the 'practical' one. My sister went to university.

Nanny at 16, office work, machinist in a factory, waitress, telephonist, evening classes in economics and geography, married at 21, mother. Suddenly: time on her hands. She knew she 'needed more'. She still burned to compete with her sister. She went to college.

She took maths and English at O level, and passed maths with an A. This was a revolution. At school her maths teacher had been her enemy, and had made her feel stupid.

Talking to the deputy-principal of the college about these results, she told him that she had always—secretly—wanted to become a teacher. 'Why not?' he said. At first she was astonished; but then she decided to take his advice and do A level. Now she is a university graduate in economics.

Her teachers at college liked and 'acknowledged' her. She talks of her maths teacher as her mentor; says that the deputy-principal who had recruited her always revelled in her success. And she had a close friend in Kerry, whose motivation was similarly coherent: she too wanted to astonish a cynical father who thought that she was wasting her time.

But her husband?

For a start he saw it as a five-minute wonder; and he was very jealous of me, particularly when I got to university.

He did a couple of O levels to shut me up! He's a plumber and heating engineer.

I do think that I've been through periods when I've got a bit kind of uppity and have thought I'm a bit superior. But I think he's been very afraid of it, because I do get absorbed in things. Once I was hooked, that was it, I didn't want to talk about anything else, and I liked being at college, I loved it. He didn't understand why. He was jealous. He would have given anything for me to stop.

There was a moment when he said, what would happen if I told you to choose between me and college? And I said, well, you'll lose. I said, if you're not decent enough to let me do something that's desperately important to me, then I don't want to be married to you!

However, he was also rather proud of what I was doing. He very much saw it as a hobby to begin with; he didn't see it as anything serious till I got a place at university, then he did realize that it was worth worrying about.

Until last summer I don't think he realized the sort of relationships that develop in a class, that male and female can be properly friends, and that there isn't anything sexual in it. He thought I was going to run off with somebody.

It's caused a lot of friction. He left for a couple of weeks. But we always seemed to come out the other side. The pressure on me to give up was always there. I was changing, and he didn't like it. I saw myself as growing but he saw it as a change for the worse. For a long time I thought, he's got to do the changing, because I'm the one who's growing and expanding and he's staying still. I think I got over that eventually, but it did take a long time, and I did go through a big patch when I was rather conceited about it all.

But he wasn't particularly impressed when I got my place at university, and I don't think he expected me to get my A level results either, so he was particularly unimpressed when I got them.

He spent a lot of time being insecure when I've been away. But he's given me a great deal more room than most men would, partly because he's had to, or it's just tough. I wanted the room and I was just taking it, and I didn't see it as unreasonable. But from his point of view it's been horrible, because he's had all his friends saying, ooh, I wouldn't let my wife do that.

I used to spend nights in town, at the student house, so that must mean I was having orgies all over the place. I wouldn't let my wife do that, what are you doing letting your wife sleep out all night? That's what he had to put up with.

But he likes people to admire him; and there was reflected glory: wasn't he wonderful, imagine putting up with Helen, she's always going off, what a wonderful husband.

He's also given me a great deal of practical support. If you've got kids and you want to do a degree, you must have practical support and he does do that. He's never been the sort of man who won't change nappies, he's always been quite sure that he's a man. He used to pick the kids up, cook their tea, bung the washing in. Without help from him and my sister it would have been practically impossible.

Things have changed a lot in the last few months since I've been teaching. The confidence I've been looking for all through university didn't come, it's only the last months in front of kids that I've lost that inferiority, the feeling that when I walk into a room I shouldn't be there because I'm not good enough. Now I just don't think about it.

His friends do see me as a raving feminist, and some men think there's something wrong with me. But he's benefited, there are very few fathers as close to their kids as him; that's because he's mothered them as well as being a dad. Sometimes I feel jealous of that, but it's fair, because he has spent many hours with them.

Dave's Account

Dave seems almost his wife's antithesis. He is calm, and gentle, and talks quietly. But he comes across as strong, too, and deeply self-possessed.

When Helen started going to college all day, I had a good govnor when I needed time off work, or if I needed to start a little later. I'd work through my lunchtime to make up for it. A lot of employers would have said, this is not on, and a wife should be at home, on your bike.

There were times when I wanted to turn the clock back. I still think that now, when I come home and Helen's still at work, or studying or marking books, and I have to cook the tea after a hard physical day.

So I do like it when it happens the old way, and I come in and my tea's there; but I couldn't be like my father now, my mum does everything. I put myself in the position of wives left at home, and all they do is clean and cook, you know. Whereas in fact they want to go out and pursue interests just as we do.

The real pressure was when she was at university. I had to

pick the kids up and cook. It was difficult to accept. We split up for a couple of weeks during that time, because of the pressure. But we missed each other.

Afterwards Helen stipulated that she wanted a career and nothing was going to change her. I work in plumbing and heating and the construction industry, and a lot of guys through these years have said, I wouldn't let my wife do that. I have got annoyed on some occasions, because these bigoted guys don't want to hear what I've got to say, they just say—I wouldn't let my wife do that. She should be in looking after the kids, cooking and cleaning.

I did feel jealous, and it got me going in a way. I went to college and took two O levels, and then I took an A level course—history, which I'd liked at school. I really wanted to see if I could do it. But I got the day of the last exam wrong and missed it, so I only did one part. But it did prove to me that I could do it as well. And I found it interesting. It got me away from all the usual conversations, the football: I'm football-mad. It was really quite a breath of fresh air.

One of the O levels was so I could understand her a little: sociology. She would talk about it, Helen always talks. She does like to come and talk about her economics, and I don't understand.

When she got an A in maths O level—I was pleased, and proud, but a bit jealous as well, I guess. It's a long time ago. But after A level, I really had to start thinking. Outwardly it was, well done, darling, but inwardly it was, oh my God, what's going to happen now? I can remember a brown envelope with a little slip in. I probably kept back what I felt. And when she had such a bad time at the interview for university and she came home and said, I don't like them and they don't like me, really I thought: well, that's handy. I'll be honest with you. I thought—perhaps it'll get it out of her system. She's not quite up to that standard: O levels—great, but getting into university when you've got kids was something different.

When she was accepted I knew then she was really going, and the onus would be on me again with the kids. People would say, how do you cope with your kids? But it's not really a matter of coping, I really love the girls.

When she was accepted for the year's teacher training, I knew there was going to be a good job at the end of it, a good career for Helen, and an income for us to enjoy as well, which would take the burden off me as the single breadwinner.

Yes, she did get big-headed. I think I accused her of that a couple of times. When we went out with people, I'm sure that she bored them stupid, talking about her subject which we knew nothing about. You're not particularly interested in that sort of thing when you go out anyway. She doesn't do it now, she doesn't feel the need to do it.

I would have heard it all before, and I'd sit there and think, I've heard all this, I'm fed up with it, how are they taking it?

Oh, it's undoubtedly true that I've been enriched by it, she's right. Perhaps I've been more involved with the kids because of this college business, though I've always been involved anyway. I love them, I'd do anything for them, I'd do anything with them. One of the objections from the guys on site was that I was doing all these things for the kids, picking them up and so on, and that wasn't my job. Which goes back through history I suppose. Some people are so rigid, and they can't see any change.

One couple we know, the woman still had to do everything, cooking and cleaning—and then staying up till two or three in the morning to study. That is a selfish reaction on the man's part, isn't it? He didn't want to know about looking after the kids or anything. It was silly, she shouldn't be doing it. He wouldn't adapt. It's short-sighted. You've got to adapt, otherwise you're in a stalemate, and that's no good for anyone, is it? But for a woman it can be another chance, not just to bring up children, not to have a humdrum life. It can be an opening, and they go for it. In the last fifteen years or so a lot of changes have taken place, haven't they, and mostly on the women's side.

Dave did not find intellectual fervour like Roger's. Nor was Helen's quest like Liz's. She wanted to prove her father wrong, who always said she was 'practical'. She wanted to prove her worth.

But his last statement shows the same principle at work in

his marriage as in Roger's: rationality. Perhaps, like Roger, he found his wife's new intellectual vigour infectious. But it is sad that so many men find it impossible to react to change with Dave's resilience, intelligence, decency.

You can detect in his account how reason had to fight prejudice: to defy the voices telling him he was a cuckold.

But he had also deliberately to refuse the option of the man at the juke-box in Peter's account. Roger too has suggested that the cheated working-class school-leaver builds a defence of pride around his 'ignorance'. Roger puts it like this:

> It's not that you don't have the capability to find out, or the opportunity. It's the fact that you don't want to know that makes it ignorance. It's the fact that you don't want to know, you don't want to find out, you don't want to see.

When the wife begins to think, that defence is sapped. No wonder then that the husband can turn on his wife in fury, and shout betrayal. And it *is* the man who has been betrayed: not by his wife, but by schooling that makes him see the educated as a race apart, and education as a threat—so that his wife's exulting mind can only frighten him.

12

The Importance of Experience

Helen, Liz, and Roger will all have been told early in their degree courses: mature students have the advantage of experience. What can this mean?

Stephanie is at an ancient university. She is a very intelligent and forthright 40-year-old woman, who used to be a residential social worker. A young man, still in the extended adolescence of his Ph.D. years, was her tutor in psychology. I suspect that she overawed him; yet he was supposed to be that most parental of figures, the wise teacher. Desperate to convince, he became unsmiling, touchy, unable to see virtue in Stephanie's still-flawed essays. She felt adulthood draining away. Her work deteriorated; her confidence ebbed. Regressing, she forgot that in order to get to university she passed three A levels in less than two years and all with A grades while bringing up three children; forgot the value and richness of her experience: that her success in her studies had drawn on ways of solving problems she had developed in her work with disturbed adolescents; on an ability to organize small amounts of time that she had learnt as a working parent.

Returners have often to face such serious assaults on their confidence when they meet their teachers at university or polytechnic. Stephanie's disastrous tuition deskilled her. Good teaching takes pains to avoid this mistake. It is not this book's job to go into the detail of good practice for adult learners. Much has already been implied, and much stated, by returners themselves. Three general principles suggest themselves.

First is that teaching should be based on the assumption that any adult's experience has already included valid learning, and that many of his or her skills are transferable to intellectual work. Instead of making Stephanie feel that she knew nothing, her tutor should have helped her to acknowledge what she already knew—like Liz's WEA tutor; should have made it his business to discover her experience and mine it for analogy and implication—not difficult, one would think, in a subject like psychology, despite its rodent tendencies.

The second principle is the importance of talk. Plenty of talk furthers the excitement of the returner's transformation, uses the energy of that excitement. Talk is important not just because discussion is an effective way of learning. Talk helps to sustain the momentum of return, because return is itself an argument: the defeat of one set of ideas by another. That is why my case about school has been central to this book. Most returners have to defeat the ideas of themselves school fostered: they have to argue themselves out of demeaning generalities. Old ghosts have to be exorcised by assertive new hopes; the delusion of stupidity has to be repeatedly countermanded. Roger and Liz are imbued with the energy of this continuing urgent argument about their own experience. Moreover, returners often come to appreciate their gifts when they find their eloquence: when they utter thoughts they never knew they had, and discover to their surprise that others are interested or persuaded by what they say. Peter's account of breaking his silence is apt illustration of this point.

The third principle may be the most important: appreciation of the importance of confidence—as Anne-Marie's case, and all the others as well, so strongly suggest. Bad experience must be acknowledged. The ghosts of school can stalk the returner's mind until graduation. Roger met a physics lecturer whose martinet technique with latecomers—though he was never one—so depressed and undermined him, he gave up the subject. He had not gone to polytechnic to meet his schoolteachers again. He was pushed back in time to when he was at his most vulnerable, most lacking in self-esteem. Liz says that his energy and his optimism drained away, as if he had been cursed. The foundations of his return were undermined. Liz had to persuade him to abandon physics: he became too demoralized to make the decision unaided. Tactless teaching—lack of respect—can turn a competent adult into a depressed schoolboy.

Most undermining is the tendency for teachers in higher

education to misinterpret technical difficulties as intellectual dearth. A spelling mistake can be corrected with such disdain that the returner gets the message: 'This don thinks I'm stupid.' Alan made the point, about essays: 'it can all be in the head; but there can be terrible difficulty about getting it on paper'. Such a difficulty is all too often seen as a sign of stupidity.

There is still in higher education lethal reluctance to think at all about teaching and learning. Dons often become as foolish as Stephanie's tutor when faced with a returner who has not yet learned the tricks of the student's trade. (Interestingly, though, the quick increase in the number of mature students in higher education is encouraging reassessment of the validity of some of those tricks: the means, methods, and techniques of demonstrating understanding.)

This third principle, about confidence, requires teachers to foster the returner's belief in her own competence. This belief is that you will be able to solve new problems: that the technical versatility life has led you to acquire will prove useful in your studies. What is vital is that the rest of life, and intellectual work, should fit together; should not be separate universes. We have seen how important it can be for those worlds to join: Vanessa's excitement at her law lecture is a good example. A connection sparked. Her life—and her competence—as a mother might be relevant in this very different world. Stephanie was undermined, because whatever she tried proved useless. Her technique for dealing with new difficulty in her ordinary life kept being condemned as fallible, when applied to her studies. Another way of expressing 'self-direction' is 'experimental confidence'. She had plenty when she began; but her tutor kept telling her that her experiments were no good. But misses should be as useful to a learner as hits. Good teaching conveys that truth. Stephanie's tutor should have offered reciprocity: should have taken as his starting-point: 'If you can achieve what you have already achieved in your life, all the complexities of psychology are within your grasp. We'll work at them together. Don't on any account be frightened of going astray: straying can be useful.' He should, in other words, have taken the position adopted by Peter's 'abbess', his first tutor-counsellor at the OU.

The returner's experience is not a plain advantage, like height in basketball. It can be used or abused; acknowledged, or disdained.

Experience does teach acceptance of difficulty. Returners are often hungry for challenges, as we have seen. Cheated of the arduous at school, they crave huge tasks. It is a vast jump to turn yourself from a writer of shopping lists to *aficionado* of the essay. It is similarly demanding for many to read a difficult book. Adult life teaches difficulty; teaches postponement while the difficult is tackled. Parenthood teaches difficulty, and postponement. Given the right support, given acknowledgement of the three principles outlined above, adults can take on huge intellectual tasks with pleasure and persistence.

Uniquely terrible experience can prompt return; and Vanessa expresses an advantage of experience in a further way: 'sometimes we make bigger, better, deeper, different connections'.

The Access students, then, could turn themselves into sophisticated learners very fast, because of their clarity of purpose; because the intellectual energy they had been storing was powerful, like compressed air in a gun; because they wanted difficulty; because they acknowledged each other and helped to sustain each other's 'experimental confidence'; and because—unlike so many adolescents—their zeal was un-distracted. At its most basic, this zeal is from bitter experience of the limitations of one sort of life, and determination to escape them. Sally's determination was from new belief in herself; but that belief made her see the limitations of the secretary's life with total clarity.

This train of thought emphasizes that an argument about improving schools does not imply that adult learning is second best, a last resort, a compensation. Adulthood may be the best time to learn since early childhood.

Adult experience—as I argued in my summary of Sally's account—itself commands thought. Maturity is a habit of reflection and interpretation; of drawing conclusions. Adult development needs intellect, gives intellect practice, because it is *integrative*. Before a crisis or a revelation makes her think of education, a returner has often been trying hard to make life coherent; to bring hopes and regrets and habits and frustrations and fears into some sort of pattern. Without knowing it, she has been using her mind in the sort of way her studies require. Return consummates the search for coherence. Think of Vanessa with her American mentor; Sally tussling with the implications of her rape. Roger before he returned was trying to *make sense* of his life; trying to bring into some sort of whole the fact of being 42, his regret at his inadequate education, the excitement he felt at his wife's experiment, and the envy and fear he felt too.

His wife's trip to Greece was also a bid for integration. Her life had become disproportionate, liked distorted physical growth. She was distorted by the overburden of motherhood. Other capacities, other possibilities deserved their due weight.

But adolescence is almost disintegrative, as the extreme case of Alan has shown. The adult world proposes for the adolescent complete patterns, formulae. One way of establishing who you are at 17 is to break them one by one, and see what is left; break the proffered personae and rearrange the bits.

Perhaps disintegration in adolescence is safer than biddable adoption of what is on offer, as Sally's history suggests. If not always disintegrative, adolescence is at least *histrionic*; and what adolescents need and so often lack in school is teachers who can direct, applaud, criticize, or even censor their enactments. Shirley had no such teacher. She gave performance after performance of her one disastrous drama. No one—in her words—'sussed her out'; no one could slow her down, suggest another act in a way that could be heard.

Shirley and Alan suggest that some adolescents are in-educable, in the formal sense (I shall chase the implications of this proposition in the last chapter). The urge to enact—in uncertainty, fear, self-doubt—does not predispose to reflective interpretation. Integration, coherence, form itself—can feel staid and uninteresting. The alarming features of adolescence are symptoms of an unappeasable desire—much more acute since teenage culture—to rearrange whatever seems settled, formed. But in adulthood, maturity may be the sense that your biography *should have a form*. Roger's mention of his sudden thoughts of mortality is suggestive here. The returner *wishes as far as possible to compose her own biography*.

Laura's and Julie's are accounts of mind serving the adult will to integrate; of very difficult adult experience commanding the service of intellect. They bring into sharper focus the relationship between experience and learning in the previous accounts.

Laura

First, an essay.

Pornography

Most mainstream pornography available is used by men and depicts women in sexually available poses. This includes page three girls. It is often argued that pornography is a harmless means of providing sexual stimulation. However, I find it disturbing to live amongst a population where pornography is enjoyed by a lot of men and some women too. What worries me is the message that a pornographic photograph, for example, gives a man.

Imagine a photo of a girl with naked breasts and erotic underwear. The girl is sexually available and looks sexually aroused. The message is that the woman is always willing to have a sexual encounter and will never say no. She also positively enjoys the experience—which must be good for male egos, not necessarily as strong and confident as society expects them to be. She also has no brain, no personality, and no choice.

Pornographic woman is not a woman at all. She is simply a male phantasy—a phantasy about sex that doesn't include an emotional relationship; a phantasy about power that gives men the right to use women sexually when they want to; and a phantasy about women: that they actually want to be, and enjoy being, like this.

Pornography corrupts our sexuality which in turn corrupts the rest of our lives. If a man thinks a woman plays the 'pornographic' role in bed, he must also assume that she will be undemanding and willing to please in all other areas of her life.

Until pornography and its implications have been abolished, a lot of men and women will continue to play roles in their relationships with each other, rather than developing as individuals to the benefit of themselves, their families, and society.

This is the first piece of considered writing its author has produced for twelve years—since she left school.

Laura is 30. She is married, with two young daughters. In a weekly class I run, she is absorbed, focused. She always says what she thinks. If she feels strongly about something she will not relent, until a finished polemic is there before her. She talks well—tersely. Laura sometimes takes the role of teacher for one of the others in the class. All the women in the group do this for each other; but—perhaps because her first education lasted longer than the schooling of the others—I notice her doing so most often. Watching the women doing this for each other gives me insight into the way the Access group worked; the way students 'acknowledged' each other, taking the role of teacher, exorcist, parent. I recall an occasion. We had read 'A Cup of Tea', a short story by Katherine Mansfield. I asked everyone to work out a statement about the story, and deliver it. Maureen has no confidence in her intellect at all. With reluctance and so many apologetic grace-notes it was hard to follow what she was saying, she delivered. Her point was sharp, like her mind. Then she said of the heroine: 'it's as if she lives in a world of trinkets . . .'. She apologized for not saying anything sensible. Three—perhaps more—women jumped. Laura among them. You could see them beefing her up; disproving her apology.

Laura has had to win adulthood; has had to fight herself for it. She and her husband have grown up together. They fell in love and into responsibility in their early twenties.

Suddenly she was pregnant and married. Then she was a mother and living in a new town.

From then on, her task was like Eleanor's. She had to map herself, and then transfigure her own territory.

When her first child was 2 years old she went back briefly to work. But when the second came, she was at home—for good, or so it felt. And she had cut herself off from the life she had led before marriage; from her circle of friends.

We went so quickly from having a baby to having a house, having a mortgage, having no money.

Her expectation that her husband should provide all that she needed became greedy. Her old dependence on parties, noise, became a new dependence on her husband; a bid for romantic thraldom.

Her husband fought against it. She wanted much more, she says, than ordinary reciprocity; ordinary love. She wanted him to make up for her isolation, her boredom, her tiredness.

Such a state of affairs is not unusual; nor was the threat for her of spiralling into depression, greater need, greater demand, greater depression, greater isolation.

But instead, she became alert to what was happening. After rows, rage, misery, came thought. She began to replace the external excitements of her old life with private intellectual pleasure.

I started reading because we stopped going out, and money was short. Almost exclusively reading female writers as well. I didn't realise at the time. And you really start to find out how women are treated when you have a child.

She had a head start, when it came to the interpretation of complexities. She had taken three A levels, though she had failed one and got only Es for the others. But she had intellectual technique at hand; some habits, some expectations—of what print might offer, for instance, though she had never been such an avid reader before—not even finishing some of the set texts for her English A level.

At A level, she was terrified of exams; and could not write essays even in her own time, because she always had too many ideas; could never sort them out. She constructed her own strategy of denial. 'None of this is really important. I will not do the work, so that I will have a good excuse for failing.' But now her subject was her life, and her need to learn her life and understand it was urgent.

I started catching up on all the feminist writers, I suppose. I can't remember—I must have read all the Doris Lessings I could get my hands on. I discovered Edna O'Brien, I really love her. Lots of writers I picked up in the library. I also read people like Sheila Kitzinger, women's health books, and—when it came to childbirth—all the alternative child care books. It's all very much about roles, and women's place, and who's having the child. All those books you read. You desperately need to know, when you're pregnant.

It was the first time I'd had a chance to be on my own. Before I'd always been socializing, and if I wasn't I was very unhappy. I was forced to be on my own, and I didn't enjoy it, not for quite a while.

It was the first time I had to think about myself. It became apparent to me that I wasn't a very happy person, but I wasn't prepared to let myself remain unhappy for ever. I was trapped in a myth about marriage, a myth about happiness.

We struggled along in our marriage for quite a while before it dawned on me: he cannot be expected to become my happiness; he cannot *give happiness*.

I think I began to see things more clearly when I started to give Robert more freedom. He really wanted to go on a week's cycling holiday, and I thought—why shouldn't he? I said yes, and he went away for a week. I suddenly realized I could cope on my own. It was a real turning-point for me, I think. I actually enjoyed coping on my own.

She began to think, to look for patterns; to try to *integrate*. Then, in supersession of her adolescent self, she wrote the first sentence of her essay, which she read out to her husband. Take a week's holiday.
She found she could plan the rest.

I started having to say what I wanted; to spell it out. Not horribly; but instead of getting angry and exploding—so that he would end up saying, what's wrong with her NOW?—I *spoke*. I decided poor Robert could not cope with me repressing all these emotions for so long, and then suddenly exploding. I used to go really over the top and say horrible things to him as you do when you're angry.

But I had to start thinking what I did want, and analysing why I was getting angry. Lots of different things nudged me towards conclusions. You're not quite sure what you've read in the end, but you realize you've somehow formed an opinion partly from what you've read.

I know what I think, whereas before I was so wishy-washy. I could see so much; but I didn't feel any of it, I really didn't. Intellectually you see something; but as a person you don't see it all, you don't feel part of it. It's almost as if learning has become essential. I'm not sure that education in a standard form is going to fit me—my education has become a sort of personal quest, and I'm not sure whether it will fit a conventional syllabus.

The class has been good, because of being part of a group; it's less hard work than being on your own. I can see why someone in prison, or in solitary confinement, must find it so hard. The process of doing things all on your own is quite a sad process, isn't it, because it doesn't spread to everybody else. I'm still essentially sociable, gregarious, whatever my own personal quest is.

The success of her authorship of her own life gives her intellectual authority; now she has a habit of taking the high ground in any subject, from which to analyse and understand it, rather than staying down amongst the details and getting lost. But her 'authorship' has also given her an intellectual limbering up. It has been good practice.

She has talked to me about the essay. Its importance arose from experience: her husband was working with an 18-year-old boy whose obsession with pornography came to disturb him, so that he and Laura found themselves talking about it a great deal. First, she sat down and wrote two pages of unconnected thoughts about the subject. She nearly panicked, as she might have done in the past, at the profusion of her ideas. But she *realized* she had reached the point at which she would have panicked. She refused to panic. She remembered her rank: marshal of her own life. So she decided on a strategy. She would move forward on one line, making one clear short set of propositions. Before, she would have advanced on a wide and cluttered front, hoping for safety in numbers, bringing with her an army of facts and examples and flashes of brilliance from bright ideas—too frightened her essay might be defeated if they did not all come too. Before, she was intellectually gregarious, noisy, chaotic; intellectually promiscuous. Now—chaste—she was in charge.

So she distilled her thoughts into the terse piece I have

already quoted. What struck me was the *authority* of its transitions from point to point.

The essay represents her stage as a learner. At first, the will to learn and to think were one and the same as the need to understand her own life, and resolve her predicament. But now she is looking outwards as well as inwards, and wants to understand much more. Learning has—in her own words— become essential. She wants to follow tracks that lead out of her life and into many different subjects. To learn enough to reach plausible conclusions was arduous. Her success has given her pride as well as authority and practice. And each conclusion has posed questions. She has looked at the economy of her own life; now she wants economics. Her analysis of herself as mother has let her understand the Mother as a set of social expectations. If motherhood, what about fatherhood? What about the state? Other states? Parenthood in other societies?

But it is sad that Laura's teachers could not unite to help her with essays. It will be very difficult for her to become a student. She lives in the country. She has no car to reach the nearest polytechnic. Despite the privacy of what she calls her 'quest' she does now want to do a degree. She may not be able to.

Julie

Julie's experience, too, restored the importance of her intellect—in the end. Her account also shows again the unexpectedness of the course of some lives; their fruitful discontinuities.

She says that she was happy at her small primary school. But:

> when I got a place at grammar school, I rushed home, I was so pleased. I thought, everybody's going to really think I'm wonderful. My mother said, well that's a shame because I've knitted you a cardigan for secondary modern.
>
> You had to wear a very big beret, like a flying saucer, no matter whether you were in school or not. You could be given a detention if you didn't. I see myself walking down the road with this bloody great thing on, feeling a nerd, and hating the school because of it.

I left the grammar school in the second year. My mum said, it's best if you go to secondary modern. I can't remember anyone asking me what I thought. Half of me felt elated, and the other half felt, I don't want them to beat me.

But her parents soon divorced. Her father was very violent. Her mother took the children to live in London. She went to a big comprehensive.

On the whole the teachers seemed to walk around in a state of despair. They seemed permanently fraught and hassled.

There wasn't much academic encouragement. I think they just tried to get you to school. They didn't mind what you did so long as you didn't bash anyone, they just wanted you to get in.

The only subject I really liked was English, and I was always good at it. Mr Robertson was brilliant. We used to skip lessons and go to see him because we were good at English. We used to go and see him and his wife after school. He took about four of us to see *Hair*. We felt really hip and adult: all those nude men!

He was great. He didn't approach us from up there, though he didn't actually come down to our level. He was interested in us. I would imagine he was very left wing, though he didn't talk about politics. He was just brilliant. He gave me lots of encouragement. He was the first adult I came across who actually made me feel good about myself and made me feel special. He was interested in our work, and he just really encouraged us.

He was so good. He accepted me as me—I don't know how to put it. I felt as if I had some sort of adult support. There weren't any demands from him, or it didn't feel as though there were. You did what you were capable of doing. You didn't feel you had to live up to his image of you.

I left at 15, despite objections from school—they thought I should have done my O levels.

Mr Robertson said I should have stayed on, and I should go into journalism or something like that.

But she could not recover so quickly from her early life, without the help of much more than one kind teacher. She had to deal with the long aftermath of her father's years of violence; with her parents' divorce; the uprooting to London; the slowness of her mother's recovery from despair.

She left school for job after job—some she liked, such as a spell at a travel agent; some she found dismal, like her time at a betting shop.

And she soon had a child, after marriage at 18 to a boy who beat her up, deserted her, and returned to beat her up again. 'I put up with it for eighteen years, so why can't you?' was her mother's comment. But Julie opted for divorce all the same.

Not long afterwards, she took her child to India, with friends who let her down, and left her on her own and penniless. Desperate, she agreed to smuggle some dope for money. She was arrested at Heathrow. Her penalty was a very large fine.

Then I met Alan. Anyway, we got married. He spent an awful lot of time going in and out of prison, and I went into a nervous breakdown, or whatever. I was quite ill for about a year. Really ill. I wouldn't answer the door, I didn't feel as though I could talk to people. If anybody came into the house I would just crack up. I didn't feel as if I could control myself, and I sat up all night, I couldn't sleep till about six. I lived with the kitchen blind drawn down to look as if I wasn't in. I just couldn't leave the house.

I went to see Alan once when he was in Wandsworth, and I got a really bad panic attack on the train. I was taking ativan in huge quantities, and giving some to Alan to sell inside.

I started to get progressively better over a period of time. The first minute we got married I knew I'd made the most tragically wrong decision of my life. But you really try to convince yourself that you like somebody. Instead I was living with a man I really didn't like and couldn't even pretend to like, let alone love.

But because I disliked him so much, I felt guilty, and so I ended up feeling really sorry for him. I did everything for him. He's one of these people who is so weak that prison is an escape for him. So in a sense, my own strength got drawn out: I was the one who was taking care of everything. I stopped hiding, started confronting things, took charge of everything. He couldn't answer the phone because it might be somebody pestering him for money—he was a cowboy fencer, so he'd get their money and run. So I would have to answer the door.

I didn't like doing it, and I started to feel—this isn't right, all this weakness being dumped on me. I was getting progressively stronger while he was getting weaker. I was actually beginning to be aware of my own intelligence. I lived on a council estate in east London. Everybody used to come to me if they had letters to write or anything to do with bureaucracy, like difficult phone calls. I used to make a point of finding out what my rights were, and the right people to contact. I enjoyed it: it was stimulating. People always treated me as a little bit different from them, because I was 'intelligent'. I wasn't quite accepted again, because I was neither one thing nor another. I didn't have family that came from the area. I was different, I'd been to India and done different things, I wasn't the same.

I don't know what it was—I just wanted to do something. I felt as though I was brain-dead, that's what it was. I used to spend hours doing crosswords, buying loads and loads of crossword books all the time—something that would tax my brain.

I think it was a whole set of circumstances. I was always aware that my mum and my sister didn't know the kind of life I was leading, with people into petty crime, cheque fraud, shoplifting, that kind of stuff. I was part of that. Again, you adapt to be accepted by the people you're living with. But then you become increasingly conscious that this isn't the way you want to live, isn't the right way to live. I was always aware of that, it was always at the back of my mind—if my parents found out what the hell would they think? But at the time I was accepted by a group of people and I had security.

I was finding it harder and harder to carry on with the way I was living. I knew it was wrong, and I was worried about Louise—she was growing older and you couldn't hide things from her. How must it be for her to have a father who's in prison—even though in the area we were in it was okay; but at school it was different, and it must have been bloody awful for her. The older she got, the more concerned I became.

I don't know—perhaps because he was so awful, I suddenly felt I'm wonderful; his badness increased my sense that I was basically okay. I'd had instilled into me an overriding sense of badness, and I'd lived up to it. But now I became aware of myself in my own right.

I'd nearly gone under—I'd had to go up to the Old Bailey as a witness in an armed robbery, that sort of thing. What worse could happen? Everything bad in life had happened to me: I'd been beaten up, homeless, everything. Nothing could get worse, it could only improve.

I thought, I want to control my life, I'm fed up with this. Supporting him just increased my own strength. I didn't need someone to look after me. I suddenly realized I was independent.

I'd undergone a lot of self-analysis over the years, after I'd been ill. I tried to work out why my mum treated me so badly, doing lots of things like when she gave my bedroom in London to friends, so I had to sleep on the sitting-room sofa. I'd felt that if she didn't love me, nobody could, so I must be totally worthless. Alan my husband helped me to think. He would let me sit and talk: if you gave him a bottle of vodka and sat him down he'd let you talk all night if you wanted to.

He'd had an awful life and he needed to talk about it as well. I spent a lot of time talking, and I went through this kind of awakening, to realize that my mum didn't really hate me. That it was maybe pressures that she'd had from her own parents that she'd transposed on to me, and that it wasn't my fault either. I stopped blaming myself and kicking myself and punishing myself.

Anyway, I left Alan.

Marrying him was like saying, I'm bad so this is the sort of person that I qualify for; and then you realize that you're not that bad. It takes a long time. Then I realized there were lots of things that I wanted to do, and do something about. And if I was going to be on my own again I had to be economically independent, because there was no way I was going to bring my kids up on social security because all that happens is that you get so bloody fed up with it you have another relationship just to make your life more comfortable; that was to be avoided at all costs. And my sister was doing the OU, so I started thinking, maybe I can do something on those lines.

She said, go and do a degree. I said, I can't for God's sake, I left school at 15. She said of course you can.

And I actually entered into it not knowing what it entailed or anything. I don't know how I knew—I just knew I needed to do it. I knew that I'd spent years in a time-warp. I'd spent 30 years trying to resolve all the problems of my childhood; and having done that I needed to go on. That's what had really happened, I just knew that I had to go on, I stopped focusing on the past and living in the past. School had played such a big part in my life, so that to go back and do some O levels or whatever would be to turn something negative into positive.

The stage I'm at now, all I'm doing is repeating the past, but I'm doing it in a positive way. This is my second go at it.

What had taken place when she talked for hours at a time to her husband was not only the piecing together of all the deranged bits and pieces of her biography—but also growing excitement at the use of her mind. I was present as she did more of the same. Her explanations had great intellectual energy, which she certainly needed, because the evidence which she had to analyse and understand was painful and taxing. Like Laura, her mind was restored to its proper place after she thought herself out of a crisis. Analysing, explaining, mastering her own history, she acquired a pattern for her future work. As she talked and talked in those crucial sessions with her drinking husband, her mind recovered vitality, and she had no choice but to go on presenting it with similarly difficult work.

In most of the lives I have touched for this book, 'return' has been an attempt to go back to the point of loss, and see what might happen if you walked from there again. Returners' will to transform, to reassess, is also at some point an urge to *retrieve*; to gamble everything on memory of a time when the garden seemed sunlit and promising.

Like Alice, you have to find the right-sized key. The gamble is risky, because if you find that your memory is a delusion, disappointment may be lethal. At some time in her childhood, before her father's violence terrorized the whole family, before her mother began to put her down, before the flying saucer beret, her malign delusion of stupidity, the divorce, the violent marriage, the drug-bust, the second marriage—Julie knew that she had been all right. The clue was an optimism she had mislaid for so long, and began to sense again. Even her London English teacher could not restore it. Perhaps her best memories of childhood were to do with her first—small—school where her teachers liked her and she felt safe, and she had a reading age of 12 when she was only 9. The point of loss was certainly when she went to grammar school; and the beginning of recovery was her Access course. It was frightening at first—the demand to express opinions, to analyse difficult books, when you had been away from school for so long. She says she felt as if she wanted to die the first time her English teacher went round the whole group asking for an opinion about a short story they had read. But the politics tutor was wonderful, she felt that he liked her, and respected her opinions even if he disagreed with them. He acknowledged her. He prompted frequent debates, in which she became more confident at saying what she thought.

Like Sally, she had become someone who needed to *know*.

Reaching the end of that road, I thought, who am I now, how can I grow? The only way I can grow is through going back to education. I need to *know*. It was just that I needed to *know*.

I benefited from going to grammar school where expectations were high, even though I failed to live up to them. But even that little bit of grounding, that little bit of extra education, was really important to me.

Louise was doing TVEI. I was hopeless at maths at school, because I was always so frightened of it, I was taught so badly. But doing maths with her, and remembering how to do algebra, and fractions and stuff, I suddenly realized that I remembered it and understood it and I could work it out; and that I get a buzz from it. So maybe I wouldn't have gone back to education if it wasn't for Louise—I don't know.

There were so many different things. My sister being at
OU was another. I looked at the syllabus of the OU and I
thought—that looks really interesting.

We always had big heavy discussions about politics, at
home with my mum. What I began to miss most was having
a conversation with somebody which was intellectually
stimulating and wasn't about the price of cabbages, or
washing powder, or all the mundane dreariness that goes on
everyday.

The small talk of the local estate revolves pretty much
around who's doing what with who, and whether the next
door neighbour's got a new freezer or whatever. You
couldn't talk about politics where I lived, they'd think you'd
gone round the bend: there was no discussion apart from
general moaning. And I wanted to discuss things again. So
much was resurfacing. It's as though I've spent all this time
trying to deal with the past, and now having dealt with it I
can pick up and carry on.

Everything in my life really revolved around grammar
school, because that's when my parents were divorcing.
That's when the overriding sense of—I don't know—gloom,
despondency, really hit me. It's as though I stopped
growing. So many things were happening in my life. It was
like going back and rewriting it, and re-establishing myself,
because everything went wrong from there onwards. Things
have only begun going right in the last two years.

I was frightened for a long time that something was going
to happen again and that would be me gone for ever, sunk to
the bottom of the abyss. Access was frightening at first, but
it was a good start. The poly still gives me fears, especially
about exams. I'm a quivering wreck, sure I'm going to be a
failure again, and they're going to put a dunce's cap on me
and drum me out of college.

Normally I get on very well with the lecturers because
they're the same age group. But a woman there reminds me
of my old headmistress, and I avoid going to her tutorial.
She's very strait-laced and schoolmarmy. I got really
intimidated because it was kind of rigid and schoolish again.

The first time I had to present a seminar I thought I was
going to die. When I get nervous I talk quickly anyway. I

stood up, and I had to sit down. I was frightened I was going
to fall over. It was supposed to last an hour and we did it in
thirty-five minutes.

I had friends of mine down on Saturday: they're real East
Enders, and they think I'm a bit odd because I'm at the poly.
I try and play it down all the time. It's as though I've stepped
over a bridge that they can't cross and we're speaking to each
other from opposite sides. I felt as if I was trying to vindicate
myself all the time, saying why I'd gone, and they're not all
bloody intellectuals there—there are nice working-class
people there too, that kind of thing.

We had a really nice evening, but I've changed much more
than they have: they haven't changed at all because they
haven't done anything different from when I last saw them.

The only way Fran remembers anything is to associate it
with what was on television at the time: I remember that
because *Sons and Daughters* was on. The television is like a
historic watch for her; she judges a sequence of events in her
own life by a sequence of events on the tele. It's like she has
two parallel lives: television and her real life.

I thought it was awful, because for the first time in my life
I seemed to understand why she felt the way she did. All she
had in her life was television, nothing else, and she was
slowly dying.

I used to spend hours in her company, and my
conversation must have revolved around the same things. I
don't think I ever watched the tele as fanatically as she does.
And I think I never lost curiosity. Everybody used to say I
stored up bits of useless information. I was always so
interested by little facts—I knew loads of 'did you know's'.

On Saturday night she gave this graphic description of
how she cooks liver and bacon, and how somebody
remarked to her how wonderful it was and when his wife
cooks liver and bacon it tastes like rubber and could she give
his wife the recipe. And I thought—she's just trying to find
justification and a sense of pride in what she does. She's at
home and she cooks, and watches the tele, and she's trying to
justify it.

I just thought it was so sad, because she doesn't know why

she feels so rotten about everything. A lot of people get so trapped, and they stop questioning, and accept, saying, this is my place, this is where I belong. They take different ways out. Normally it's the pools: I'm going to win, and all that money's going to change my life. Or they read Mills and Boon and hope the milkman's going to whisk them away.

He's a retired bank robber, and they're really nice people, but I felt sort of alienated, because it's really difficult to bring yourself back on to that level. They were reminding me about things I'd forgotten, because it seemed such a long, long time ago: in a previous incarnation.

All Fran's done is add a few more memories to the ongoing catalogue. But I'd switched off two years ago from that, and my mind now is full of everything else, it's not full of those memories any more. It's quite difficult to realize that you've outgrown people, and they haven't outgrown you.

Nobody teaches us in school how to understand ourselves. People who need help don't get it. Where are they going to go? What's Fran going to do—she doesn't know there's a way out for her, and there is a way out; but she doesn't know that. She did say at one point, oh you're so clever, I couldn't do that. And I said, of course you could, anyone can, go and find if there are any Access courses you can do. But it's beyond her comprehension.

I sometimes think people need to go through a pain threshold, like marathon runners. Once you've gone through all your worst nightmares, you can say, right, the way is clear for free choice.

You take control, you start being powerful instead of being powerless. I know at the end of these three years I'm going to be totally different. I know in the last year I've changed radically. I think with education, the more you know, the more you understand why things are the way they are. Sociology for instance helps you to understand the way people are. It also gives me an added insight into my own circumstances, and the way my parents were. The more knowledge you have the more in control you feel, because you know why things operate the way they do. You might be powerless to do anything about it, but you know what's going on.

Education does an awful lot in so many different ways, so that it's difficult to be precise about it.

There's the joy of learning something and understanding it. You realise you're actually a free-thinking person, with your own opinions, and with insights about the world that don't come from television. They're independent, drawn on your own resources, from analysing, thinking. Nobody's telling you how to think; they do, but it doesn't make any difference. And you don't accept things either: I think that's one thing that knowledge gives you: you question all the time; whereas most people with a little education don't.

Talking to people who don't is frustrating. It's like talking to the blind. That sounds really pretentious, I don't mean it like that. It's as though your eyes have been opened. You want to rush round and do it for everybody else, but you know that you can't. Even to try would be insulting. But it's sad, because some people live in a world within a world within a world: trapped in this bubble, and they don't or can't think or see outside it.

You can equate it with young children when they have lots to say but they don't know how to say it: the frustration of knowing what you want but not being able to articulate it. It's the same when you're uneducated: you know you need something, but you don't know how to put into words exactly what it is. It's only when you've got some kind of knowledge that you can speak, and understand what it is you want, and what you're fighting for.

When you get a decent education you realize that your frustrations aren't personal frustrations, they're shared by everyone.

But anything that gives me pleasure or which enriches my life to any degree shouldn't be examined, it should be for personal fulfilment, not to suit a job or anything else.

Years ago I used to refuse to write to my sister when I was in India, because I knew that when she got the letter she would notice that I hadn't punctuated it properly, or that I'd misspelt something. And because of that I was too intimidated to write to her. She was powerful in her possession of knowledge, and I was vulnerable in my lack of it. That was a big gulf, because if you haven't got knowledge, it is really awe-inspiring.

Knowledge isn't regarded as something personal, or personally enriching. If you think of school as exams and being tested, and having others judge you all the time—whereas it shouldn't be like that, it shouldn't be how other people judge you, it should just be about knowledge for your own growth. There are so many people who will never realize their full potential. We need to know. I know more about me the more I learn about everything else.

Inside all of us is a fully rounded human being desperately trying to form. And the more you learn, the more bits you fill in. It's the gaps that cause the problems.

In a sense it's a kind of spiritual thing, only I don't believe in God. But it's finding peace with yourself, clearing out all the cobwebs in your mind and all the bits that don't belong there—and replacing them with valid things. The only way to go on is by learning; the more we learn and know the more we know about ourselves. The foundation of everything's got to be self-awareness.

Julie's is a clear statement about 'integration'—about learning in adulthood serving the returner's need to give form to her life: 'I know more about me the more I learn about everything else.'

Her own experience enriches her learning and is given coherence by it. She, like other returners, believes that explanation can take her anywhere: she has become a true pioneer. Cheated of intellectual freedom before, she's going to make up for lost time by going anywhere she wants.

Of course schools should be so empowered that they become far less likely to miss so many of their pupils—so that Julie's friend Fran could have had an education. But the irony, for the small minority of those cheated by their schooling who do manage to find their way back, is that when they do so, a profound adventure awaits them. Education becomes as essential, as seriously enthralling, as it is for a very young child, for whom each new day extends her range. Schools should make that serious enthralment last into later childhood and adolescence. But their power to do so is being steadily taken away.

13

The End of School as we Know it

In this final chapter, I bring my argument to a conclusion. I write at a time when the whole country is concerned about the state of education; and when there is dangerous talk—for instance—of making it possible again for a 13-year-old to slam the door on physics and poetry and opt for vocational training instead. But that door *must not close*, then or ever, not least because it is so difficult to open later, in spite of Access, in spite of returners' courage and determination. Training is vital; but it must never be an alternative to education, and certainly not at school. When training begins, it should accompany education, never replace it.

'Trainees to the left, scholars to the right' presupposes a god-like ability on the part of schools to judge early and accurately. But this is not possible. Returners tell us that the choices made for (never truly *by*) 13-year-olds are more likely to be the fulfilment of sociological fate than the picking of an appropriate future after infallible testing.

Selection of any sort before adulthood tends to ratify theft of opportunity; to make cheating systematic.

Fun Now: A New Way to Cheat

The people in this book were cheated. They have made their case for the importance of the right to return. The right exists, and has existed for some time; but it is still not easy to take it up. Nor is it widely seen as the same right as a child's to education. Access does help; as does the dearth of 18-year-olds. Universities and polytechnics have to recruit mature students. As it becomes evident to more and more people that vast numbers of talented and intelligent people have been missed by their schools, so will the right to return become more widely understood as a proper part of any educational provision.

Another sign of necessary shift may be for hospitality to adults to become a common rather than unusual feature of school fifth and sixth forms. Even if Access spreads its provision much more widely, in most places the secondary school will continue to be the most accessible institution where learning to an advanced level takes place. I take the ideal of the community school to be a good one: I would welcome the proliferation of schools that provide for all ages, flexibly and imaginatively. More often than not, provision for adults in schools is tacked on, subsidiary; seen by school staff as an irritant. Local management of schools may well confirm this tendency.

Wherever adults do enter school classes, all benefit. The mix of ages works. Nothing is a better symbol of education as a lifelong right. A large influx of adults into schools would perhaps provide pressure for change unlikely to be applied while private education continues to flourish. If the Access students in this book had moved from a 'Return-to-Learn' course into a sixth form—had their Access course not existed—they would have been outraged by some of the insufficiencies commonly to be met in schools.

If those insufficiencies become graver still, adults would be advised to give schools a wide berth.

Recent correspondence in the *Guardian* (1 June 1990) followed a piece by Edward Pearce—a set of variations on the theme presented to him the preceding week, of the illiteracy of so many school-leavers. He lamented this fact. On his first lament he balanced another: his belief that people are not taught to read any more. He recalled that when he had to read two Shakespeare plays for A level, he read widely in the works of other playwrights of the time, such as Massinger. He extolled Smollett and Fielding as good stuff to give them at school if you want your pupils to write well. He did not blame teachers.

One letter two days later was from a pained and troubled teacher from the Midlands. She wrote as follows:

Oh dear. I do wish journalists would do a bit of real reading,

never mind Smollett and Fielding, before they launch forth
with their simplistic views of what creates and sustains
literacy. I can just imagine really engaging the committed
and critical interest of the young people I teach (industrial
working class . . .) with the works of Middleton, Massinger,
and friends.

But this book suggests that in ten years' time, given the chance,
those same resistant pupils may wish they had read Smollett,
and may—who knows?—feel cheated that Massinger was not
offered them at school. She asks, by implication, the same
wrong question that we all asked in the 1960s and 1970s: how
can we teach without 'relevant' texts? What we should have
asked, and what the teacher I have quoted above should have
asked, is why we felt powerless to bring pupils to the remote
and strange and difficult and persuade them to *wait to see the
point.*

Schools have accepted that they are powerless to offer
abeyancy, a necessary deferment of understanding. It does not
wildly caricature new wave history teaching, for instance, to
say that it has allowed a self-respecting 15-year-old to think of
herself—unpersuaded of the need to know what happened
before, what comes next—as equally qualified to construe a
document relating to a particular event or circumstance as any
professor. Steps between The Beginner and The Master have
been magically removed. There she is, pal and partner of
Schama or Hobsbawm, construing cleverly and led to believe
in the unimportance of her ignorance. It is more fun to
construe than to learn; to use your critical faculties, rather than
wait for mastery like a novice string player, or like 18-year-old
Charlie Parker alone in his room practising, practising,
practising.

Neil Postman is the prophet of what is happening in our
schools. We offer FUN NOW:

television's principal contribution to educational philosophy
is the idea that teaching and entertainment are inseparable.
This entirely original conception is to be found nowhere in
educational discourses, from Confucius to Plato to Cicero to

John Locke to John Dewey. In searching the literature of education, you will find it said by some that children learn best when they are interested in what they are learning. You will find it said—Plato and Dewey emphasized this—that reason is best cultivated when it is rooted in robust emotional ground. You will even find some who say that learning is best facilitated by a loving and benign teacher. But no one has ever said or implied that significant learning is effectively, durably and truthfully achieved when education is entertainment. Education philosophers have assumed that becoming acculturated is difficult because it necessarily involves the imposition of restraints. They have argued that there must be a sequence to learning, that perseverance and a certain measure of perspiration are indispensable . . . that learning to be critical and to think conceptually and rigorously do not come easily to the young but are hard-fought victories. Indeed, Cicero remarked that the purpose of education is to free the student from the tyranny of the present, which cannot be pleasurable for those, like the young, who are struggling hard to do the opposite—that is, accommodate themselves to the present. (Neil Postman, *Amusing Ourselves to Death* (Methuen, 1985), 150–1)

Returners seem often to sense they have been cheated—apart from anything else—of the *difficult*. Leaving school early, some know that in all their hours at school the highest awkwardness they attained was the *slightly tricky*. Sally is a good example. When she began her return, she was prepared to take anything on: to learn huge intractable chunks of stuff, to batter away at what she did not understand until it gave in. But at school she met nothing arduous. Now we may be cheating children even more comprehensively. Perhaps adulthood will become the only time for education if we continue to weaken our teachers and our schools with our refusal to acknowledge that what they need is to be made as powerful as possible, in order to overwhelm pupils' prejudice against education; to beguile the reluctant, to commandeer the patience of the too easily bored. Instead, steady erosion. We pay teachers less and less—I was much better off as a young teacher in 1974 than a novice today—and we give them more and more work to do. We neglect the buildings in which they work. In order to cope with the reluctance of young graduates to enter the profession, we fill newspapers with dishonest recruiting advertisements rather than doing anything serious about the conditions in which those sufficiently gullible to respond will be expected to work.

I spoke approvingly of GCSE in my first book as antidote to what I called stuffing, education-as-taxidermy. Nothing is worse. Anything is better. Talk and do, practise and experiment: those are the principles behind the new exam. Sound theory backs them: doing and talking are better means to understanding than *being told*. Most returners love discussion, not because they like chatting for its own sake, but because discussion releases into the intellectual air flight after flight of interpretations, from which choices can be made. Discussion leads to intellectual sophistication. It gives conceptual practice, and leads away from simple right-and-wrong thinking to acceptance of plurality.

But behind the sound principles of GCSE lies a deception. Imagine a well-paid and rewarded history teacher with enough time to think about what she is doing before she does it, and enough time to make fine distinctions between her pupils, enough time to be inventive, enough time to sustain her own intellectual vitality, free of the tormenting need to control the disruptive. A teacher—in other words—in a good public school. She will be able to teach a group of 14 in such a way that it will give her pupils a most satisfying two years. The syllabus is a recipe that can be cooked plainly or richly. Comfortably provided with time and reward, free of the need to control a large number, sure of her authority, she will let her pupils have their construing fun with documents, and learn as they do so one of the examinable skills. But at the same time she will cook that part of the syllabus that admits the importance of knowledge, and require her pupils to learn a great deal. She will probably ask them to know more than the recipe officially asks. They will groan as they are told to read books the syllabus does not mention. They will mutter as she takes them on apparent diversions into the history of different countries, other epochs. She will constantly bypass and supersede the recipe, relying on its active ingredients to give her pupils intellectual pleasure to keep them going; but making

all work done take its place in an enterprise far larger than a
mere exam. The principle of abeyancy will hold.

An ill-paid, demoralized history teacher in a pollarded
comprehensive can just about cook GCSE richly for a class of
24. But he will probably only be able to do so on the sly with
some pupils—those whose parents can collude with his secret
cookery. At home they will be serious patient students,
working in silence in a room upstairs. At school they will join
the rest, having fun with documents in groups. The favoured
minority become serious students *elsewhere*; the majority can go
through their fourth and fifth school years thinking *if it's not fun
it's boring so it's useless*. GCSE enforces an educational apartheid
between those with homes that favour education, and those
with homes that do not, just as effectively as the old apparatus
of grammar school and secondary modern.

The cheated ones will be working-class children like
Andrew. He bunked off to wars in the library. The new
cheated stay in the classroom, because it's a good laugh. Life
later may teach postponement, may prompt return; but it may
not. If children leave school with no capacity to cope with the
very difficult, and no willingness to stalk understanding
through long bafflement—they have been cheated. Recall the
tiler in Chapter 1 note 1: he knew his schooling in the early
1970s had sold him a pup. He knows that no one respected him
enough to give him Shakespeare to study, and to say, 'This is
incomprehensible at the moment, but I promise you that it's
worth working at, because it's great art.'

The fun-room is the sign. Schools have become powerless to
ask for contemplation. Instead, in room after room, the normal
state is fun. The wise—backed by educated parents, favoured
by their teachers—make intellectual fun, as Sally learnt to do in
maths. Others, whose 'rules' debunk education, are cheated by
being allowed to browse and gossip their way through lessons,
doing enough to perform averagely well—having presented to
their teachers a credibly average persona—confident that their
chit-chat is impossible to distinguish from productive discussion.

But if browsers talk to good purpose for an eighth of their
time, they are probably better off than their stuffed silent
forebears. At least fun—with a nice friendly teacher—will not

put you off history or physics for life. I am not proposing retreat. But until *all* schools are powerful enough for *all* their teachers to work like the public school historian I have just invented, so that very few pupils will be tempted to browse and fritter and gossip, we will have to make it easier for the cheated browsers to return. Nor is the power I am proposing the power to bully—but the power to create the sort of urgent seriousness that returners crave when they begin. Make no mistake: children and adolescents are capable of that seriousness. Sit in a classroom with one of the many wonderful comprehensive teachers not allowed to appear in this polemic, and you will see that seriousness. But it is not the norm. We do not give schools what they need to make it so.

The powerful teacher is a pluralist: able—for instance—to make the enlightened opportunities for intellectual fun instituted by GCSE take their place beside the old indispensable rigours. She is powerful enough to *solve the problem of credible authority*. When she says, 'Be still and know that this will be good in the end', her pupils believe her. She can hold that rich fermenting peace you feel in a room where young minds are taking ten minutes' silence to think. Instead, in class after class, thinking is gregarious, thinking is social, thinking is chatty, thinking is fun. Talk is vital, talk is indispensable, talk should be fun; but there must be peace to think as well. Thinking sometimes should be serious enthralment and nothing to do with fun.

It is possible to see the fun-room as failure to solve the problem of authority; as appeasement of the teenager, aggrandized since the 1950s. Teenage culture, cultivated by those who make money out of it, makes authority difficult. That difficulty has become graver as teenage culture has become ever more monolithic. Teenagers have a life of their own, over which adults have no authority, because they belong to a different order of being. Boring old bears do not legislate for sharply dressed young tigers. Every day in every classroom, teachers have to challenge adolescents' haughty scepticism. James Dean knows it all: that is what his beautiful sneer and his pocketed hands and his denim shoulders are saying. His inheritor prances into the classroom waiting to be bored, confident that his pout and his swagger are sanctified.

Since the 1960s we have missed our chance to make all schools so powerful that they can enchant and overwhelm James Dean, encouraging him to wait until his capacity for heroism and decency, and his imagination and his intelligence, have been properly nurtured, so that he will not allow them to be burned out in a crashed Porsche.

A teacher, then, should be able to say to her pupils, 'Believe me, *Hamlet* is worth struggling to understand. Join me, be patient, we will work at it together . . .' So what might she offer them instead? A video of *Neighbours* to 'criticize'? To ask teenagers to be 'critical' can be good intellectual practice; and it can be a challenge to their pseudo-omniscience, a bluff-calling—if refereed by a powerful very intelligent teacher, confident of her Socratic agility. But it can also be an evasion of responsibility, the parent saying, 'Let me be your pal.'

Ideologues attack the vision of the enchantment of *Hamlet* postponed. Middle-class deferred gratification, they will bluster: rank élitism. But their prescriptions mean that the suborned troopers suggested in Roger's account are cheated just the same—but in the newest right-on way.

I saw the new at its worst and best in one day not long ago. First, I sat in a room in the company of twenty-three 15-year-olds taking GCSE English: a 'second group' in a streamed year. Their teacher was a sensitive, bright, warm man. He had devised a module based on four science-fiction films, all of which his class had seen, and about which they were—as I watched—solicited in groups to talk, prompted by a written agenda. Discussion would lead to writing of one from a choice of assignments: a range of different ways of responding to the films. Writing would be done at home, or could be started there and then if a pupil so chose.

I could see the wise few in one group. I eavesdropped. They were talking to the point—though off it as well. Other groups were whiling their time away until the bell, with gossip and argument—of a most seductive geniality—that sometimes became disruptive. The teacher—not authoritative—asked for good behaviour with the utmost civility. Briefly he was obeyed. The wrong sort of fun was then restored. It was clear that even if he had wanted to be a pluralist, to demand twelve minutes' silence while he taught—say—the felicity in prose argument of the occasional short sentence, he stood no chance of being allowed so to do. I sat there crying woe to myself at the waste of this good man's mind, at the waste of the time of these children, at the barbarous fatuity of such frittering, at the certainty that many of those I was watching would need to return because they were being cheated of their first chance. And yet that classroom could have been observed, and the FORM of what was happening therein approved as what should be.

On the same day I saw this class I wrote a report after observing another:

I watched French with a high-stream class of 28. Fourth-year GCSE. It was active and talkative and enjoyable to watch. First a tense was being practised. In pairs, pupils had to ask and answer questions (Have you eaten your toast? Yes I have eaten my toast . . .).

This part of the lesson took 16 or 17 minutes. Some of the pairs were far more assiduous than others. There was a lot of discreet larking about. But as use of class time—by a very effective teacher—it had advantages: pupils were talking French; and an enthusiastic, energetic atmosphere was created. But in 16 minutes prime time, each pair was at most asking and answering four questions. Some pairs managed far less. It was clear that there were far too many pupils for the teacher to monitor the rigour and seriousness of what they were saying to each other. With affable reasonable pupils such as these how do you distinguish between the sort of talk you want and the sort you don't? To make talkative lessons succeed you have to create just the sort of relaxed atmosphere that is perfect camouflage for teenage chat.

The teacher then 'tested' some of the pairs—the best of whom did a beautiful job. This—again very lively—part of the lesson lasted about 10 minutes; its liveliness good camouflage again for those with urgent things to tell each other in English.

Finally, in a more and more festive atmosphere, a game was played. There were two sets of cards, each with one half of a sentence which had to be completed by finding the matching half in the other pack. The class was divided into two teams.

Surely this sort of learning will create irresistible pressure for smaller numbers? 28 pupils writing in silence or near silence can be just about monitored by one adult. But the same number talking and emoting and role-playing and experimenting?

Is it enough to say, at least they're enjoying themselves and not being PUT OFF—if many of those thus contented are covering in one subject in two years an amount of material easily covered by a well-motivated adult (with a job and a family) in 6 months of evening classes and private study?

I was left with an itchy suspicion that what I had watched was a superb teacher presiding very effectively over 45 minutes' largely wasted time. Or, to put it another way, 10 minutes was very well spent indeed by a third—say—of the class, and the rest of the time wasted; 5 minutes well spent by another third of the class—and the rest of the lesson agreeably wasted; and for the final third of the class, the entire lesson was wasted.

At present adolescence may well be the worst time of all for education. Teachers are not to blame. It is not the fault of the teacher I quoted at the beginning of this chapter that she holds her hands up in horror at the incongruity of the combination: my pupils : the works of Fielding. But working-class children are being cheated, all the same: those children to whom in the 1960s the comprehensive held out the promise: an education of the best quality for all.

The comprehensive has scored many successes. It is probably true that many more people of moderate rather than outstanding ability have been educated to a higher level as a result of the ending of selection—to the crudity and iniquity of which returners bear witness. But that higher level again and again will be nothing near a measure of what they could have achieved if their expectations had been higher. An irony of the comprehensive is that it sanctions 'average' as well as high attainment. So if you, your parents, and your teachers all agree that your goals should be modest, so long as you pleasantly attain them you will be honoured—much as Sally's school honoured her few fatuous CSEs. Ability—particularly in women—is constantly pretending to be moderate.

It is probably also true that many people acquire in the comprehensive a breadth of social sympathy unknown before in the regime of grammar school and secondary modern. It may well be true that fewer able adolescents miss out on their first—and for most their only—chance of education than before. In a comprehensive the possibility for a pupil who has begun badly to make good is preserved until she leaves, though it will be extraordinarily difficult for her to do so, because harassed teachers with no time to think stick their labels on firmly—to save time.

It is true—too—that comprehensive education has been associated with the debunking of didactic taxidermy as good enough on its own. Pupils *should* do, and speak; not sit and be stuffed. They must emote and create. They must express themselves: they are capable of independent understanding, and have opinions worth hearing. Such freedom is fine, if teachers are powerful enough to be pluralist: if it does not kill the willingness to learn and does not countermand the principle of abeyancy. Utterance is fine if it can be challenged; activity is fine if it can be made difficult as well as instantly gratifying. But passivity is worse than anything. In the elementary school Peter attended the utterance of a scholar's own thoughts was not encouraged. Nor, much later, was Sally's mental life thought to be of interest.

However, both, when they returned, did not just want to talk and be more active and expressive; they were prepared—while they learned to utter—to accept the wisdom and expertise and counsel of their tutors. Peter's first tutor at the OU was not a pal—but an arduous, demanding, invigorating, challenging mentor-friend. I am not talking about didactic authoritarianism: the deadly stance of the teacher who never doubts that she knows it all, and that her charges are infallibly ignorant. I am not talking about Gradgrind: taxidermy from the dominie with chalk in one hand and tawse in the other. I am talking about teachers empowered to feel confident that their adult experience is worth respect; confident that their knowledge and their thinking has depth and richness that their charges cannot yet have; sure enough of themselves to offer that depth and richness with authority. Ill-paid, too briefly trained, denigrated, and belittled, teachers in comprehensives at present are not helped to find that confidence.

It is hard not to see a dark side of change since the 1960s, when so many good developments in education gained momentum. A romantic child of my time, I went into teaching in 1972 because I believed that children were wise, and that culture was repressive and stupefying. Of course I did not spell out such a thought to myself; but it was in the air I breathed. I was absurdly attentive to my charges' utterance. This attention was beyond decent respect for pupils' ideas, the decent expectation that pupils should understand rather than be told, and that they should make things.

My subject was English. I awaited the poems of some of my pupils with excitement: the next haiku might well be just as *important* as anything Hopkins wrote. Science, perhaps, went on much as before; but in the humanities we believed in creation; in the probable wisdom and the certain and sacred uniqueness of a child's thoughts. To have criticized the cult— for that is what it was—of creative originality would have been blasphemous. If in 1974 I had heard someone recommend prolonged prophylaxis against 'the violation of the idea',[1] or the value of a little imitation, I would have reached for my Blake or my e.e. cummings and thrown the book at them.

When we did not get what we believed in, we tried to be friendlier, to see if that helped. Still baffled, we would make deeper and deeper incursions into Their Territory, making it valid subject-matter. We became like that regular tenant of early *Private Eye*: the Ton-Up Vicar, encouraging his boys to bring their bikes to church. Our textbooks were full of images that bespeak this accommodation: images of Their World; grinning boys up to no good; clinched couples in discos; a girl laughing with her boyfriend's arm around her shoulders. The sort of phantasy we encouraged was teenage daydream, the

[1] See Philip Rieff, *Fellow Teachers* (University of Chicago Press, 1985), 12–13, a book that is the nearest thing I have known intellectually to swallowing a useful poison that you just about survive. Required reading for anyone of my generation in the education game.

wherewithal for more class discussion, in which closeness was the aim, a confessional geniality.

Much of this was sensible. To write about what you knew might make writing urgent and interesting—could encourage the act of writing itself. But what we took to be respect for authenticity was just as much the fear that they would not let us offer them anything else. We retreated in confusion from the truth about good schools private and state: they are, in some indefinable way, other-worldly. You enter them as a pupil, and something is being set against the rest of the world. Not necessarily critical, not better than, not superior; but *other*. I think—for quick instance—of a comprehensive with an outlandish addition to the normal curriculum from third year upwards: philosophy in half-class groups held by teachers whose belief in the importance of their work was moving.

Only teachers can overwhelm pupils with the importance of what their schools offer, and challenge them when they resist. Powerful teachers are clever pluralists in their determination to educate. Their authority has a large repertoire. Powerless teachers in pollarded schools offer only two sorts of authority, the martinet and the caring pal.

The martinet does not need attention. A little totalitarian, he or she is always outnumbered nowadays.

The headmaster as caring pal says, 'Your child may not succeed academically, but he will be treated in a friendly and caring manner so that his personality will flourish. He will come to school and relax in the friendly atmosphere generated by his teachers who will become like big brothers and sisters to him. My school is really a drop-in centre on a large scale, a youth club that sells a little learning on the side. Your boy will not feel uncomfortable here: far from it.'

The caring pal is the biggest thief of a child's right to education. I was a caring pal in a very difficult city school in the late 1970s. It was beyond my resources and those of most of my colleagues to be anything else.

Many of the teachers at such an academy now, as then, will have a devotedness that impresses all who meet them. Amid the patronizing hilarity of their charges—charges in charge—they remain decent, reasonable; representing reason in their behaviour. Even the ones who have gone under or are going under will keep kindness as their stock in trade until the day their breakdown begins or they finally escape the profession altogether. Schools are full of harassed, demeaned, ill-paid, devoted heroes and heroines.

But inside every retreating one, there was once, or still is, a teacher who wants to say, 'Listen, listen, this is important, this truly is important. Glaciation is more enthralling than anything you've so far met in your life; Chaucer is worth waiting to understand.'

I remember a boy I call Hamish in my book *Invisible Children*. I met him at my first school. I can see him now with his fist of cards in the back row. 'Shut up and gie's a bit of peace', he said, when I asked him to put them away. There was nothing wrong with his mind—though much wrong with his life. I was nice to him and he liked me, and in his 15-year-old mess a friendly big brother might well have been helpful. But I cheated him none the less.

The cheated, like returners, are all around us. Many in this book met someone in their childhood or adolescence, like Peter's Aunt Liz, who left them with an idea of education, a hope, which they could not then realize. But many of the cheated have nothing good to retrieve, no loved figure to go back to find. A decent society would reach out to them as well as offer opportunities to those who do manage to return to claim their right to education.

A New Kind of Education

Secondary schools have to become more powerful, because they will go on offering most people their main chance of intellectual fulfilment, for the immediate future.

The power schools need is to catch each pupil, challenging her 'rules' if necessary. This needs accurate response to individual difference—rather, for instance, than weakly submitting to Shirley's recalcitrance, and relegating her as unteachable. Pupils respond to teachers' authority if they feel deeply known and liked; if teachers are powerful enough to understand and respect them as individuals. Then, the promise of later fruition can become credible; and pupils will wait, learn—and even allow themselves to slog through patches of boredom.[2]

Adults make their own promises to themselves. But we have seen how important it is for the returner to meet the mentor's sensitivity and optimism from her first teachers. If education for cheated adults is to be successful it has to be able to offer the same respect for individuality needed in schools.

Adults can take up the right to education only when they realize that what is offered them respects, touches, transforms their experience; when they sense the reciprocity felt by Vanessa when she went to a law lecture that mentioned thalidomide. The 'acknowledging' teacher, too, offers reciprocity—by showing deep respect for the returner, as Peter's first tutor managed to do. After such respect, the student begins to become autonomous, and knows that anything she studies will enter and affect her own life; move her on.

Schooling in so many returners' accounts sounds like instruction, and they lament their silence, their thoughts unexpressed; the sense that their schooling was designed to complete them for a certain sort of life; to make them serviceable. Sally expressed this regret when she said she thought her teachers were preparing her to leave school early and get married.

Returners' influence is exciting—and their experience important—because they stress a quite different idea of education. Liz, for instance, Julie, Eleanor, and Peter confound 'education' and 'life' altogether when they talk about their return. They cannot think in a utilitarian way about education. Education is opening out to the world; is growth; is—in a

---

[2] As an indication of what I mean by power, the following from a letter I wrote recently will help. 'Giving power to teachers is the answer. I mean giving them decent money and more arduous training that continues while they work. I mean never expecting them to teach more than two lessons on the trot without time to take stock, think, absorb what's happened. I mean giving them the aid of ancillaries: some paid to do the paper work; retired volunteers to tutor groups or individuals; student mentors from nearby colleges to help disturbed pupils. I mean giving teachers the circumstances that encourage confidence and authority—so when they say, "this is difficult, but it's wonderful when you get the hang of it" they are believed, not scorned.

Well-paid, confident, enthusiastic teachers of smallish classes can be irresistibly persuasive' (from *The Sunday Times*, 16 Sept. 1990).

sense—biography itself. Returners reclaim education for their lives—not just for its power to get you a good job with a reasonable salary. Liz goes so far as to say that she would go back quite readily to waitressing, now that her mind is free.

Too many lives are shut before their time. Schooling-as-instruction fits lives to boxes too soon; dropping in a few appropriate skills, like the weapons and ornaments left in a tomb for the use of its corpse. 'Rules' can allow a box to be accepted, and snugly kitted out by its inhabitant. The snugger the fit, the more the prisoner will defend himself against rumours of larger scope beyond the tomb; the greater her dependence on explosive crisis for a chance to break out. It is for the sake of the prematurely entombed that the idea of return has to become easier to think—even if school becomes less likely to train for the tomb in the first place.

But return should be easier for the educated as well as the cheated. We would all gain if our system of education could make better use of the crises, the sudden irregularities in people's lives.

Such are the turning-points that returners use—when an unsuspected faculty appears; when intellect finally springs its trap. Education needs to cater to change and unpredictability. Making serviceable lives should not be its aim. Education needs to be a door easy to open throughout life—rather than opening at 5 and closing all too often at 16.

Crises produce energy, determination, devotion. Return makes use of them; and shows what might be the result if our entire system of education were better attuned to the unruliness of biography. Eleanor will now give to the world fifteen years of energetic, supercharged work.

So returners teach us what education should be like: a system that takes as its premiss that life is learning; that when life lurches or explodes, learning is what it needs; a system that stands on Julie's exalted belief: 'the only way to go on is by learning'.

Education's claims must not be overstated. People retain curiosity—if they are lucky—and openness, and the will to learn, without formal education after school years. But many do not. Ignorance can be entrenched with pride. Minds can close in defensive determination to miss out for good on what returners enjoy.

Schools have to become more powerful to stop cheating, the waste of minds, as soon in life as possible. But schools will never catch all—as Alan's account suggests. It could also be argued that the adolescent makes less of higher education than the adult returner. The best time for higher learning may be after, rather than before, adult experience.

The greatest educational change since the war has been the arrival of the Open University. Gradually, we are learning its lessons and putting them into practice. It may finally come to be seen as the prime mover of a subtle and—with luck—irreversible shift in structures and expectations associated with work and learning, towards greater acknowledgement of what I have called biography's unruliness. Even once-chaste collectivists are beginning to tempt themselves with the thought that groups are made up of individuals who should not be too easily generalized; individuals full of surprises, and endlessly varied in their speed of development. Perhaps social science will show new interest in exceptions, disobedience, aberration; in human quirks and quarks.

Returners teach us the validity of this change, and the need for it—which is this book's conclusion. Their stories are chastening, because they suggest that so many of the generalized, so much of the apparently immutable, might be quite different. How many fingers flickering over tills might be drumming a boardroom table, or pointing at a blackboard, or making an alteration to an engineer's drawing?

Returners teach so much. Where their numbers are high, institutions benefit: good practice follows. A thorough infection of returners attacks bad teaching, because staff have to think hard about what they are doing and how they are doing it. Returners ask questions; they will not take thoughtless methods for granted; their irreverence is useful. Once over their early lack of confidence, they will not put up with taxidermy; they will demand the sort of methods that served them so well in their earlier courses.

But most of all—if their influence is not resisted—they can sustain for those that teach them the sense that learning is as vital as air, food, love.

Paula was the last person I interviewed. At first, she seemed demure, a bit saddened, not sure that what she says is worth hearing. But by the end of the interview, I had forgotten this glimpse of her old manner. I guess that she retreats to it still for safety's sake; that it is a useful precaution for meetings with strangers. Just before I left, she was telling me about non-Euclidean geometry, her dissertation subject.

'But they never meet, do they?' I said, of parallel lines.

'Why shouldn't they? We can't know; it's an axiom, that's the whole point. Get rid of the axiom, and everything's different. Besides, we couldn't draw lines long enough, anyway.'

'But—'

'Think of a globe,' she said, peremptorily.

'Okay—'

'The equator as a band across the middle, yes? Now think of two parallel lines intersecting it at right angles. They'll meet at the poles, won't they?'

Soon we were talking about a geometry I never knew.

'You can go to any point inside a circle in any direction, can't you?'

'Er—yes—'

'But you couldn't in a doughnut—'

She could see I did not understand, so she explained, and told me there was a geometry of such shapes, defining things as one or the other, so a car would be a circle, and a teacup a doughnut. And thus she took me to the heart of this book, which is about mutability; about the axing of axioms, and the revelation that there might be limits to the authority of even the most godlike voices of your education. Paula has at last discarded the axiom 'I am stupid', and is working to a new one: 'I am clever.'

Her first education ended at 16, at which the decision was made—on inadequate and misconstrued evidence—that she should train in cartography. Now at last she is becoming the mathematician she should always have been. At school she was shy, did not speak up for herself, asked few questions. Now in her seminars she and another mature student talk more than the youngsters.

Outside her kitchen stands her shiny, red, 500 cc motorbike.

Another doughnut, capable of 120 m.p.h., she said, but she had only managed 95. 44 years old, divorced, the bike is one of many new freedoms. She can go anywhere she likes on it, in any direction.

Suggestions for Further Reading

This is a book for a general readership. It is not an academic book. It does not seek to *demonstrate*, but to *suggest*. My approach has been to let themes and patterns emerge from the accounts of those I interviewed. I did not begin by reading, but by interviewing. I did not want my witnesses to exemplify ideas suggested by the literature or by my interpretation of it. What they say is essence, as well as illustration; what I say is a mixture of interpretation and polemic.

But this book has been constantly nourished by reading— some of a kind not obviously relevant, as my citations may have suggested. I suspect that Richard Holmes has had more influence on me than any other writer. I came across this book some time after I had begun to write:

Footsteps: Adventures of a Romantic Biographer, Hodder and Stoughton, 1985. On page 208 he writes:

> Once known in any detail and any scope, every life is something extraordinary, full of particular drama and tension and surprise, often containing unimagined degrees of suffering or heroism, and invariably touching extreme moments of triumph and despair, though frequently unexpressed.

Tony Parker has been just as important. I admire his work immoderately: for instance, *The People of Providence*, Hutchinson, 1983. Anyone trying to write my sort of book is likely to hold Tony Parker in awe.

But for anyone wishing to pursue the academic literature of the subject of this book, below—a few are already cited in the text—are some books and articles, often with invaluable bibliographies, which offer a useful beginning.

M. J. Abercrombie, *The Anatomy of Judgement*, Pelican, 1969.

M. J. Abercrombie and P. M. Terry, *Talking to Learn*, Society for Research into Higher Education, 1978.

Stephen D. Brookfield, *Understanding and Facilitating Adult Learning*, Open University Press, 1986. This book contains a bibliography which, taken with the bibliography mentioned below (Davies and Thomas), will provide a very good guide indeed to the literature of adult education.

N. Costello and R. Richardson, *Continuing Education for the Post-industrial Society*, Open University Press, 1982.

J. H. Davies and J. E. Thomas (eds.), *A Select Bibliography of Adult and Continuing Education*, National Institute of Adult and Continuing Education, 1988.

N. Evans, *Post Education Society*, Croom Helm, 1985.

O. Fulton (ed.), *Access and Institutional Change*, The Society for Research into Higher Education, and the Open University Press, 1989. See in particular chapter 8 by Susan Warner Weill.

R. Goldman (ed.), *Breakthrough*, RKP, 1968.

M. Knowles, *The Modern Practice of Adult Education*, Association Press, 1970.

A. T. McLaren, *Ambitions and Realizations*, Peter Owen, 1985. (This book is, in a way, a scholarly close relative of my own, in that it sets out to explore and respect the individual experiences of a group of women returners. Of great interest.)

J. Mezirow, *A Critical Theory of Adult Learning and Education*, Adult Education, Volume 32, Number 1, Fall, 1981, 3–24.

J. Rogers, *Adults Learning*, Open University Press, 1977.

I also mention the following, to do with education:

A. S. Neill, *Neill, Neill, Orange Peel*, Hart, 1972.

N. Postman, *Amusing Ourselves to Death*, Methuen, 1985.

P. Rieff, *Fellow Teachers: of Culture and its Second Death*, University of Chicago Press, 1985.

Anyone thinking of return should approach their nearest college of education, secondary school, polytechnic, or university. But there are some 'how to' books; and browsing in a shop would lead to books such as:

J. Perkin, *It's never too late: A Practical Guide to Continuing Education for Women of all Ages*, Impact Books, 1984. (It is interesting that I have not come across a similar book aimed specifically at men.)

D. Barker, *Fresh Start: your Guide to Changing Careers*, Rosters, 1990.

J. Bell, S. Hamilton, G. Roderick, *Mature Students' Entry to Higher Education. A Guide for Students and Advisers*, Longman, 1986.

A. Reed, *Returning to Work*, Reed Employment, 1989. Chapters 4 and 6 deal respectively with confidence, and training or education.

Finally, most essential of all, I have mentioned:

Arnold Wesker, *Roots*, The Wesker Trilogy, Longman, 1984.

Willy Russell, *Educating Rita, Stags and Hens and Blood Brothers*, Methuen, 1988.

Willy Russell, *Shirley Valentine and One for the Road*, Methuen, 1988.

Index of Characters

Page references in bold type are to characters' main appearances. Page references in light type are to their earlier or subsequent mentions.

Index

OXFORD

MORE OXFORD PAPERBACKS

Details of a selection of other Oxford Paperbacks follow. A complete list of Oxford Paperbacks, including The World's Classics, Twentieth-Century Classics, OPUS, Past Masters, Oxford Authors, Oxford Shakespeare, and Oxford Paperback Reference, is available in the UK from the General Publicity Department, Oxford University Press (RS), Walton Street, Oxford, OX2 6DP.

In the USA, complete lists are available from the Paperbacks Marketing Manager, Oxford University Press, 200 Madison Avenue, New York, NY 10016.

Oxford Paperbacks are available from all good bookshops. In case of difficulty, customers in the UK can order direct from Oxford University Press Bookshop, 116 High Street, Oxford, Freepost, OX1 4BR, enclosing full payment. Please add 10 per cent of the published price for postage and packing.

OXFORD REFERENCE

Oxford is famous for its superb range of dictionaries and reference books. The Oxford Reference series offers the most up-to-date and comprehensive paperbacks at the most competitive prices, across a broad spectrum of subjects.

THE CONCISE OXFORD COMPANION
TO ENGLISH LITERATURE

Edited by Margaret Drabble and Jenny Stringer

Based on the immensely popular fifth edition of the *Oxford Companion to English Literature* this is an indispensable, compact guide to the central matter of English literature.

There are more than 5,000 entries on the lives and works of authors, poets, playwrights, essayists, philosophers, and historians; plot summaries of novels and plays; literary movements; fictional characters; legends; theatres; periodicals; and much more.

The book's sharpened focus on the English literature of the British Isles makes it especially convenient to use, but there is still generous coverage of the literature of other countries and of other disciplines which have influenced or been influenced by English literature.

From reviews of *The Oxford Companion to English Literature Fifth Edition:*

'a book which one turns to with constant pleasure . . . a book with much style and little prejudice' Iain Gilchrist, *TLS*

'it is quite difficult to imagine, in this genre, a more useful publication' Frank Kermode, *London Review of Books*

'incarnates a living sense of tradition . . . sensitive not to fashion merely but to the spirit of the age' Christopher Ricks, *Sunday Times*

Also available in Oxford Reference:

The Concise Oxford Dictionary of Art and Artists
edited by Ian Chilvers
A Concise Oxford Dictionary of Mathematics
Christopher Clapham
The Oxford Spelling Dictionary compiled by R. E. Allen
A Concise Dictionary of Law edited by Elizabeth A. Martin

ANTHONY TROLLOPE IN THE WORLD'S CLASSICS

Anthony Trollope (1815–1882), one of the most popular English novelists of the nineteenth century, produced 47 novels and several biographies, travel books, and collections of short stories. The World's Classics series offers the best critical editions of his work available.

THE THREE CLERKS

Anthony Trollope
Edited with an Introduction by Graham Handley

The Three Clerks is Trollope's first important and incisive commentary on the contemporary scene. Set in the 1850s, it satirizes the recently instituted Civil Service examinations and financial corruption in dealings on the stock market.

The story of the three clerks and the three sisters who become their wives shows Trollope probing and exposing relationships with natural sympathy and insight before the fuller triumphs of Barchester, the political novels, and *The Way We Live Now*. The novel is imbued with autobiographical warmth and immediacy, the ironic appraisal of politics and society deftly balanced by romantic and domestic pathos and tribulation. The unscrupulous wheeling and dealing of Undy Scott is colourfully offset by the first appearance in Trollope's fiction of the bullying, eccentric, and compelling lawyer Mr Chaffanbrass.

The text is that of the single-volume edition of 1859, and an appendix gives the most important cuts that Trollope made for that edition.

Also in the World's Classics:

The Chronicles of Barsetshire
The Palliser Novels
Ralph the Heir
The Macdermots of Ballycloran

PAST MASTERS

General Editor: Keith Thomas

Past Masters is a series of concise and authoritative introductions to the life and works of men and women whose ideas still influence the way we think today.

'Put end to end, this series will constitute a noble encyclopaedia of the history of ideas.' Mary Warnock

SHAKESPEARE *

Germaine Greer

'At the core of a coherent social structure as he viewed it lay marriage, which for Shakespeare is no mere comic convention but a crucial and complex ideal. He rejected the stereotype of the passive, sexless, unresponsive female and its inevitable concommitant, the misogynist conviction that all women were whores at heart. Instead he created a series of female characters who were both passionate and pure, who gave their hearts spontaneously into the keeping of the men they loved and remained true to the bargain in the face of tremendous odds.'

Germaine Greer's short book on Shakespeare brings a completely new eye to a subject about whom more has been written than on any other English figure. She is especially concerned with discovering why Shakespeare 'was and is a popular artist', who remains a central figure in English cultural life four centuries after his death.

'eminently trenchant and sensible . . . a genuine exploration in its own right' John Bayley, *Listener*

'the clearest and simplest explanation of Shakespare's thought I have yet read' Auberon Waugh, *Daily Mail*

Also available in Past Masters:

PAST MASTERS

General Editor: Keith Thomas

The people whose ideas have made history . . .

'One begins to wonder whether any intelligent person can afford not to possess the whole series.' *Expository Times*

JESUS

Humphrey Carpenter

Jesus wrote no books, but the influence of his life and teaching has been immeasurable. Humphrey Carpenter's account of Jesus is written from the standpoint of an historian coming fresh to the subject without religious preconceptions. And no previous knowledge of Jesus or the Bible on the reader's part is assumed.

How reliable are the Christian 'Gospels' as an account of what Jesus did or said? How different were his ideas from those of his contemporaries? What did Jesus think of himself? Humphrey Carpenter begins his answer to these questions with a survey and evaluation of the evidence on which our knowledge of Jesus is based. He then examines his teaching in some detail, and reveals the perhaps unexpected way in which his message can be said to be original. In conclusion he asks to what extent Jesus's teaching has been followed by the Christian Churches that have claimed to represent him since his death.

'Carpenter's *Jesus* is about as objective as possible, while giving every justifiable emphasis to the real and persistent forcefulness of the moral teaching of this charismatic personality.' Kathleen Nott, *The Times*

'an excellent, straightforward presentation of up-to-date scholarship' David L. Edwards, *Church Times*

Also available in Past Masters:

Muhammad   Michael Cook
Aquinas   Anthony Kenny
Cervantes   P. E. Russell
Clausewitz   Michael Howard

HISTORY IN OXFORD PAPERBACKS

Oxford Paperbacks offers a comprehensive list of books
on British history, ranging from Frank Stenton's *Anglo-
Saxon England* to John Guy's *Tudor England*, and from
Christopher Hill's *A Turbulent, Seditious, and Factious
People* to Kenneth O. Morgan's *Labour in Power: 1945–
1951*.

TUDOR ENGLAND

John Guy

Tudor England is a compelling account of political and religious developments from the advent of the Tudors in the 1460s
to the death of Elizabeth I in 1603.

Following Henry VII's capture of the Crown at Bosworth
in 1485, Tudor England witnessed far-reaching changes in
government and the Reformation of the Church under Henry
VIII, Edward VI, Mary, and Elizabeth; that story is enriched
here with character studies of the monarchs and politicians
that bring to life their personalities as well as their policies.

Authoritative, clearly argued, and crisply written, this comprehensive book will be indispensable to anyone interested in
the Tudor Age.

'lucid, scholarly, remarkably accomplished . . . an excellent
overview' *Sunday Times*

'the first comprehensive history of Tudor England for more
than thirty years' Patrick Collinson, *Observer*

Also in Oxford Paperbacks:

John Calvin   William J. Bouwsma
Early Modern France 1515–1715   Robin Briggs
The Spanish Armada   Felipe Fernández-Armesto
Time in History   G. J. Whitrow

PHILOSOPHY IN OXFORD PAPERBACKS

Ranging from authoritative introductions in the Past Masters and OPUS series to in-depth studies of classical and modern thought, the Oxford Paperbacks' philosophy list is one of the most provocative and challenging available.

THE GREAT PHILOSOPHERS

Bryan Magee

Beginning with the death of Socrates in 399, and following the story through the centuries to recent figures such as Bertrand Russell and Wittgenstein, Bryan Magee and fifteen contemporary writers and philosophers provide an accessible and exciting introduction to Western philosophy and its greatest thinkers.

Bryan Magee in conversation with:

A. J. Ayer	John Passmore
Michael Ayers	Anthony Quinton
Miles Burnyeat	John Searle
Frederick Copleston	Peter Singer
Hubert Dreyfus	J. P. Stern
Anthony Kenny	Geoffrey Warnock
Sidney Morgenbesser	Bernard Williams
Martha Nussbaum	

'Magee is to be congratulated . . . anyone who sees the programmes or reads the book will be left in no danger of believing philosophical thinking is unpractical and uninteresting.'
Ronald Hayman, *Times Educational Supplement*

'one of the liveliest, fast-paced introductions to philosophy, ancient and modern that one could wish for' *Universe*

Also by Bryan Magee in Oxford Paperbacks:

Men of Ideas
Aspects of Wagner 2/e

MUSIC IN OXFORD PAPERBACKS

Whether your taste is classical or jazz, the Oxford Paperbacks range of music books is in tune with the interests of all music lovers.

ESSAYS ON MUSICAL ANALYSIS

Donald Tovey

Tovey's *Essays* are the most famous works of musical criticism in the English language. For acuteness, common sense, clarity, and wit they are probably unequalled, and they make ideal reading for anyone interested in the classical music repertory.

CHAMBER MUSIC

Chamber Music contains some of Tovey's most important essays, including those on Bach's 'Goldberg' Variations and *Art of Fugue*, and on key works by Haydn, Mozart, Beethoven, Schumann, Chopin, and Brahms.

CONCERTOS AND CHORAL WORKS

Concertos and Choral Works contains nearly all the concertos in the standard repertory, from Bach's for two violins to Walton's for viola—fifty concertos in all. The choral works include long essays on Bach's B minor Mass and Beethoven's Mass in D, amongst other famous works.

SYMPHONIES AND OTHER ORCHESTRAL WORKS

Symphonies and Other Orchestral Works contains 115 essays: on Beethoven's overtures and symphonies (including Tovey's famous study of the Ninth Symphony), all Brahms's overtures and symphonies, and many other works by composers from Bach to Vaughan Williams.

Also in Oxford Paperbacks:

Singers and the Song   Gene Lees
The Concise Oxford Dictionary of Music 3/e
Michael Kennedy
Opera Anecdotes   Ethan Mordden